Antonin Artaud

Addicted to drugs from an early age and incarcerated in a series of mental asylums throughout his adult life, Antonin Artaud was nevertheless one of the most brilliant artists to emerge from the twentieth century. His writing influenced entire generations, from the French post-structuralists to the American beatniks. He was a key figure in the European cinema of the 1920s and 1930s, and his drawings and sketches have been displayed in some of the major art galleries of the Western world. Possibly best known for his concept of a 'theatre of cruelty', his legacy has been to redefine the functions and possibilities of live performance.

This unique resource brings together for the first time a selection of the best critical writing available on the key themes of Artaud's life and work from critics such as Jacques Derrida, Julia Kristeva, Maurice Blanchot, Herbert Blau, Leo Bersani and Susan Sontag.

Containing some of the most intellectually adventurous and emotionally passionate writings on this classic and controversial figure, this book is an essential read for Artaud scholars working in a number of arts disciplines, including theatre, film, philosophy, literature and fine art.

Edward Scheer is a Senior Lecturer in the School of Theatre, Film and Dance at the University of New South Wales in Sydney, Australia. He is the editor of *One Hundred Years of Cruelty: Essays on Artaud* (2000) and has published work on Butoh, narrative theatre and performance art. He is Secretary of the Board of Directors of The Performance Space in Sydney, Australia.

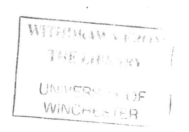

Antonin Artaud

A critical reader

Edited by Edward Scheer

LONDON AND NEW YORK

First published 2004
by Routledge
11 New Fetter Lane, London, EC4P 4EE

Simultaneously published in the USA and Canada
by Routledge
29 West 35th Street, New York, NY 10001

Routledge is an imprint of the Taylor & Francis Group

Typeset in Times by
Rosemount Typing Services, Barjarg Tower, Auldgirth, Dumfriesshire
Printed and bound in Great Britain by
MPG Books Ltd, Bodmin

British Library Cataloguing in Publication Data
A catalogue record for this book is available from the British Library

Library of Congress Cataloging in Publication Data
Antonin Artaud : a critical reader / Edward Scheer.
   p. cm.
Includes bibliographical references and index.
 1. Artaud, Antonin, 1896–1948–Criticism and interpretation. I.
Scheer, Edward, 1964–
   PQ2601.R677Z566 2003
   848' .91209–dc21

                                        2003005178

ISBN 0–415–28254–3 (hbk)
ISBN 0–415–28255–1 (pbk)

Contents

Acknowledgements   vii
A note on the text   ix

Introduction: on Antonin Artaud – a beginner's guide
to cruelty   1

PART I
On biography: madness and language   9

1   André Breton with André Parinaud: from *Conversations:
    The Autobiography of Surrealism*   11

2   André Breton, 'Homage to Antonin Artaud'   14

3   Georges Batailles, from 'Surrealism from day to day'   16

4   Sylvère Lotringer, from an interview with
    Jacques Latrémolière   21

5   Gilles Deleuze, 'Thirteenth series of the schizophrenic
    and the little girl'   27

PART II
Theatre: acts and representations   37

6   Jacques Derrida, from 'The theatre of cruelty and
    the closure of representation'   39

7   Helga Finter, from 'Antonin Artaud and the impossible
    theatre: the legacy of the theatre of cruelty'   47

8   Jerzy Grotowski, 'He wasn't entirely himself'   59

9   Jane Goodall, 'The plague and its powers in
    Artaudian theatre'   65

10 Herbert Blau, from 'The dubious spectacle of collective
    identity'   77

11 Susan Sontag, from 'Approaching Artaud'   83

12 Leo Bersani, 'Artaud, defecation and birth'   96

PART III
On writing and fine arts   107

13 Maurice Blanchot, 'Artaud'   109

14 Julia Kristeva, from 'The subject in process'   116

15 Jacques Derrida, from 'To unsense the subjectile'   125

16 Umberto Artioli, from 'Production of reality or hunger
    for the impossible?'   137

PART IV
Beyond words: on film and radio   149

17 Allen S. Weiss, 'K'   151

18 Denis Hollier, 'The death of paper, part two: Artaud's
    sound system'   159

19 Mikhail Yampolsky, from 'Voice devoured: Artaud
    and Borges on dubbing'   169

20 Francis Vanoye, 'Cinemas of cruelty?'   178

    Notes   184
    Bibliography   192
    Index   198

Acknowledgements

For copyright material reprinted in this volume thanks are due to the following:

Mark Polizzotti for the excerpt from his translation of André Breton with André Parinaud, *Conversations: The Autobiography of Surrealism*, New York: Paragon House, 1993.

Methuen for Jerzy Grotowski, 'He wasn't entirely himself', from *Towards a Poor Theatre*, trans. M. Buszewicz and J. Barba, London: Methuen, 1968.

Allen S. Weiss for 'K', in *Art and Text*, 37, September 1990.

Denis Hollier for 'The death of paper, part two: Artaud's sound system', *October*, 80, Spring 1997.

Herbert Blau for the extracts from 'The dubious spectacle of collective identity', in *The Dubious Spectacle: Extremities of Theatre, 1976–2000*, Minneapolis/London: University of Minnesota Press, 2002; originally in Teresa Alves, Teresa Cid and Heinz Ickstadt (eds) *Ceremonies and Spectacles: Performing American Culture*, Amsterdam: Vrije Universiteit Press, 2000.

Sylvère Lotringer for the extracts from his interview with Jacques Latrémolière and the accompanying essay 'I talked about God with Dr L', in S. Lotringer (2002) *Antonin Artaud und der gute Mensch von Rodez*, Vienna: Schlebrügge.

Routledge for the extracts from Julia Kristeva, 'The subject in process', in ffrench, P. and Lack, R.-F. (eds) *The Tel Quel Reader*, London and New York: Routledge, 1998; and for extracts from Jacques Derrida, 'The theatre of cruelty and the closure of representation', trans. Alan Bass, in *Writing and Difference*, London: Routledge, 1978.

The editors of *Modern Drama* for Jane Goodall, 'The plague and its powers in Artaudian theatre', 33, December 1990.

MIT Press Journals for the extracts from Helga Finter, 'Antonin Artaud and the impossible theatre: the legacy of the theatre of cruelty', trans. Matthew Griffin, *TDR*, 41.4, Winter 1997; and for the sections from Mikhail Yampolsky, 'Voice devoured: Artaud and Borges on dubbing', trans. Larry P. Joseph, *October*, 64, Spring 1993.

Éditions Desjonquères for Francis Vanoye, 'Cinémas de la cruauté ?', in Camille Dumoulié (ed.) *Les Théâtres de la cruauté: Hommage à Antonin Artaud*, Paris: Desjonquères, 2000.

Little, Brown and Co. for Leo Bersani, 'Artaud, defecation and birth', in *A Future for Astyanax: Character and Desire in Literature*, Boston and Toronto: Little, Brown and Co., 1976.

MIT Press for Jacques Derrida, from 'Forcener le subjectile', trans. Mary Ann Caws, in *The Secret Art of Antonin Artaud*, Cambridge, MA, and London: MIT Press, 1998.

University of Nebraska Press for André Breton, 'Homage to Antonin Artaud', in *Free Rein*, trans. Michel Parmentier and Jacqueline d'Amboise, Lincoln: University of Nebraska Press, 1995.

Verso for Georges Bataille, from *The Absence of Myth: Writings on Surrealism*, trans. and ed. Michael Richardson, London and New York: Verso, 1994.

Columbia University Press for Gilles Deleuze, 'Thirteenth series of the schizophrenic and the little girl', in *The Logic of Sense*, trans. Mark Lester with Charles Stivale, ed. Constantin V. Boundas, New York: Columbia University Press, 1990.

All reasonable efforts have been made to seek permissions from relevant copyright holders. If any copyright holders have been inadvertently overlooked, they are invited to contact the publishers, who will be pleased to make the necessary arrangements.

Thanks to Agnese Trocchi and Candida TV for the image; to Allen S. Weiss for the example; Sylvère Lotringer for the brio; Jane Goodall for the practicalities, the thoughtfulness and the intellectual friendship; The College of Arts, Education and Social Sciences at the University of Western Sydney for their timely and generous support for this project; The School of Theatre, Film and Dance at the University of New South Wales for the boost at the end; Sam Spurr for enthusiasm and grace; to my colleague John Golder for selflessness personified and collegiality beyond the call; Talia Rodgers for persistence and vision, and Rosie Waters for getting this over the line; to Isabel and Rosa, for those quotidian joys, and for keeping an Artaud scholar sane (well, sort of) – this book is dedicated to you.

A note on the text

Due to the fragmented nature of Artaud's writings, the profusion of letters and short pieces, and to the fact that no complete edition of Artaud's works exists in English, the convention is usually to refer to the various published collections of the works in English and French. References in this volume to *OC* are to Artaud's *Oeuvres Complètes – Nouvelle édition revue et augmentée*, vols I to XXVI, Paris: Gallimard, 1976–, with the exception of the essay by Julia Kristeva (pp. 116–24), which uses the first edition, Paris: Gallimard 1956–. Vols I and XIV are in two parts designated by an asterix * for part one, and ** for part two.. The citations are made in parentheses, with the volume number in Roman numerals followed by the page number in Arabic numerals. References to *SW* are to *Antonin Artaud Selected Writings*, trans. Helen Weaver, ed. Susan Sontag, Los Angeles: University of California Press, 1988. References to *CW* are to *Collected Works*, vols 1–4, trans. Victor Corti and Alastair Hamilton, London: Calder and Boyers, 1961. References to *AA* are to *Artaud Anthology*, ed. Jack Hirschman, San Francisco: City Lights Books, 1965. References to *TD* are either to *Le Théâtre et son double*, Paris: Gallimard, 1964, or to *The Theatre and its Double*, trans. Mary Caroline Richards, New York: Grove Press, 1958 (see individual chapters). All other references are made according to the Harvard system.

There is no standard form of usage regarding the phrase 'theatre of cruelty'. I would argue that it was only to have been an institution, i.e. the 'Theatre of Cruelty', prior to the production of *The Cenci* in May 1935. Thereafter, the institutional aims vanished and the expression has entered the language of theatre studies and cultural history and so needs no capitalisation.

Any endnotes referring to authors' translations are, of course, referring to the individual authors of the respective chapters. Any editorial interventions on my part are noted in the text as '(ES)'.

Introduction: on Antonin Artaud

A beginner's guide to cruelty

Edward Scheer

Committee work – Artaud's legacy

In Rome, on 15 January 1998, the 'Committee for the Beatification of Antonin Artaud' began collecting signatures. They were demanding, not unreasonably, that Antonin Artaud be made not a saint, but one of the blessed. They chose this day to make their first public appearance to take advantage of the occasion of a meeting between the Mayor of Rome, Francesco Rutelli, and Pope John Paul II. They took photographs of nuns and priests with their banner, images which later circulated widely on CH99 (independent television of the future) and on local TV broadcasts. Media activists Candida TV joined the movement and helped promote the Committee's cause through installations, happenings and video-perfomances. The petition was later presented to the Church but the request was denied.[1] Remembering Artaud's 1925 letter to the Pope on behalf of the surrealists, which includes references to the Pope as a 'dog' and his 'Roman masquerade', this is perhaps unsurprising (*CW* 1: 180).

The apparent failure of the campaign notwithstanding, this conjunction of performance, activism, religion and power, at once parodic and deeply serious, suggests something of Artaud's legacy and how it continues to leave tracks in contemporary culture. The committee's activity can be seen as a dramaturgy of a particularly Artaudian kind, a performative testament to his memory, but reliving rather than remembering him. This collection of writings on and around Artaud, while far from an exercise in culture jamming, is intended as a testament of another kind, tracing Artaud's tracks in the intellectual life of the last 50 years.

Should Artaud be beatified? Artaud's life (1896–1948) was certainly scandalous and often interrupted by long periods of sickness, but was perhaps not sufficiently miraculous to justify beatification. As is well known, Artaud was drug addicted from a relatively early age, suffered psychotic episodes throughout his adult life and endured an eight-year, eight-month incarceration in the asylums of France. What seems truly miraculous is that he was also immensely productive and worked at an elite level in a number of different fields and across various media. So to refer to him simply as a prominent screen actor, writer and artist would be insufficient and would require re-imagining those professions in the light of his immense, sometimes amorphous and often perverse, output. For instance, he wrote some of the seminal theatre essays of the twentieth century yet he clearly failed as a practitioner. Similarly, as an author of texts whose poetry had been rejected, he nonetheless influenced an entire generation of writers and thinkers in France (the post-structuralist generation) and in the USA (John Cage and the beats). Again, he was a popular figure in the cinema of the 1920s, but he turned his back not only on popular cinematic forms but on the cinema itself. Instead, he strove to reinvent the very concept of form in text and sound experiments which would finally scandalise France in the controversy surrounding his 'obscene' studio recording for radio in 1947, which was, typically, banned by the very institution that commissioned it. Finally, he was an artist who rejected the tag 'fine art' but whose drawings have been shown at some of the major galleries in the Western world.

Artaud's practice of theatre, painting and film, as much as his writings about and through them, stand as a testament not to any notion of the disciplinary history of these practices but to the relentless passion for aesthetic innovation and for personal re-invention which, despite or because of his perversity, underlies his legacy. This is why it is time to gather in one place some of the flak of this explosion called Artaud and so begin to comprehend the effects of Artaud's opus since his death in 1948 at the age of 51.

As the example which the 'Committee for the Beatification of Antonin Artaud' provides, and as this collection affirms, Artaud has inspired many writers, thinkers and artists. He is frequently referenced, less often quoted, but the singularity of his work, heterodox, complex and variegated as it is, is sometimes overlooked. What doubles for it are, as Jane Goodall points out, the myths about his life and character which developed in the 1960s (Goodall 1994: 1), notably the myth of the counter-cultural guru of a holy and violent theatre and that of the mad writer whose experience is exoticised as the purest form of autobiography, i.e. of a person unable to separate themselves from their own obsessions sufficiently to develop a strategy for representing them. Yet it is more accurate to say that whatever we know of his life, it is in his writing that we discern a variety of positions which have 'opened the way to new ideas of subjectivity as multiple or heterogeneous, as *en proces* (in process/on trial)' (Goodall 1994: 2). Artaud's thought cannot be identified with a particular philosophy, yet it has been of great significance, for example to some of the central texts of that set of discourses known in the anglophone world as post-structuralism, providing them with much of their poetic resonance and conceptual power. Similarly, his writing on theatre and the arts cannot be said to be embodied in any particular practice, though it has fed into most of the major experiments in anti-representational performance since the Second World War. This collection of critical essays attempts to reflect these influences while working against the constructions of the doubles that have taken over Artaud's legacy. It is, then, intended as a demythologising project undertaken through a series of encounters with his work.

His work consists of letters, glossolalia (invented language for speech), theatre, art and film reviews and criticism, essays, texts on theatre, manifestos, poems, screenplays (notably 'La Coquille et le clergyman', 1927), a novel, translations from English to French, including texts by Lewis Carroll and Shelley's *The Cenci*, fragments, spells, sketches, portraits, recordings, acting roles in cinema and on stage. There are 26 volumes of his *Oeuvres Complètes* in French *chez* Gallimard. His writing on the theatre constitutes only a fraction of his total output but its influence on contemporary performance practice has been immense, helping substantively to redefine the functions and the possibilities of live performance. As Josette Feral has argued: 'Conceived as an art form at the juncture of other signifying practices as varied as dance, music, painting, architecture and sculpture, performance seems paradoxically to correspond to the new theatre invoked by Artaud' (quoted in Wright 1989: 115).

It is in the theatre writings that his central aesthetic strategies are all, in some form, in evidence. Artaud uses terms like 'plague', 'cruelty', 'athleticism', 'appetite for life', which indicate the urgency and the energy he both brought to his writing and sought from its subjects and which come together in his phrase 'the theatre of cruelty'. In what follows here I will outline some of these key themes of his thought and suggest ways in which we can read these concepts at work in the various media with which Artaud worked and in those writers whose encounters with him are the subject of this collection.

Force/form – beyond acting

The key texts in relation to the theatre of cruelty are those written between 1931 and 1937 and first published together as *Le Théâtre et son double* in February 1938 (several months after Artaud had been interned in a psychiatric hospital in Rouen in the north of France). In *Le Théâtre et son double* Artaud employs several important images that function as metonyms for his theatre of cruelty, since it resists any positivist definition or formulation. Artaud approaches his idea of the theatre lyrically through comparisons with the plague, alchemy, Balinese dance, the Seraphim (the highest order of angels) and even a Dutch painting, *Lot and his daughters* by Lucas Van Leyden.[2] These metonyms combine in Artaud's book in the manner of a Cubist painting to constitute not an image of aesthetic unity, not one clear image as in a conventional essay, but an accumulation of partial images, each substituting for the whole and each of which itself demands a multiplicity of perspectives from the viewer or reader. This is how much of Artaud's writing proceeds.

In the opening essay to *Le Théâtre et son double*, 'Le Théâtre et la culture', Artaud explores the idea of life in culture as 'true culture' which wakens 'the gods that sleep in museums' through the intensity of a form which only exists 'to seduce and captivate a force' (*TD*: 16). This is a key to understanding how language, art and theatre function for Artaud not as ends in themselves, but as temporary forms for channelling forces. It is less a matter of representation and more a concern with the actions which approach the limits of the representable. If this sounds like the familiar art/life conjunction, it is important to remember that Artaud's idea of life is by no means obvious: 'Moreover, when we say the word life, one must understand that it's not a matter of life as recognised by external facts, but by that kind of frail, shifting source which forms never attain. And if there is still something infernal and truly damned in these times, it is this dithering artistically over forms, instead of being like those tortured at the stake, signalling through the flames' (*TD*: 19–20). It is life considered as an inchoate pre-symbolic yearning for the essence, and the actor can bring us close to this force by finding and maintaining the urgency of the impulse to action, an impulse which must be found in the moment of the body's fatal crisis.

Instances of cinematic immolation in some of Artaud's film roles supplied him with examples of how this might work. The immolation sequences at the end of *La Passion de Jeanne d'Arc* (Carl Dreyer 1927), in which Artaud plays the monk whose task it is to hold the crucifix up to Jeanne as she burns, and his role as Savonarola in *Lucrèce Borgia* (Abel Gance 1935) are suggestive of the power of this concept for Artaud. The ritual destruction of the body, the staging of its radical moment of crisis, are for Artaud instructive of how theatre broaches the limit of representation since, for him, actors do not strike poses or construct gestures; they respond to events out of necessity. Artaud sees actors as brutalised by representation and advises them to hang on to the moment through an 'inner force' which 'sustains' them and by which they rejoin 'that which survives forms and produces their continuation'. Similarly, language for Artaud has a secondary function in theatre. Instead of realising a text on stage, Artaud would drive language itself to its limit and stage its dismantling, its disintegration: 'To smash language to touch life is to make or remake the theatre' (*TD*: 19). One does not give a speech, one destroys the forms it might take and which might hide the true force of the moment.

Artaud himself gave three notorious examples of this quintessentially theatrical approach to the text in three public lectures given by him at the Sorbonne in 1933, in Brussels in 1937 and after his release from the asylums in 1947 at the theatre of the Vieux-Colombier. The first of these lectures was supposed to have been a reading of 'The theatre and the plague' as part of a series of lectures organised by the prominent psychoanalyst René Allendy.[3] A similar performance followed in Artaud's lecture at the Maison d'Art in Brussels in May 1937 on the subject of 'the decomposition of Paris'. His parents-in-law-to-be were in the audience and were so appalled by what they saw that the wedding was cancelled. Ten years later in front of a huge audience of artists, writers and public figures, Artaud gave a three-hour lecture/performance which began with him reading some of his poems before launching into a 'wild improvisation', and ended with him insulting the audience and 'abruptly leaving the stage' (Barber 1993: 137).

These three abortive lectures are perhaps the best live examples Artaud would give of his plans for the theatre. (His theatre-of-cruelty production of *The Cenci* in May 1935 was a failure and only ran for seventeen performances.) Even though Artaud demanded egress, an exit from the closed circuit of representation, the despatialising of the frame of the stage so that theatre would become life and assume the force of history, these lectures showed a body on stage pointing to the force contained within the constricted space, reanimating rather than abolishing the frame of the stage. But they also suggest the manner in which representation itself can be hijacked, as in certain forms of cultural activism, such as the activities of the beatification committee.

Beyond theatre?

On 28 February 1947, after this last performance, Artaud wrote to André Breton, the surrealist chief, who had reminded Artaud that he had been in a theatre throughout his performance at the Vieux-Colombier and had therefore failed to realise his ideas of a pure theatre: 'So yes, I appeared on a stage, once again, and for the LAST TIME, at the Vieux-Colombier theatre, but with the visible intention of leaping out of its framework, leaping out from the inside, and I do not believe that the spectacle of a man who wails and roars with fury to the point of puking up his intestines is a very theatrical spectacle' (Artaud 1968: 20).

There is a crucial problem delineated in this correspondence with Breton, as his two short texts in this collection suggest: whether Artaud's theatre is in any sense possible and, if not, why did he and why do we write about it and try to produce it on stage? Looking at the attempts in the 1960s, especially the 1964 Season of Cruelty at the RSC directed by Peter Brook, and the improvisations of the Living Theatre (also Artaud inspired), one can see that it has generated a suitably diverse range of approaches to theatre (see also Blau in this volume). But although these are necessarily reductions of Artaud's thinking, for whom cruelty denoted rigour, discipline and necessity, they would not have been possible without Artaud, and they provoke the question of the very possibility of a correct reading of Artaud or, as Jacques Derrida puts it, a 'faithful' rendering.

This idea of 'faith' is interesting, not only in relation to the performance strategies of the 'Committee for the Beatification of Antonin Artaud', but also in the sense that *Le Théâtre et son double* has become a bible of modern theatre of which all interpretations are necessarily blasphemous, a sacred text 'at the same time unchangeable and impracticable in its purity' (Virmaux and Virmaux 1980: 233). Alain and Odette Virmaux, who have written several studies of Artaud and the theatre, argue that such betrayals are legitimate 'not because this discourse is impossible to apply or is concretely unrealisable, but because its principal power is in constituting an inexhaustible seeding (une semence inépuisable)' (Virmaux and Virmaux 1980: 234). This is persuasive, but Artaud himself has best indicated the parameters of the debate: 'The crucial thing is not to believe that this action must remain sacred, that's to say, set apart, but that not just anyone can do it and that there has to be a preparation for it. This leads us to reject man's usual limitations and powers and infinitely extends the frontiers of what we call reality' (*TD*: 19).

Jerzy Grotowski's theatre laboratory gets close to this kind of thinking, as his essay here indicates, for example in regard to what he called the 'total act', defined as 'an extreme solemn gesture' which does not 'hold back before any obstacle set by custom and behaviour'. It is 'modelled in a living organism, in impulses, a way of breathing, a rhythm of thought and the circulation of blood' and must be 'ordered and brought to consciousness, not dissolving into chaos and formal anarchy'. In this way it is possible to learn to 'respond totally, that is to begin to exist. For each day we only react with half our potential' (Grotowski 1968: 92–3). This total commitment exceeds the notion of acting and demands a different conception of theatre. Grotowski himself went beyond theatre in his search for genuinely transformative rituals that needed no audience.

Artaud would also eventually reject theatre for radio, which provided an alternative and concrete means for exploring the aesthetics of cruelty and so exceeding the physical limitations of space/time. In a recording of 'Pour en finir avec le jugement de dieu' ('To have done with the judgement of god') from 1947/48, Artaud's voice can be heard screeching glossolalia and intoning a bizarre and politically volatile text concerning American imperialism and the power of religious cliché. This combination effected the banning of the piece by the director of the station that had commissioned the work in the first place on the grounds that it was 'inflammatory, obscene and blasphemous' (Barber 1993: 157). In this piece Artaud calls for a reworking of the human body, a body without organs, in other words a self-made body without the hierachical emplacement of organs, a body made not in the image of god and which will liberate man, who can then be retaught to 'dance inside out . . . and that inside out will be his true side out' (*OC* XIII: 79).

Artaud died in March 1948, two months after completing this recording, which became one of his most successfully subversive pieces and which continues to resist aesthetic recuperation. Yet it continues to seed new initiatives in fields such as philosophy, for example Deleuze and Guattari's writings on the 'BwO', and performance, for example the intonation techniques used in the theatre of Robert Wilson, the wild choreographies of Butoh or the apocalyptic dramaturgy of Romeo Castellucci's 'Societas Raffaello Sanzio'. This piece, along with his Vieux-Colombier recital and the two lectures, were perhaps the closest Artaud himself came, outside of his theoretical writings, to indicating what precisely was at stake in a performance based on cruelty and what its 'unique language' would sound like.

Theoretical encounters

Artaud's oeuvre poses some unique problems for criticism and for the organisation of critical material. Suspicious of any particular genre, discourse or aesthetic, Artaud's written works embody the trajectory outlined by Roland Barthes as the passage from work to text, from the conceptual unity of a work to the text considered as 'methodological field' whose 'constitutive movement is that of cutting across' (Barthes 1977: 157). As argued above, Artaud's career as a writer is characterised from the very beginning by this 'cutting across' the boundaries of the genre or form: of poetry, drama, criticism and biography; in manifestos, letters, pamphlets as well as more conventional publications. The Gallimard volumes are testament to his expanded concept of work as an art of traversals.

Any collection of critical material which takes Artaud as its subject must therefore account for the multiplicity and perversity of his enterprise, for the fact that it is an art and a textual practice which cuts across the gaze of the viewer or reader, interrupting it, disorientating it. The function of a collection such as this one must be to maintain a sense of the fluidity of the subject while providing a way through the critical material without losing the reader. But *cruelty* is Artaud's name for an encounter which leaves no category secure. To read Artaud is to realise that we still do not know what reading is, what writing is, what the cinema or theatre is. We are on foreign ground which is constantly slipping beneath our feet. To return to the tracks left in this soil by the generation of writers and intellectuals which followed that of Artaud is not quite a return to the familiar but constitutes one often spectacular route through what at times appears to be impenetrable terrain.

The organisation of this material is therefore necessarily contingent but designed to suggest some of the areas of scholarship that Artaud has affected, destabilised and threatened. The four parts of this collection are not intended to reflect particular disciplines but rather to suggest the ways in which Artaud's challenges have been refracted through a variety of lenses, a multiplicity of forms. So Part I, 'On biography: madness and language', deals with the problems that biography and theory face when dealing with Artaud's written performances of a more *and* less strategic madness. 'Theatre: acts and representations' questions the theatrical frame Artaud chose to encompass many of his aesthetic interventions. It must be in the form of a question since, as Brian Singleton points out, just as Artaud 'theatricalised his life', it is equally the case that he 'loathed the theatre' (Artaud 1989; 2nd edn 2001: xi).[4] 'On writing and fine arts' deals with the convergence of these practices in both Artaud's writings about art and his artworks themselves, and 'Beyond words: on film and radio' suggests the manner in which Artaud sought the breakdown of words in these media.

All critical commentary is pigshit

> The whole literary scene is a pigpen, especially this one . . . Those for whom certain words have a meaning, and certain manners of being; those who are so fussy; those for whom emotions are classifiable, and who quibble over some degree or other of their hilarious classifications; those who still believe in 'terms'; those who brandish whatever ideologies belong to the hierarchies of the times . . . those who still believe in some orientation of the spirit; those

who follow paths, who drop names, who fill books with screaming headlines
. . . are the worst kind of pigs.[5]

Maybe it's not very Artaudian, this collection of academic essays. In defence of
a project like this, one could say that in the absence of beatification this is at least
a start. Anyway, this series of encounters is not intended to exhaust the
possibilities of others and, while something is inevitably lost in the transference
with academic language, there is always the relaunching of an engagement. In
'La Parole soufflée', an essay not represented here but one to which the reader is
strongly recommended, Derrida theorises the process by which commentary
makes a case of unique experiences and thereby destroys the uniqueness of the
experience under scrutiny. He writes that Artaud's 'adventure' is the 'protest itself
against exemplification itself' (Derrida 1967b/1978: 175). It is evidently the case
that although Artaud's topics do not entirely disappear in Derrida's work on
Artaud, they are nonetheless subordinated to Derrida's own concerns.

In this regard Derrida is the paradigmatic case of Artaud commentary. His
essays reveal that, although it is possible to write about the function of language
or representation in Artaud without also talking about evil spirits, food, disease
and the most intimate bodily functions, it is achieved through a process of
elaborate editing and cutting – sculpting Artaud, if not to fit a particular critical
paradigm, then certainly to correspond to the calm syllogisms of academic prose
and to imbricate with its themes. For instance, Derrida's work on Artaud is
characterised by a desire to affirm Artaud as a protodeconstructor when he is
more of a two-headed Heideggerian destroyer – a desire to affirm Artaud as a
writer of and at the limit, but also and conspicuously by a desire not to get his
hands too dirty with Artaud's demonological dramaturgy, his body rages and
syphilitic language.[6]

As the Derrida case suggests, the Artaud of the Academy is often a polite, if
slightly barmy, theorist of the arts. The furious bursts of his writing, the logical
disjunctions and violent changes of direction, the hysterical games become *non-
sequiturs* and *éclats*. The energy and the drama, the wild rhythms, the noise and
the dissonance of Artaud are suffused in a placid academic *legato*. Nevertheless,
the writings that figure here facilitate the perception of these difficult, perhaps
indigestible, things in the work of Artaud. This is at least partly because these
discourses have been conceived in the wake of Artaud. They have been informed
by the risk that he took, the experiments that he made and, to paraphrase
Foucault, they grew out of the soil of his language (Foucault 1972 [1961]: 582).
It is a debt perhaps not clearly acknowledged until now.

Part I

On biography

Madness and language

The first section deals with the crucial question, in relation to Artaud, of whether or not it is possible to separate the life of an artist from their work. Of particular concern is the insistence with which Artaud's periods of illness haunt the construction of his oeuvre and construct it, in some commentaries, as a more or less undifferentiated document of mental disorder. Each of the following texts addresses this in its own way, though only Breton and Bataille ever met Artaud.

1 André Breton with André Parinaud

From *Conversations: The Autobiography of Surrealism**

André Breton, the organiser and chief strategist of the surrealist group in Paris in the 1920s, had a long and difficult relationship with Artaud. Always suspicious of the products of genuine madness, however artfully constructed, he felt uneasy about Artaud's very visible and very eccentric persona. He was also critical of Artaud's various theatrical experiments, and he included Artaud's various public readings in this category of work, in particular Artaud's benefit evening at the Vieux-Colombier theatre after Artaud's return to Paris from the asylum at Rodez in 1947. Breton responded to the organisers of the event by reading a brief 'Homage to Antonin Artaud', which we reproduce here (in Chapter 2). It must be placed in the context of the frequent conflicts the two had had since the mid-1920s, when Breton banished Artaud among others from the company of the surrealists, describing him in the 'Second Manifesto of Surrealism' (1930) as 'an actor looking for lucre and notoriety' and by the words: 'It is M. Artaud, whom I will always see in my mind's eye flanked by two cops, at the door of the Alfred Jarry Theatre, sicking twenty others on the only friends he admitted having as lately as the night before, having previously negotiated their arrests with the commissariat' (Breton 1969: 130, 131). Breton also conducted a series of interviews with André Parinaud for Radiodiffusion Français between 1947 and 1952, which were broadcast from March to June 1952. In one of the later interviews, parts of which are reproduced here, Breton speaks openly about his relationship with Artaud in the surrealist years.

AB: Very little time had passed since Antonin Artaud had joined us, but no one had put all his abilities, which were considerable, so spontaneously in the service of the surrealist cause as he had. In the past his great reference – in this he would have agreed with Eluard – was Baudelaire; but if Eluard took his inspiration from 'The fine ship', Artaud much more darkly savoured 'The murderer's wine'. Perhaps he was at even greater odds with life than the rest of us were. He was very handsome back then, and when he moved he dragged behind him a gothic landscape pierced throughout by lightning. He was possessed by a kind of fury that spared no human institution, but that

occasionally dissolved into laughter containing all the defiance of youth. Be
that as it may, his fury, by its astonishing power of contagion, profoundly
affected the surrealist procedure. It enjoined the lot of us truly to take every
risk to attack, *without restraint*, what we couldn't abide.

AP: And how was this will to combat expressed? Were you in complete
agreement over it?

AB: The tone of various individual or collective texts published during the year
1925 bears witness to a hardening in our positions. A 'Bureau of Surrealist
Research' was opened at 15 rue de Grenelle, its initial aim being to collect
every communication touching on the forms that the mind's unconscious
activity was liable to take. Given the number of busybodies and intruders
who besieged it, we were soon forced to close its doors to the public. Artaud,
who took over running the bureau from Francis Gérard, strove to make it a
centre for 'rehabilitating' life. On the walls hung several of De Chirico's
early paintings, which enjoyed an unparalleled prestige in our eyes, along
with casts of women's bodies. It wasn't rare to see Valéry and Léon-Paul
Fargue in that room, among others who weren't scared away by subversive
activities.

Under Artaud's influence, collective texts of great violence were published
at the time. Whereas the 'surrealist stickers' [*papillons*: literally, butterflies]
that had flown two or three months earlier from the Bureau of Research still
seemed to hesitate as to the best route to take (poetry, dreams, humour) and,
all things considered, were highly inoffensive, these collective texts were
suddenly filled with an insurrectional ardour. This was the case with the
'Declaration of January 27, 1925', with the one called 'Open the Prisons!
Disband the Army!' with addresses 'to the Pope' and 'to the Dalai lama', and
with letters 'to the rectors of European universities', 'to the Buddhist
schools', or 'to the heads of insane asylums'. Their language had been
stripped of all ornaments; it eschewed the 'wave of dreams' that Aragon had
spoken of;[1] it meant to be sharp and gleaming, but gleaming like a weapon.
I love these texts, in particular the ones that most strongly bear Artaud's
imprint. Once again, I'm judging by his eventual destiny, the large measure
of suffering behind his almost total refusal – which was also ours, but which
he formulated more aptly and more heatedly than anyone.

Still . . . if I completely shared in the spirit behind these texts – moreover,
they were the fruit of long discussions between several of us – and if I had
few reservations as to their content, I soon began to worry about the
atmosphere they were creating. The very fact of their rapid succession, and
the fact that this highly polemical activity necessarily tended to subordinate
all the others, gave me the impression that, without our quite realising it, we
had been seized by frenzy, and that the air had rarefied around us. Looking
at the situation more closely today, I better understand my resistance, which
at the time remained obscure. That half-libertarian, half-mystical path was
not really mine, and I came to see it as more of a dead end (I wasn't the only

one). The space that Artaud led me into always strikes me as abstract, a hall of mirrors. For me, there's always something 'verbal' about it, even if that verb is very noble, very beautiful. It's a place of lacunae and ellipses in which, personally, I lose all my means of communication with the innumerable things that, despite everything, give me pleasure and bind me to this earth. I forget too easily that surrealism has had an enormous capacity for love, and that what it violently condemned were precisely the things that impaired love.

Finally, I distrusted a certain fever pitch that Artaud was definitely trying to reach – just as Desnos must have been trying to reach it on another level. I felt it entailed an expenditure of energy that we would not subsequently be able to offset. In other words, I saw all too clearly how the machine was running full steam ahead, but not how it could keep fuelling itself . . .

AP: This no doubt explains the abrupt change in course of *La Révolution surréaliste*, which you took over at that moment.

AB: Yes, it was for those reasons – and a few others – that, not without great misgivings, I put a stop to the experiments Artaud was initiating and decided to assume the editorship of *La Révolution surréaliste* myself. In the rather confused text in which I announced this – where it's clear that I was holding back from saying certain things – I tried with uneven success to explain that we still wanted very much to 'do away with the ancien régime of the mind', but that, in order to do this, it was not enough to try to 'intimidate the world by banging it over the head with brutal demands'. I recommended returning to earlier positions – in other words, essentially and above all, that we restore language's effervescence, as we had done with automatic writing and the sleeping fits – and counting blindly on the eventual results.

2   André Breton

'Homage to Antonin Artaud'*

Ladies and gentlemen,

It is somewhat reluctantly that I have responded to the appeal of the organisers of tonight's event. Were it not for the pressing moral obligation to be among them in order to pay homage to a most exceptional individual and to celebrate the return of an especially dear friend to less horrific living conditions, I would have preferred not to be called upon to deliver this preamble. I have only been back in Paris a short while and I was away too long to know whether I am already once more attuned to this city, whether I am fully aware of all the emotional currents that flow through it, whether I will immediately be able to find the right *pitch*. Above all, I confess that I am somewhat troubled by this new tendency which I am discovering, to track with a circus spotlight – or to tolerate as much – some of those intellectual investigations that we used to believe were best conducted in twilight.

Unless we let our own essence dissolve within the norm, today more unacceptable, more revolting than ever, unless we allow a series of individual defections to create the impression of a collective spiritual bankruptcy that, after so many other failures, will inflate the arrogance of what we have despised and loathed, it is my opinion that we must react in an implacable fashion. Make no mistake, it is not in the limelight that in 1946 the movement that has been trying and is, I hope, still *genuinely* trying to find itself under the name of surrealism will come into its own. The evil spell cast upon the conditions to which thought and action are presently subjected on a universal scale, and the threat of annihilation hanging over the world, are such that we can feel but pity for those who persist in begging for public recognition or in making retrospective claims to a dubious fame. Especially in view of the events of these past few years let me add that I find laughable any kind of so-called engagement that falls short of this indivisible threefold objective to transform the world, to change life, to reshape the human mind.

Antonin Artaud, recklessly and on his own, has gone farther in that direction than anyone else today, and yet my previous remarks preclude my commenting openly on his most tragic message as well as my recounting his exceptionally painful social experience. If I were to do so, it seems that I would be betraying the very cause that is common to us both, that I would be disclosing sacred stakes to all and sundry. More than twenty years have elapsed, but I can still feel that burst of impossible hope that gave a few of us purpose and lifted us above ourselves. I am thinking of all that possessed us at that time, of that torrent that propelled us ahead of ourselves as its cascading laughter swept aside all the opposition with which we met. Each time I happen to recall – nostalgically – the surrealist rebellion as expressed in its original purity and intransigence, it is the personality of Antonin Artaud that stands out in its dark magnificence, it is a certain intonation in his voice that injects specks of gold into his whispering voice. And it is, as well, *Le Pèse-nerfs* (*The Nerve-scale*), *L'Ombilic des limbes* (*The Umbilicus of Limbo*), and that third issue of *La Révolution surréaliste*, for which he was solely responsible and which, among all other issues, is the one that reaches the highest phosphorescent point: reading it always makes me feel what true life is like by showing me man braving lightning itself as he ascends the highest peaks. Antonin Artaud: I do not have to account in his stead for what he has experienced nor for what he has suffered. I do not wish to cast the blame upon any particular individual, least of all on a man who is known to some of us and who, by all accounts, has been very understanding and has shown great compassion toward Artaud. The clinical methods about which our friend may have cause to complain must be ascribed to an institution that we will never cease to denounce as a barbaric anachronism, the very existence of which – with its potential for concentration camps and torture chambers – is in itself a decisive indictment against so-called civilisation as we know it today.

Let us not forget that beneath skies other than the empty sky of Europe, the constantly inspired voice of Antonin Artaud would have been heard with the utmost deference, that it would likely have led the community quite far (I am thinking particularly of the welcome and the status given to extraordinary seers of his calibre by various Indian communities). I am still too far removed from the old rationalism that we decried when we were young to dismiss extraordinary accounts under the pretext that common sense goes against them. This reassurance I want to impart to Antonin Artaud himself when I see how distressed he is, because my recollections of what happened during the more or less atrocious decade we have just experienced do not exactly corroborate his own. I know that Antonin Artaud *saw*, the way Rimbaud, as well as Novalis and Arnim before him, had spoken of *seeing*. It is of little consequence, ever since the publication of *Aurélia*, that what was *seen* this way does not coincide with what is *objectively visible*. The real tragedy is that the society to which we are less and less honoured to belong persists in making it an inexpiable crime to have gone over to the *other side of the looking glass*. In the name of everything that is more than ever close to my heart, I cheer the return to freedom of Antonin Artaud in a world where freedom itself must be reinvented. Beyond all the mundane denials, I place all my faith in Antonin Artaud, that man of prodigies. I salute Antonin Artaud for his passionate, heroic negation of everything that causes us to be dead while alive.

1946

3   Georges Bataille

From 'Surrealism from day to day'*

Another difficult and transgressive voice from the surrealist period is that of writer and surrealist ethnographer, Georges Bataille. Bataille's sometimes painful reflections of the circumstances in which he encountered Artaud, recorded in his journals from the surrealist period, comprise just a few pages of commentary on Artaud from one of the very few who can be said to be in any way a fellow traveller with Artaud – not simply because he was expelled from the group at the same time, but because his theoretical writings echo some of Artaud's concerns. Bataille was determined to explore the limit of his culture through tracking extreme behaviours and practices in other cultures. His work in *Inner Experience* and *Eroticism* provides an important discursive frame for considering some of Artaud's considerably less systematic formulations about madness and the limit of the social and about the place of theatre in the world. In Bataille's opus the notion of transgression can be seen as a key to explicating some of Artaud's strategies.

Bataille uses this idea to develop a social analysis, later extended by Foucault, which is based on the exclusions at the heart of the social. The function of taboo, as Freud conceived it, was that it guaranteed civilisation through the incest prohibition, in his story of the primal hordes. In Bataille it is transgression which brings taboo or excluded elements of the system into focus: 'transgression does not deny the taboo, but transcends it and completes it' (Bataille 1987: 64–5).

For Bataille transgression participates in the structure of social life as much as taboo does in redistributing the boundaries around excluded behaviours, practices and representations. This involves testing the limits, violating protocols and established genres, inserting differences, constructing hybrids. It does not deny the rule of law, but affirms it through the denial of the absolute sovereignty of taboo. For Artaud the theatre should be a place where excluded behaviours can be performed and taboos violated. Perhaps the theatre of cruelty is exactly what Bataille had in mind with the notion of transgression. In any event, these brief observations from Bataille give no sense of the proximity of their thinking. One insight, however, is telling. In describing his reaction to reading Artaud's *Letters from Rodez*, Bataille says: 'The unique thing about these writings is their shock, the violent shaking of ordinary boundaries, the cruel lyricism that cuts short its own effects, not tolerating even the very thing it is so clearly expressing' (Bataille 1987: 45). Here the sense of Artaud's doubling of the text, the sense of a need for two complete readings of Artaud's delirious prose, is acute and the economy of its expression does not diminish its significance as a reading of Artaud's writing from Rodez.

Section 7. Antonin Artaud

I soon got to know Antonin Artaud to *some extent*. I met him in a brasserie in rue Pigalle with Dr Fraenkel.[1] He was handsome, dark and emaciated. He had some money, for he worked in the theatre, but he still looked half-starved. He didn't laugh, was never puerile and although he didn't say very much, there was something emotionally eloquent in his rather grave silence and terrible edginess. He was calm; this mute eloquence was not convulsive but, on the contrary, sad, dejected, and it gnawed away inside him. He looked like a caged bird of prey with dusty plumage which had been apprehended at the very moment it was about to take flight, and had remained fixed in this posture. I have said that he was silent. It must be said that Fraenkel and I were just about the least loquacious people in the world, and perhaps it was contagious. In any event, it did not encourage conversation.

Artaud was consulting Fraenkel about his nervous complaints. He was in pain and asked for drugs, and Fraenkel was trying to make his life bearable. The two of them had a private consultation. Then no conversation followed. So Artaud and I knew each other fairly well without ever having spoken.

One evening, about ten years later, I suddenly came across him at the corner of rue Madame and rue de Vaugirard. He gripped my hand energetically. It was at the time when I was involved in trying to set up political activity. He told me point-blank: 'I know you are doing important things. Believe me: we need to create a Mexican fascism'! He went on his way without insisting.

The incident gave me a rather disagreeable feeling, but only partly: he frightened me, but not without giving me a strange feeling of sympathy.

A few years before I had attended a lecture he gave at the Sorbonne (without seeking him out afterwards). He talked about theatrical art, and in the state of half-somnolence in which I listened I became aware that he had suddenly risen: I understood what he was saying, he had resolved to personify the state of mind of Thyestes when he realised he had devoured his own children. Before an auditorium packed with the bourgeoisie (there were hardly any students), he grasped his stomach and let out the most inhuman sound that has ever come from a man's throat: it created the sort of disquiet that would have been felt if a dear friend had suddenly become delirious. It was awful (perhaps the more so for being only *acted out*).

In time I learned what happened during his trip to Ireland, which was followed by his internment. I could have said that I did not like him . . . and had the feeling that someone was walking over my grave. I felt sad at heart, and preferred not to think about it.

At the beginning of October 1943 I received an enigmatic and rather crude letter. It arrived at Vézelay at a time when I was both unhappy and cheerful, and today leaves me with a memory of anguish and marvel. I saw the signature was that of Antonin Artaud, whom I barely knew, as you have seen. It had been written at Rodez, where he had read *L'Expérience intérieure*, which had been published at the beginning of the year. The letter was more than half-mad: it was about the cane and manuscript of St Patrick (his delirium on his return from Ireland was all about St Patrick). This manuscript, which would change the world, had vanished. But he had written to me because his reading of *L'Expérience intérieure* had shown him that I needed to be converted, that I must return to God. He had to warn me . . .

I am sorry I no longer have this letter. I sent it to someone who was working on a collection of Artaud's letters and had asked me if I had any documents of his. I had loaned my letter despite there being little likelihood of publication . . . I simply told him what I thought: it was obviously the letter of a madman. But I cannot with absolute precision recall who it was who had asked me for it – it was a long time ago – and the only person I mentioned it to said he had never seen it. I regret it. I was very affected when I received it. I am sorry I have to leave its contents vague. I cannot even exactly state whether what I have reported it as saying about St Patrick is accurate. It would be amazing if I had really distorted it, but memory, even when it has the object at hand, is always a little unstable and fleeting. The entreaty to become pious, which was addressed to me in moving – even urgent – terms, has remained clearly in my mind.

Section 8. Anticipation of the shipwreck

I caught sight of Artaud on the terrace of the Deux Magots after his return from Rodez. He did not recognise me and I did not seek to make myself known: he was in such a state of decay it was frightening: he looked like one of the oldest men I had ever seen. I have been unable to read some of the writing that was published at that time without a feeling of poignancy. And though I think that what happened was the best that could be done in the circumstances, it was still for me, in spite of everything, something atrocious – atrocious and inevitable. A little earlier, Henri Parisot had shown me one day a long, indignant and grandiloquent telegram from Dr Ferdière forbidding the publication of the documents under the title *Letters from Rodez*. Parisot did not have words black enough to denounce the attitude of the director of the Rodez asylum. I found myself in agreement: it was necessary to go ahead – the more so in that publication of the book would yield a little money that would help the poor fellow to live. But how could one not be worried, as a rule, about the idea of publishing writings by a madman who might be cured, when these writings would always bear witness to his madness? One might think that, in this case, Artaud was beyond the categories of reason and madness. But is anything ever so clear? Would forgetfulness not be one of the conditions for a lasting cure? In any event, the abuse generally heaped upon Dr Ferdière seems to me unwarranted. Where Antonin Artaud himself was concerned, it is easy to understand: Ferdière had cared for him, resorting to electric shock treatment, and the patient often had reason to disagree with his doctor's decisions. But were Artaud's friends to believe him about something that happened when he was sick? I used to know Ferdière, and I can only too easily imagine him exasperating his patients in spite of himself. He is a very kind person, as secret anarchists often are, often drowning in arrogant verbalism, something of a chatterbox, and finally getting on one's nerves. He must have done his best, and if he might be criticised for applying an unsuitable treatment (but no one else will ever know; he alone would be able to say, and he would not have done what he thought inappropriate), it is certain that he greatly improved Antonin Artaud's condition. These suffocating writings, which are like the last gleams of the setting of shipwrecked surrealism (and have not ceased to bear witness to the exorbitant and stupendous aspect of the movement), would not, perhaps, have seen the light of day without Ferdière, in spite of the unreasonable telegram I have mentioned.

The unique thing about these writings is their shock, the violent shaking of ordinary boundaries, the cruel lyricism that cuts short its own effects, not tolerating even the very thing it is so clearly expressing. Maurice Blanchot has quoted him, in speaking of himself (1946): 'I began in literature by writing books in order to say that I could write nothing at all; it was when I had something to say or write that my thought most refused me. I never had ideas, and two very short books, each of seventy pages, turned on this profound (ingrained and endemic) absence of all ideas.' Commenting on these lines, Maurice Blanchot wrote: 'It is difficult to see what it would be proper to add to such words, for they have the frankness of the knife and surpass in clairvoyance anything a writer could ever write about himself, showing what a lucid mind it is which, in order to become free, undergoes the proof of the Marvellous.' For me, this last phrase by Maurice Blanchot seems to be the precise epilogue to the surrealist adventure as a whole, considered from the moment it falteringly articulated its ambitions. I think that Maurice Blanchot is right to use these last words to implicate the basic principle of a movement which has most often avoided the reef and the spectacular shipwreck that the last years of Antonin Artaud's life show us in a glimmer of disaster.

Besides, Artaud's excitement was no less significant at the dawn than it was, I believe, in the twilight of the surrealist evening. In any case, to my knowledge it was Antonin Artaud who drafted the essential part of the Declaration of 27 January 1925, which was not, perhaps, the most remarkable expression of developing surrealism, but retains a special place for me because it was the first text communicated to me (by Leiris, on his return from the South, in the circumstances I mentioned) and the occasion for an accord I conceived without reserve and which, in truth, was due to a misunderstanding.

Maurice Nadeau reproduces this Declaration in the _Surrealist Documents_, and I will quote the second paragraph: 'Surrealism is not a new or an easier means of expression, nor even a metaphysic of poetry; it is a means towards the total liberation of the mind and _all that resembles it_.' The ninth paragraph adds: '[Surrealism] is a cry of the mind which turns back on itself and is determined desperately to tear off its shackles.'

I read this Declaration in a café, in a greatly disordered and lethargic state of mind in which I was – just about – _surviving_. Reading it again today, I feel the same; I feel as though I misread it as 'of the mind which turns *against* itself'. Even forewarned, I fell into the trap, so strong has my hatred remained – not only of the intelligence and reason but of the 'mind'; also of the capital entity opposing its clouds to what is inextricably filthy. In the same way, I read 'liberation of the mind' as if it were a question of a 'deliverance from evil'! Besides, perhaps I was not entirely deceived, or only partly, and this is why I have spoken fairly about Artaud who, if he wrote what preceded in 1925, wrote in 1946: '. . . and the garlic mayonnaise contemplates you, mind, and you contemplate your garlic mayonnaise: And finally let's say shit to infinity! . . . ' But in the end it is as open-ended, as empty, and equal to the sound which resolutely fades away and can finally be heard no longer.

4 Sylvère Lotringer

From an interview with Jacques Latrémolière*

This sensational interview[1] suggests the intensity of the 'Artaud affair' that flared up after he returned to Paris in 1946, complaining about the brutal treatment he had received at the asylum of Paraire in Rodez. He had been transferred from Ville-Evrard, in the Occupied Zone, and arrived in an emaciated state in February 1943. Rodez proved a more humane institution in some ways, given the context of the war, but Artaud still had to endure 51 electro-shock treatments between June 1943 and June 1944. He later publicly denounced this treatment and the director of the asylum, Gaston Ferdière. The affair involved his family, friends, his publisher Gallimard and his psychiatrists in a very bitter and public debate, which has resulted in the suspension of the publication of the last volumes of his *Oeuvres Complètes* due to litigation.

The interview took place in July 1983 at the home of Dr Jacques Latrémolière in Figeac, a small town in southern France. Latrémolière, the psychiatrist responsible for administering the shock treatments, died a few years later.

In general terms it constitutes a debate between a scholar (Lotringer) and a psychiatrist (Latrémolière) about the relative merits of humanist epistemology versus empiricist truth, and *centres*, of course, on the case of Artaud. The psychiatrist claims to have reinvented Artaud through electro-shock therapy and further that Artaud's work is of no value because he was 'no longer viable' and 'couldn't take care of himself'. Lotringer counters with assertions of the value of different types of experience and points out the influence of Artaud's ideas for contemporary theatre and performance. The encounter raises the epistemological questions to which Artaud always returned: how do we think we know things? with what certainty and authority? what guarantees our sanity? why is it important to think otherwise? It also reveals much of what Artaud was trying to make visible in his work, not just about the carceral conditions of psychiatric institutions, but the broader bad faith of a society which maintains them. The arguments expressed by Lotringer in this piece, regarding the importance of a particular kind of critical attention in reading Artaud's texts, viewing the drawings and cinema performances and listening to his radio experiments and not simply reading the madness of Artaud as the determining trait of his work, are essential considerations in regard to the reception of that work. Their passionate framing in these exchanges gives an insight into the fierce loyalties that Artaud seems so frequently to provoke.

In his text 'Van Gogh, the man suicided by society' (1947) Artaud attacks psychiatry in general and a certain 'Dr L.' in particular:

> And I do not believe that the rule of the confirmed erotomania of psychiatrists admits of a single exception. I know one who objected, a few years ago, to the idea of my accusing wholesale the whole gang of high flying scoundrels and patented quacks to which he belonged. I, Mr Artaud, am not an erotomaniac, he told me, and I defy you to show me a single piece of evidence on which you can base your accusation.
>
> As evidence, Dr L., I need only show yourself, you bear the stigma on your mug, you rotten bastard. You have the puss of someone who inserts his sexual prey under his tongue and then turns it over like an almond as a way of showing contempt for it.

As Lotringer has argued elsewhere, Latrémolière 'wasted no time identifying himself as the object of the poet's wrath: "I am this Doctor L., and this address constitutes the last personal message I received from Artaud alive; those he wrote in Rodez, of course, were quite different."' Sadly, as Lotringer also points out, the real Dr L. is none other than Dr Jacques Lacan, who had treated Artaud in 1938 and who had made use of erotomania in his study of paranoia.[2]

LATRÉMOLIÈRE: I have to tell you that when you called me to set up this meeting I wasn't very enthusiastic about it. Raising the issue of Artaud's life again, thirty years on, seems slightly ludicrous to me.

LOTRINGER: You were personally in charge of Antonin Artaud throughout his stay at the asylum at Rodez, isn't that right?

LATRÉMOLIÈRE: I worked with Dr Ferdière, the director of the asylum. I was Artaud's friend for two years. Have you read the article I wrote about all that?[3] In it I said just about everything I had to say about Artaud at the time and since then I've been thinking of other things. The studies of Artaud seem to be multiplying, which is something I find regrettable. Artaud had no message to communicate, never had. He was a distinguished paranoiac with absolutely extraordinary delusions of grandeur and persecution.

LOTRINGER: You were Artaud's friend . . .

LATRÉMOLIÈRE: His friends were those he could take advantage of and he turned to them every time he needed opium. We never gave him any, but he certainly asked for it. We were his friends, but the moment we disappeared from view we became his enemies and that happened to a lot of us. I consider his written work as a kind of scream, a scream of horror from a man who had no sense. No sense at all of others. He placed himself at the centre of the world. It was just him and the little birds.

LOTRINGER: At least there were the little birds.

LATRÉMOLIÈRE: Which is better than nothing, but, in any case, I find the distinction attributed to him a little exaggerated.

LOTRINGER: But isn't it precisely the horror at the heart of paranoia that makes what he says so important? What he felt, which caused him to write in the way he did, as well as what he actually wrote, which caused such a shock . . .

LATRÉMOLIÈRE: How was it possible that he could feel all these different things at almost the same time? It didn't come from the inner depths of himself. I myself saw him screaming, I heard him. Not screaming against me, never. He only yelled at me after he had left Rodez, right? So I don't think people will find anything in Artaud's work. It won't advance civilisation. Just the opposite. . . . Those shouts behind the curtain, that terrible evening that was held in Paris . . .[4] We heard him scream there, too. He had lost his notes and yet continued to vociferate. Screaming was all he could do and I believe that someone who can't control himself has nothing to offer anyone else. I have his complete works here. I have the first editions of his works. He gave them to me . . . and I read them bit by bit. Well, when you read the totality of what he says, you see that there is very little that's intelligible. It contributes nothing to civilisation. Nothing at all.

LOTRINGER: Do you really think that civilisation makes very much sense in itself? I link Artaud with Dada. They belong in the same period in history: the first great slaughter . . .

LATRÉMOLIÈRE: Well, Artaud was a surrealist.

LOTRINGER: Of course, but his sensibility seems to me much more chaotic and anarchistic, more out of control, like the Dadaists. Artaud for me is a resonance of that great rupture in civilisation which was Dada. If you can give the name civilisation to that global craze for annihilation . . . So Artaud may well be paranoiac, narcissistic, megalomaniacal, whatever you want, but that also gives him a certain perception of things. Some would say an inhuman perception.

LATRÉMOLIÈRE: If he is inhuman, it is truly that he has nothing to contribute to humans.

LOTRINGER: We are perhaps not being sufficiently aware of the inhumanity of the kind of civilisation that we are in the process of constructing.

LATRÉMOLIÈRE: And you imagine that he, Artaud, was sensitive to this civilisation? On that score I can guarantee you that he was not. Not at all. He was only interested in himself. The whole time I knew him he was the Christ, the centre of the world. So don't tell me that he has advanced humanity when the opposite is the case.

LOTRINGER: What was it like to be Artaud's friend?

LATRÉMOLIÈRE: Oh, we had conversations that went on for hours . . . about God. And God only knows, his ideas about religion were debatable. It was a kind of myth for him, centred on himself.

LOTRINGER: Did Artaud think he had a privileged relationship with God?

LATRÉMOLIÈRE: Privileged? He was the one who was going to take power before the final appearance of God on this earth. So you understand why I laugh when people talk about his message. There's nothing there at all. It's hollow, like this [he knocks on the table] and, besides, it's unintelligible. How many people read him? No one. No one reads him except a few intellectuals here and there.

LOTRINGER: His work has had an enormous influence on our culture. All the great theatre directors of the last twenty years – Jerzy Grotowski, Peter Brook, the Living Theatre – from all over the world: Poland, the UK, the USA, all see Artaud as a seminal figure.

LATRÉMOLIÈRE: Listen, don't talk about the theatre. He never had any theatrical success. Everything he wrote for the theatre was a flop. And don't try to tell me that Artaud's ideas in *The Theatre and its Double* have any importance whatsoever. It's all about the plague. The proof is that the practical applications were a failure. So I'm sorry . . . when something weird appears, it always gets taken up.

LOTRINGER: It's no accident that everything important in modern art since the beginning of the twentieth century turned to primitive societies, just as Artaud did. Our civilisation was already losing its substantiality, everything was appearing and disappearing again at incredible speed. There was a strong sense that people needed to reconnect with the force of the traditional, to get back to our roots in the earth and to rediscover serious rituals. That is what Artaud's theatre is about and that is what drew him to Mexico and to Ireland. And you find that weird? I see it as a complete refusal to compromise.

LATRÉMOLIÈRE: In everyday life we don't mind making compromises. But you don't have to tell me stories. I knew him personally. He came to our place and began to read out loud from books. He was good at that, as you'd expect from a man of the theatre, but no more than that. He was wrapped up in himself.

LOTRINGER: Perhaps as a result of being wrapped up in yourself, there comes a time when you become more open to things.

LATRÉMOLIÈRE: Listen, I'm sorry but I have practised psychiatry for many years and I'm telling you that what you are saying is absurd. The more wrapped up in oneself a person is, the less open they are to others. They don't listen to others and they can no longer love others. That's why Artaud was trashed. He was no longer capable of having a proper relationship with anyone. He was no longer sociable. And if we treated him – something for which we have been criticised – it was to protect him from himself. And we saw him come around. Eventually he could write and draw and talk with us again. It was us who gave him that. All my life I'll remember my friend Ferdière admitting to me, 'If I'd known what was to come, I'd never have let him leave Rodez. I regret it *infinitely*' . . .

LOTRINGER: It allowed him to write piles of important texts.

LATRÉMOLIÈRE: Come on! He wrote some letters to a few people. So what? One letter to Hitler and there you are.

LOTRINGER: When you read Artaud's texts, don't you ever try to forget the man you knew? To read them like you would read Racine, for example . . .

LATRÉMOLIÈRE: Oh no, in his texts he speaks to me. He doesn't say much but at least he speaks to me.

LOTRINGER: And what does he say?

LATRÉMOLIÈRE: Oh! Images . . . he throws images around. It's of no value. In 30 or 50 years I'm convinced that no one will talk about him any more.

LOTRINGER: Then what is the value of this thing called literature? Why do people wrack their brains to write and not just put things simply?

LATRÉMOLIÈRE: Because they hope to be able to make money.

LOTRINGER: Why do we teach these things at school, if people only write to make money or because they are a bit weird?

LATRÉMOLIÈRE: Which people? Artaud is clearly not taught at school.

LOTRINGER: I teach him at Columbia University and I'm not the only one.

LATRÉMOLIÈRE: OK, well, I feel sorry for your students, because that will not make them happy in life. It won't empower them. It will leave them crawling.

LOTRINGER: So why is his work published? Maybe the world has gone a bit mad to allow such stuff to be published in an esteemed publishing house like Gallimard.

LATRÉMOLIÈRE: [silence] I didn't say there wasn't anything in it. I said it wouldn't leave any trace.

LOTRINGER: Who will leave a trace? Which writer of Artaud's generation will remain?

LATRÉMOLIÈRE: I don't do literature for fun. I'm hoping to find an essential form of civilisation. That's all.

LOTRINGER: In literature?

LATRÉMOLIÈRE: No, in life! I didn't have a literary experience with Artaud, I had a life experience with him. I couldn't care less about the worth of his texts and in any case, as I've said before, I don't think they will be remembered for long. He will sink without a trace.

LOTRINGER: When a mad person writes and that writing is read, it becomes literature. What are we going to do with this genre of literature? Why should we read it . . . why should we not read it? What is this if not culture?

LATRÉMOLIÈRE: Really Artaud will be forgotten very quickly. [. . .] You know, for a psychiatrist, when you see the root of the problem, the base of the problem . . . the patient's habits of thought, which you know to be paranoiac or delirious, the doctor doesn't react . . . You don't judge a man on first impressions, but on their whole attitude. I was obliged to pass judgement on Artaud in order to treat him.

LOTRINGER: Why is it necessary to judge people?

LATRÉMOLIÈRE: You judge people in order to be able to return them to normal. It's the role of a doctor to return them to normal. To allow them to live in a milieu outside the clinic without embarrassing anyone. OK? But him, I tell you, Ferdière bitterly regretted letting him go. He would have kept him three or four years longer but he couldn't . . . To think he was entrusted to a doctor who gave him the keys to the clinic, so he could come and go when he pleased. It's curious to say the very least.

LOTRINGER: This happened when he went back to Paris [in 1946] . . .

LATRÉMOLIÈRE: Yes, at Ville-Evrard.[5] He had a key to the clinic and a room a little bit set back from it. It is for this reason, moreover, that he died alone.

LOTRINGER: You mean that Artaud should not have been allowed to go free.

LATRÉMOLIÈRE: Basically, yes. Ferdière demanded that he be kept under surveillance.

LOTRINGER: Why? Was he afraid that Artaud would commit suicide?

LATRÉMOLIÈRE: No, no, no, not at all. He was afraid that he'd do stupid things. That he'd do whatever he wanted. After he'd left Rodez, he'd go to the cathedral and fall to his knees in the middle of the aisle and make these bizarre gestures like this . . .

LOTRINGER: Frankly, Artaud could have crawled along the sidewalk in New York and no one would have taken the slightest notice . . . and anyway there has to be a society which is sufficiently open not to be embarrassed or menaced whenever someone shaves their head or changes their mind or screams out loud. And we are talking about what society is because it seems that the problem with Artaud is that he presents a danger to society.

LATRÉMOLIÈRE: He was no longer viable you see. He was not fit. He really should have stayed with us. I protected society from him.

LOTRINGER: But why? What were you afraid of?

LATRÉMOLIÈRE: That he'd do stupid things.

LOTRINGER: What kind of stupid thing can place society in danger?

LATRÉMOLIÈRE: You had to be there. Then you wouldn't ask this question. He walked up and down the corridor making noises, 'Pfff! Pfff! Pfff!' He spat on the ground at the demons that were chasing him . . . So please don't exaggerate! To my wife, whenever he crossed her path, he would greet her very softly and then make his noises, 'Pfff! Pfff! Pfff!', because the wives of his friends were demons for him.

LOTRINGER: So what does this mean for you, this period of four years in your life?

LATRÉMOLIÈRE: Four years, of which three were with Artaud. [. . .] Well, on the one hand it wouldn't have meant anything, if there hadn't been so much noise about it. He was a patient like any other . . . On the other, if you really want to know what it represents for me: it gave me the idea of the normal man. I mean the man who is capable of living in society.

LOTRINGER: Wasn't Artaud capable of living in society?

LATRÉMOLIÈRE: No. If he hadn't been thrown back into it, he would have lived a lot longer.

5 Gilles Deleuze

'Thirteenth series of the schizophrenic and the little girl'*

To chart the parallel trajectories of Artaud's thought and the work of Gilles Deleuze prior to, during and after his collaborations with Felix Guattari, one would need to examine four central texts by Gilles Deleuze: 'Pour en finir avec le jugement' from 1993,[1] the earlier *Logique du sens*, and Deleuze's work with Felix Guattari in the two volumes of *Capitalisme et schizophrénie*. This controversial text on Artaud's 'madness' – which has also been published under the title 'The schizophrenic and language: surface and depths in Lewis Carroll and Antonin Artaud' (Deleuze 1979) – caused something of a furore in France in the late 1960s (see below). In it, Deleuze tries to track the language of schizophrenia in analysing a text by Artaud which purports to be a translation of Lewis Carroll's poem 'Jabberwocky' and examines the specifics of Artaud's language in search of a paradigm of schizophrenic writing. Deleuze deploys this encounter between Artaud and Carroll as a paradigm for the logic of sense, that sense only makes sense in relation to 'non-sense' and that it participates in a geographical play of depths and surfaces that 'non-sense' can never master, confined as it is to the depths. This essay is important, as it raises the question (central to Artaud studies) of madness and the work – how can a schizophrenic be an artist, when they are 'out of control'? What is the status of art that risks nonsense, etc.? It does so in terms which affirm the specificity of each experience (artistic breakthrough and psychic collapse), but attempts to account for more than the blank paradox of the co-existence of madness and literature, for example. Deleuze tries to explain how the mad text functions and attempts to reveal the inner logic of Artaud's madness in an engagement *with*, rather than a rejection *of*, this kind of 'outsider' textuality.

Paule Thévenin, the editor of the Gallimard edition of Artaud's *Oeuvres Complètes* and one of his closest confidants at the time of his death, has written an extensive critique of this essay (Thévenin 1969: 35–44). In it she points out that Deleuze reads Carroll's text as exploring the surface terrain of sense, while Artaud is confined to the depths of schizophrenia, and suggests that Artaud had already pulled the rug from under Deleuze's feet by not translating Carroll but rather appropriating him. Thévenin later relented somewhat and, in the light of Deleuze's subsequent engagements with Artaud's ideas, described this polemic as 'a little bit exaggerated' (Thévenin 1993: 189).

In his later work with Guattari, Deleuze is conspicuously less judgemental in his approach to the question of Artaud's schizophrenia. In the two volumes of *Capitalisme et schizophrénie* they actively romanticise this experience and systematically chart the territories that Artaud opened up beyond sense and beyond the life of the good citizen.[2] Deleuze's late work, in the essays collected in *Critique et clinique*, imbricates with that of Artaud in the active struggle to unseat judgement, including the judgement he once made in relation to Artaud and the logic of sense, and to put judgement itself *en procès*. They both identify its traces, for Artaud in the history and organisation of the human body, and for Deleuze in the history of philosophy. Artaud's cruelty, as he says at the end of 'To have done with the judgement of God', would redesign the body as a 'body without organs', a favourite phrase of Deleuze and Guattari, and teach it to 'dance inside out'. Deleuze channels Artaud's de-sublimated rage into an alternative version of the possibility of consciousness as a 'making exist' rather than a passing judgement on what already exists. For both Deleuze and Artaud, judgement designates more than a limit on creative power, but rather a negation of the creative disposition. Their work shares a 'slash and burn' approach to literary and philosophical history, clearing a path towards this disposition, this figure of vitality, in the name of Artaud's cruelty and Deleuze's notion of combat.

Nothing is more fragile than the surface. Is not this secondary organisation threatened by the monster even more awesome than the Jabberwocky – by formless, fathomless nonsense, very different from what we previously encountered in the two figures still inherent in sense? At first, the threat is imperceptible, but a few steps suffice to make us aware of an enlarged crevice; the whole organisation of the surface has already disappeared, overturned in a terrible primordial order. Nonsense no longer gives sense, for it has consumed everything. We might have thought at first that we were inside the same element, or in a neighbouring element. But now we see that we have changed elements, that we have entered a storm. We might have thought we were still among little girls and children, but we are already in an irreversible madness. We might have believed we were at the latest edge of literary research, at the point of the highest invention of languages and words; we are already faced by the agitations of a convulsive life, in the night of a pathological creation affecting bodies. It is for this reason that the observer must be attentive: it is hardly acceptable, under the pretext of portmanteau words, for example, to run together a child's nursery rhymes, poetic experimentations, and experiences of madness. A great poet may write in a direct relation to the child that she was and the children she loves; a madman may carry along with him an immense poetical work, in a direct relation to the poet that he was and which he does not cease to be. But this does not at all justify the grotesque trinity of child, poet and madman. With all the force of admiration and veneration, we must be attentive to the sliding which reveals a profound difference underlying these crude similarities. We must be attentive to the very different functions and abysses of nonsense, and to the heterogeneity of portmanteau words, which do not authorise the grouping together of those who invent or even those who use them. A little girl may sing '*Pimpanicaille*'; an artist may write 'frumrious'; and a schizophrenic may utter 'perspendicace'.[3] But we have no reason to believe that the problem is the same in all of these cases and the results roughly analogous. One could not seriously confuse Babar's song with Artaud's howl-breaths (*cris-souffles*), 'Ratar ratara ratar Atara tatara rana Otara otara datara . . . ' We may add that the mistake made by logicians, when they speak of nonsense, is that they offer laboriously constructed, emaciated examples fitting the needs of their demonstration, as if they had never heard a little girl sing, a great poet recite, or a schizophrenic speak. There is a poverty of so-called logical examples (except in Russell, who was always inspired by Lewis Carroll). But here still the weakness of the logician does not authorise us to reconstruct a trinity against him. On the contrary, the problem is a clinical problem, that is, a problem of sliding from one organisation to another, or a problem of the formation of a progressive and creative disorganisation. It is also a problem of criticism, that is, of the determination of differential levels at which nonsense changes shape, the portmanteau word undergoes a change of nature, and the entire language changes dimension.

Crude similarities set their trap. We would like to consider two texts in which these traps of similarity can be found. Occasionally Antonin Artaud confronts Lewis Carroll: first in a transcription of the Humpty Dumpty episode; and again in a letter, written from the asylum at Rodez, in which he passes judgement on Carroll. As we read the first stanza of 'Jabberwocky', such as Artaud renders it, we have the impression that the two opening verses still correspond to Carroll's criteria and conform to the rules of translation generally held by Carroll's other French translators, Parisot and Brunius. But beginning with the last word of the second line, from the third line onward, a sliding is produced, and even a creative, central collapse, causing us to be in another world and in an entirely different language.[4] With horror, we recognise it easily: it is the language of schizophrenia. Even the portmanteau words seem to function differently, being caught up in syncopes and being overloaded with gutturals. We measure at the same moment the distance separating Carroll's language and Artaud's language – the former emitted at the surface, the latter carved into the depth of bodies. We measure the difference between their respective problems. We are thus able to acknowledge the full impact of the declarations made by Artaud in his letter from Rodez:

> I have not produced a translation of 'Jabberwocky'. I tried to translate a fragment of it, but it bored me. I never liked this poem, which always struck me as an affected infantilism . . . I do not like the poems or languages of the surface which smell of happy leisures and of intellectual success – as if the intellect relied on the anus, but without any heart or soul in it. The anus is always terror, and I will not admit that one dumps an excrement without . . . thereby losing one's soul as well, and there is no soul in 'Jabberwocky'.

... One may invent one's language, and make pure language speak with an extra-grammatical or a-grammatical meaning, but this meaning must have value in itself, that is, it must issue from torment . . . 'Jabberwocky' is the work of a profiteer who, satiated after a fine meal, seeks to indulge himself in the pain of others . . . When one digs through the shit of being and its language, the poem necessarily smells badly, and 'Jabberwocky' is a poem into which every great poet has plunged, and having been born from it, smells badly. There are in 'Jabberwocky' passages of fecality, but it is the fecality of an English snob, who curls the obscene within himself like ringlets of hair around a curling iron . . . It is the work of a man who ate well – and this makes itself felt in his writing . . .

(*OC* IX: 184–6)

Summing this up, we could say that Artaud considers Lewis Carroll a pervert, a little pervert, who holds onto the establishment of a surface language, and who has not felt the real problem of a language in depth – namely, the schizophrenic problem of suffering, of death, and of life. To Artaud, Carroll's games seem puerile, his food too wordy, and even his fecality hypocritical and too well-bred. [. . .]

In Carroll's works [. . .], the basic oral duality (to eat/to speak) is sometimes displaced and passes between two kinds or two dimensions of propositions. Some other times it hardens and becomes 'to pay/to speak', or 'excrement/language' (Alice has to buy an egg in the Sheep's shop, and Humpty Dumpty pays [sic] his words; as for fecality, as Artaud says, it underlies Carroll's work everywhere). Likewise, when Artaud develops his own antinomic series – 'to be and to obey, to live and to exist, to act and to think, matter and soul, body and mind' – he himself has the impression of an extraordinary resemblance with Carroll. He translates this impression by saying that Carroll had reached out across time to pillage and plagiarise him, Antonin Artaud, both with respect to Humpty Dumpty's poem about the little fishes and with respect to 'Jabberwocky'. And yet, why did Artaud add that his writing has nothing to do with Carroll's? Why is this extraordinary familiarity also a radical and definite strangeness? It suffices to ask once more how and where Carroll's series are organised. The two series are articulated at the surface. On this surface, a line is like the frontier between two series, propositions and things, or between dimensions of the same proposition. Along this line, sense is elaborated, both as what is expressed by the proposition and as the attribute of things – the 'expressible' of expressions and the 'attributable' of denotations. The two series are therefore articulated by their difference, and sense traverses the entire surface, although it remains on its own line. Undoubtedly, this immaterial sense is the result of corporeal things, of their mixtures, and of their actions and passions. But the result has a very different nature than the corporeal cause. It is for this reason that sense, as an effect, being always at the surface, refers to a quasi-cause which is itself incorporeal. This is the always mobile nonsense, which is expressed in esoteric and in portmanteau words, and which distributes sense on both sides simultaneously. All of this forms the surface organisation upon which Carroll's work plays a mirror-like effect.

Artaud said that this is only surface. The revelation which enlivened Artaud's genius is known to any schizophrenic, who lives it as well in his or her own manner. For him, *there is not, there is no longer, any surface.* How could Carroll not strike him as an affected little girl, protected from all deep problems? The first schizophrenic evidence is that the surface has split open. Things and propositions have no longer any frontier between them, precisely because bodies have no surface. The primary aspect of the schizophrenic body is that it is a sort of body sieve. Freud emphasised this aptitude of the schizophrenic to grasp the surface and the skin as if they were punctured by an infinite number of little holes.[5] The consequence of this is that the entire body is no longer anything but depth – it carries along and snaps up everything into this gaping depth which represents a fundamental involution. Everything is a mixture of bodies, and inside the body, interlocking and penetration. Artaud said that everything is physical: 'We have in our back full vertebrae, transfixed by the nail of pain, which through walking, the effort of lifting weights, and the resistance to letting go, become cannisters by being nested in one another' (Artaud qtd. in *La Tour de feu*, 1961). A tree, a column, a flower, or a cane grow inside the body; other bodies always penetrate our body and coexist with its parts. Everything is really a can – canned food and excrement. As there is no surface, the inside and the outside, the container and the contained, no longer have a precise limit; they plunge into a universal depth or turn in the circle of a present which gets to be more contracted as it is filled. Hence the schizophrenic manner of living the contradiction; either in the deep fissure which traverses the body, or in the fragmented parts which encase one another and spin about. Body-sieve, fragmented body, and dissociated body – these are the three primary dimensions of the schizophrenic body.

In this collapse of the surface, the entire world loses its meaning. It maintains perhaps a certain power of denotation, but this is experienced as empty. It maintains a certain power of manifestation, but this is experienced as indifferent. And it maintains a certain signification, experienced as 'false'. Nevertheless, the word loses its sense, that is, its power to draw together or to express an incorporeal effect distinct from the actions and passions of the body, and an ideational event distinct from its present realisation. Every event is realised, be it in a body. The procedure is this: a word, often of an alimentary nature, appears in capital letters, printed as in a collage which freezes it and strips it of its sense. But the moment that the pinned-down word loses its sense, it bursts into pieces; it is decomposed into syllables, letters, and above all into consonants which act directly on the body, penetrating and bruising it. We have already seen that this was the case for the schizophrenic student of languages. The moment that the maternal language is stripped of its sense, its *phonetic elements* become singularly wounding. The word no longer expresses an attribute of the state of affairs; its fragments merge with unbearable sonorous qualities, invade the body where they form a mixture and a new state of affairs, as if they themselves were a noisy, poisonous food and canned excrement. The parts of the body, its organs, are determined in virtue of decomposed elements which affect and assail them.[6] In this passion, a pure language-affect is substituted for the effect of language: 'All writing is PIG SHIT' (that is to say, every fixed or written word is decomposed into noisy, alimentary, and excremental bits).

For the schizophrenic, then, it is less a question of recovering meaning than of destroying the word, of conjuring up the affect, and of transforming the painful passion of the body into a triumphant action, obedience into command, always in this depth beneath the fissured surface. The student of languages provides the example of the means by which the painful explosions of the word in the maternal language are converted into actions relative to the foreign languages. We saw a little while ago that wounding was accomplished by means of *phonetic elements* affecting the articulated or disarticulated parts of the body. Triumph may now be reached only through the creation of breath-words (*mots-souffles*) and howl-words (*mots-cris*), in which all literal, syllabic, and phonetic values have been replaced by *values which are exclusively tonic* and not written. To these values a glorious body corresponds, being a new dimension of the schizophrenic body, an organism without parts which operates entirely by insufflation, respiration, evaporation, and fluid transmission (the superior body or body without organs of Antonin Artaud).[7] Undoubtedly, this characterisation of the active procedure, in opposition to the procedure of passion, appears initially insufficient; fluids, in fact, do not seem less harmful than fragments. But this is so because of the action–passion ambivalence. It is here that the contradiction lived in schizophrenia finds its real point of application: passion and action are the inseparable poles of an ambivalence, because the two languages which they form belong inseparably to the body and to the depth of bodies. One is thus never sure that the ideal fluids of an organism without parts do not carry parasitic worms, fragments of organs, solid food, and excremental residue. In fact, it is certain that the maleficent forces make effective use of fluids and insufflations in order to introduce bits of passion into the body. The fluid is necessarily corrupted, but not by itself. It is corrupted only by the other pole from which it cannot be separated. The fact, though, is that it represents the active pole and the state of perfect mixture. The latter is opposed to the encasing and bruising of the imperfect mixture which alters the body, and the total and liquid mixture which leaves the body intact. In the fluid element, or in the insufflated liquid, there is the unwritten secret of an active mixture which is like the 'principle of the Sea', in opposition to the passive mixtures of the encased parts. It is in this sense that Artaud transforms Humpty Dumpty's poem about the sea and the fish into a poem about the problem of obedience and command.

What defines this second language and this method of action, practically, is its consonantal, guttural, and aspirated overloads, its apostrophes and internal accents, its breaths and its scansions, and its modulation which replaces all syllabic or even literal values. It is a question of transforming the word into an action by rendering it without articulation. [. . .] Rather than separating the consonants and rendering them pronounceable, one could say the vowel, once reduced to the soft sign, renders the consonants indissociable from one another, by palatalising them. It leaves them illegible and even unpronounceable, as it transforms them into so many active howls in one continuous breath. These howls are welded together in breath, like the consonants in the sign which liquefies them, like fish in the ocean-mass, or like the bones in the blood of the body without organs. A sign of fire, a wave 'which hesitates between gas and water', said Artaud. The howls are gurglings in breath.

When Artaud says in his 'Jabberwocky', 'Until rourghe is to rouarghe has rangmbde and rangmbde has rouarghambde', he means to activate, insufflate, palatalise, and set the word aflame so that the word becomes the action of a body without parts, instead of being the passion of a fragmented organism. The task is that of transforming the word into a fusion of consonants – fusion through the use of soft signs and of consonants which cannot be decomposed. Within this language, one can always find words which would be equivalent to portmanteau words. For '*rourghe*' and '*rouarghe*', Artaud himself indicates '*ruée*', '*roue*', '*route*', '*règle*' or '*route à régler*'. To this list, we could add 'Rouergue', that section of Rodez in which Artaud was at the time. Likewise when he says '*Uk'hatis*', with an internal apostrophe, he indicates '*ukhase*', '*hâte*', and '*abruti*', and adds 'a nocturnal jolt beneath Hecate which means the pigs of the moon thrown off the straight path'. As soon as the word appears, however, as a portmanteau word, its structure and the commentary attached to it persuade us of the presence of something very different. Artaud's '*Ghoré Uk'hatis*' are not equivalent to the lost pigs, to Carroll's 'mome raths', or to Parisot's '*verchons fourgus*'. They do not compete with them on the same plane. They do not secure the ramification of series on the basis of sense. On the contrary, they enact a chain of associations between tonic and consonantal elements, in a region of infra-sense, according to a fluid and burning principle which absorbs and reabsorbs effectively the sense as soon as it is produced: *Uk'hatis* (or the lost pigs of the moon) is K'H (*cahot* = jolt), 'KT (nocturnal), and H'KT (Hecate).

The duality of the schizophrenic word has not been adequately noted: it comprises the passion-word, which explodes into wounding phonetic values, and the action-word, which welds inarticulate tonic values. These two words are developed in relation to the duality of the body, fragmented body and body without organs. They refer to two theatres, the theatre of terror or passion and the theatre of cruelty, which is by its essence active. They refer to two types of nonsense, passive and active: the nonsense of the word devoid of sense, which is decomposed into phonetic elements; and the nonsense of tonic elements, which form a word incapable of being decomposed and no less beneath sense and far from the surface. Sub-sense, a-sense, *Untersinn* – this must be distinguished from the nonsense of the surface. According to Hölderlin, language in its two aspects is 'a sign empty of meaning'. Although a sign, it is a sign which merges with an action or a passion of the body.[8] This is why it seems entirely insufficient to say that schizophrenic language is defined by an endless and panic-stricken sliding of the signifying series toward the signified series. In fact, there are no longer any series at all; the two series have disappeared. Nonsense has ceased to give sense to the surface; it absorbs and engulfs all sense, both on the side of the signifier and on the side of the signified. Artaud says that Being, which is nonsense, has teeth. In the surface organisation which we called secondary, physical bodies and sonorous words are separated and articulated at once by an incorporeal frontier. This frontier is sense, representing, on one side, the pure 'expressed' of words, and on the other, the logical attribute of bodies. Although sense results from the actions and the passions of the body, it is a result which differs in nature, since it is neither action nor passion. It is a result which shelters sonorous language from any confusion with the physical body. On the contrary, in this primary order of schizophrenia, the only duality left is that between the actions and the passions of the body. Language is both at once, being entirely reabsorbed into the gaping depth. There is no longer anything to prevent propositions from falling back onto bodies and from mingling their sonorous elements with the body's olfactory, gustatory, or digestive affects. Not only is there no longer any sense, but there is no longer any grammar or syntax either – nor, at the limit, are there any articulated syllabic, literal, or phonetic elements. Antonin Artaud could have entitled his essay 'An antigrammatical effort against Lewis Carroll'. Carroll needs a very strict grammar, required to conserve the inflection and articulation of bodies, were it only through the mirror which reflects them and sends a meaning back to them.[9] It is for this reason that we can oppose Artaud and Carroll point for point – primary order and secondary organisation. The *surface series* of the 'to eat/to speak' type have really nothing in common with the *poles of depth* which are only apparently similar. The two *figures of nonsense* at the surface, which distribute sense between the series, have nothing to do with the two *dives into nonsense* which drag along, engulf, and reabsorb sense (*Untersinn*). The two forms of stuttering, the clonic and the tonic, are only roughly analogous to the two schizophrenic languages. The break (*coupure*) of the surface has nothing in common with the deep *Spaltung*. The contradiction which was grasped in an infinite subdivision of the past-future over the incorporeal line of the Aion has nothing to do with the opposition of the poles in the physical present of bodies. Even portmanteau words have functions which are completely heterogeneous.

One may find a schizoid 'position' in the child, before the child has risen to the surface or conquered it. Even at the surface, we can always find schizoid fragments, since its function is precisely to organise and to display elements which have risen from the depth. This does not make it any less abominable or annoying to mix everything together – the child's conquest of the surface, the collapse of the surface in the schizophrenic or the mastery of the surfaces in the person called, for example, 'pervert'. We can always make of Carroll's work a sort of schizophrenic tale. Some imprudent English psychoanalysts have in fact done so: they note Alice's telescope-body, its foldings and its unfoldings, her manifest alimentary, and latent excremental, obsessions; the bits which designate morsels of food as well as 'choice morsels', the collages and labels of alimentary words which are quick to decompose; her loss of identity, the fish and the sea . . . One can still wonder what kind of madness is clinically represented by the Hatter, the March Hare, and the Dormouse. And one can always recognise in the opposition between Alice and Humpty Dumpty the two ambivalent poles: 'fragmented organs – body without organs', body-sieve and glorious body. Artaud had no other reason for confronting the text of Humpty Dumpty. But, at this precise moment, we could listen to Artaud's warning: 'I have not produced a translation . . . I have never liked this poem . . . I do not like the surface poems or the languages of the surface.' Bad psychoanalysis has two ways of deceiving itself: by believing that it has discovered identical materials, that one can inevitably find everywhere, or by believing that it has discovered analogous forms which create false differences. Thus, the clinical psychiatric aspect and the literary critical aspect are botched simultaneously. Structuralism is right to raise the point that form and matter have a scope only in the original and irreducible structures in which they are organised. Psychoanalysis must have geometrical dimensions, before being concerned with historical anecdotes. For life, and even sexuality, lies within the organisation and orientation of these dimensions, before being found in generative matter or engendered form. Psychoanalysis cannot content itself with the designation of cases, the manifestation of histories, or the signification of complexes. Psychoanalysis is the psychoanalysis of sense. It is geographical before it is historical. It distinguishes different countries. Artaud is neither Carroll nor Alice, Carroll is not Artaud, Carroll is not even Alice. Artaud thrust the child into an extremely violent alternative, an alternative of corporeal action and passion, which conforms to the two languages in depth. Either the child is not born, that is, does not leave the foldings of his or her future spinal cord, over which her parents fornicate (a reverse suicide), or she creates a fluid, glorious, and flamboyant body without organs and without parents (like those Artaud called his 'daughters' yet to be born). Carroll, on the contrary, awaits the child, in a manner conforming to his language of incorporeal sense: he waits at the point and at the moment in which the child has left the depths of the maternal body and has yet to discover the depth of her own body. This is the brief surface moment in which the little girl skirts the surface of the water, like Alice in the pool of her own tears. These are different regions, different and unrelated dimensions. We may believe that the surface has its monsters, the Snark and the Jabberwock, its terrors and its cruelties, which, although not of the depths, have claws just the same and can snap one up laterally, or even make us fall back into the abyss which we believed we had dispelled. For all that, Carroll and Artaud do not encounter one another; only the commentator may change dimensions, and that is his great weakness, the sign that he inhabits no dimension at all. We would not give a page of Artaud for all of Carroll. Artaud is alone in having been an absolute depth in literature, and in having discovered the vital body and the prodigious language of this body. As he says, he discovered them through suffering. He explored the infra-sense, which is still unknown today. But Carroll remains the master and the surveyor of surfaces – surfaces which were taken to be so well known that nobody was exploring them anymore. On these surfaces, nonetheless, the entire logic of sense is located.

Part II

Theatre

Acts and representations

This section gathers the disparate voices of Jacques Derrida, Helga Finter, Jerzy Grotowski, Jane Goodall, Herbert Blau, Susan Sontag and Leo Bersani to account for the substance of Artaud's theatrical influence, its possible uses, its theoretical limits, as well as its extant effects on the field. The wide range of approaches in evidence in this section – from abstract theoretical formulations of Artaud's ideas to the more direct statement of the usefulness of those ideas for the performer (in Grotowski's essay for example) – is indicative of the way Artaud worked as both a practitioner and as a theoretician. 'Acts and representations' also refers to the two central strategies he sought to expose in the theatre, its forces and forms.

6   Jacques Derrida

From 'The theatre of cruelty and the closure of representation'*

Derrida's essays are all close readings of Artaud's texts, though, of course, they are tied to some of Derrida's favourite themes. This earlier piece appeared alongside 'La Parole soufflée' in his groundbreaking book *L'Écriture et la différence* in 1967. Both essays are deserving of inclusion in a reader such as this, but in my view 'La Parole soufflée', if anything, lacks the intense and concrete focus of the theatre piece.

In both essays, Derrida's argument is that Artaud enables the aims of Western metaphysics to emerge in all their naive glory – self-presence, unity, self-identity – through his war on language and representation. Derrida is careful to point out that Artaud's only weapons in this struggle *are* language and representation and that Artaud's project is itself metaphysical and therefore not likely to succeed.

Thus Derrida identifies two coexistent but contradictory trajectories in Artaud's work: one which would restore to language the unity of thought, object and sign in the flesh of the speaker, hence the theatre, and the other, an acknowledgement of the impossibility of achieving this pure presence from within the system of representation of which language and theatre are part. This problem is essential in understanding what Artaud was trying to do with the theatre of cruelty, which is not at all about blood and guts but about staging metaphysics, a point he makes repeatedly in his letters explaining the idea of cruelty in *Le Théâtre et son double*.

Perhaps we now can ask, not about the conditions under which a modern theatre could be faithful to Artaud, but in what cases it is surely unfaithful to him. What might the themes of infidelity be, even among those who invoke Artaud in the militant and noisy fashion we all know? We will content ourselves with naming these themes. Without a doubt, foreign to the theatre of cruelty, are:

1   All non-sacred theatre.
2   All theatre that privileges speech or rather the verb, all theatre of words, even if this privilege becomes that of a speech which is self-destructive, which once more becomes gesture of hopeless reoccurrence, a *negative* relation of

speech to itself, theatrical nihilism, what is still called the theatre of the absurd. Such a theatre would not only be consumed by speech, and would not destroy the functioning of the classical stage, but it also would not be, in the sense understood by Artaud (and doubtless by Nietzsche), an *affirmation*.

3   All *abstract* theatre which excludes something from the totality of art, and thus, from the totality of life and its resources of signification: dance, music, volume, depth of plasticity, visible images, sonority, phonicity, etc. An abstract theatre is a theatre in which the totality of sense and the senses is not consumed. One would incorrectly conclude from this that it suffices to accumulate or to juxtapose all the arts in order to create a total theatre addressed to the 'total man' (*TD*: 123).[1] Nothing could be further from addressing total man than an assembled totality, an artificial and exterior mimicry. Inversely, certain apparent exhaustions of stage technique sometimes more rigorously pursue Artaud's trajectory. Assuming, which we do not, that there is some sense in speaking of a fidelity to Artaud, to something like his 'message' (this notion already betrays him), then a rigorous, painstaking, patient and implacable sobriety in the work of destruction, and an economical acuity aiming at the master parts of a still quite solid machine, are more surely imperative, today, than the general mobilisation of art and artists, than turbulence or improvised agitation under the mocking and tranquil eyes of the police.

4   All theatre of alienation. Alienation only consecrates, with didactic insistence and systematic heaviness, the non-participation of spectators (and even of directors and actors) in the creative act, in the irruptive force fissuring the space of the stage. The *Verfremdungseffekt*[2] remains the prisoner of a classical paradox and of 'the European ideal of art' which 'attempts to cast the mind into an attitude distinct from force but addicted to exaltation' (*TD*: 10). Since 'in the theatre of cruelty the spectator is in the centre and the spectacle surrounds him' (*TD*: 81), the distance of vision is no longer pure, cannot be abstracted from the totality of the sensory milieu; the infused spectator can no longer *constitute* his spectacle and provide himself with its object. There is no longer spectator or spectacle, but *festival* (*TD*: 85). All the limits furrowing classical theatricality (represented/representer, signified/ signifier, author/director/actors/spectators, stage/audience, text/interpretation, etc.) were ethico-metaphysical prohibitions, wrinkles, grimaces, rictuses – the symptoms of fear before the dangers of the festival. Within the space of the festival opened by transgression, the distance of representation should no longer be extendable. The festival of cruelty lifts all footlights and protective barriers before the 'absolute danger' which is 'without foundation': 'I must have actors who are first of all beings, that is to say, who on stage are not afraid of the true sensation of the touch of a knife and the convulsions – *absolutely* real for them – of a supposed birth. Mounet-Sully believes in what he does and gives the illusion of it, but he knows that he is behind a protective barrier, me – I suppress the protective barrier' (letter

to Roger Blin, September 1945). As regards the festival, as invoked by Artaud, and the menace of that which is 'without foundation', the 'happening' can only make us smile: it is to the theatre of cruelty what the carnival of Nice might be to the mysteries of Eleusis. This is particularly so due to the fact that the happening substitutes political agitation for the total revolution prescribed by Artaud. The festival must be a political act. And the *act* of political revolution is *theatrical*.

5   All non-political theatre. We have indeed said that the festival must be a political act and not the more or less eloquent, pedagogical, and superintended transmission of a concept or a politico-moral vision of the world. To reflect – which we cannot do here – the political sense of this act and this festival, and the image of society which fascinates Artaud's desire, one should come to invoke (in order to note the greatest difference within the greatest affinity) all the elements in Rousseau which establish communication between the critique of the classical spectacle, the suspect quality of articulation in language, the ideal of a public festival substituted for representation, and a certain model of society perfectly present to itself in small communities which render both useless and nefarious all recourse to *representation* at the decisive moments of social life. That is, all recourse to political as well as to theatrical representation, replacement, or delegation. It very precisely could be shown that it is the 'representer' that Rousseau suspects in *The Social Contract*, as well as in the *Letter to M d'Alembert*, where he proposes the replacement of theatrical representations with public festivals lacking all exhibition and spectacle, festivals without 'anything to see' in which the spectators themselves would become actors: 'But what then will be the objects of these entertainments? . . . Nothing, if you please . . . Plant a stake crowned with flowers in the middle of a square; gather the people together there, and you will have a festival. Do better yet; let the spectators become an entertainment to themselves; make them actors themselves' (Rousseau 1960: 126).[3]

6   All ideological theatre, all cultural theatre, all communicative, *interpretive* (in the popular and not the Nietzschean sense, of course) theatre seeking to transmit a content, or to deliver a message (of whatever nature: political, religious, psychological, metaphysical, etc.). That would make a discourse's meaning intelligible for its listeners;[4] a message that would not be totally exhausted in the *act* and *present tense* of the stage, that would not coincide with the stage, that could be repeated without it. Here we touch upon what seems to be the profound essence of Artaud's project, his historico-metaphysical decision. *Artaud wanted to erase repetition in general.*[5] For him, repetition was evil, and one could doubtless organise an entire reading of his texts around this centre. Repetition separates force, presence, and life from themselves. This separation is the economical and calculating gesture of that which defers itself in order to maintain itself, that which reserves expenditure and surrenders to fear. This power of repetition governed

everything that Artaud wished to destroy, and it has several names: God, Being, Dialectics. God is the eternity whose death goes on indefinitely, whose death, as difference and repetition within life, has never ceased to menace life. It is not the living God, but the God that we should fear. God is Death. 'For even the infinite is dead, infinite is the name of a dead man who is not dead' (*84* [1967c]). As soon as there is repetition, God is there, the present holds on to itself and reserves itself, that is to say, eludes itself. 'The absolute is not a being and will never be one, for there can be no being without a crime committed against myself, that is to say, without taking from me a being who wanted one day to be god when this is not possible, God being able to manifest himself only all at once, given that he manifests himself an infinite number of times during all the times of eternity as the infinity of times and eternity, which creates perpetuity' (September 1945). Another name of repetition: Being. Being is the form in which the infinite diversity of the forms and forces of life and death can indefinitely merge and be repeated in the word. For there is no word, nor in general a sign, which is not constituted by the possibility of repeating itself. A sign which does not repeat itself, which is not already divided by repetition in its 'first time', is not a sign. The signifying referral therefore must be ideal – and ideality is but the assured power of repetition – in order to refer to the same thing each time. This is why Being is the key word of eternal repetition, the victory of God and of Death over life. Like Nietzsche (for example in *The Birth of Philosophy*), Artaud refuses to subsume Life to Being, and inverts the genealogical order: 'First to live and to be according to one's soul; the problem of being is only their consequence' (September 1945), 'There is no greater enemy of the human body than being' (September 1947). Certain other unpublished texts valorise what Artaud properly calls 'the beyond of being' (February 1947), manipulating this expression of Plato's (whom Artaud did not fail to read) in a Nietzschean style. Finally, Dialectics is the movement through which expenditure is reappropriated into presence – it is the economy of repetition. The economy of truth. Repetition *summarises* negativity, gathers and maintains the past present as truth, as ideality. The truth is always that which can be repeated. Non-repetition, expenditure that is resolute and without return in the unique time consuming the present, must put an end to fearful discursiveness, to unskirtable ontology, to dialectics, 'dialectics [a certain dialectics] being that which finished me' (September 1945).

Dialectics is always that which has finished us, because it is always that which *takes into account* our rejection of it. As it does our affirmation. [...]

The possibility of the theatre is the obligatory focal point of this thought which reflects tragedy as repetition. The menace of repetition is nowhere else as well organised as in the theatre. Nowhere else is one so close to the stage as the origin of repetition, so close to the primitive repetition which would have to be erased, and only by detaching it from itself as if from its double. Not in the sense in which Artaud spoke of *The Theatre and its Double*,[6] but as designating the fold, the interior duplication which steals the simple presence of its present act from the theatre, from life, etc. in the irrepressible movement of repetition. 'One time' is the enigma of that which has no meaning, no presence, no legibility. Now, for Artaud, the festival of cruelty could take place only *one time*: 'Let us leave textual criticism to graduate students, formal criticism to aesthetes, and recognize that what has been said is not still to be said; that an expression does not have the same value twice, does not live two lives; that all words, once spoken, are dead and function only at the moment when they are uttered, that a form once it has served, cannot be used again and asks only to be replaced by another, and that the theatre is the only place in the world where a gesture, once made, can never be made the same way twice' (*TD*: 75). This is indeed how things appear: theatrical representation is finite, and leaves behind it, behind its actual presence, no trace, no object to carry it off. It is neither a book nor a work, but an energy, and in this sense it is the only art of life. 'The theatre teaches precisely the uselessness of the action which, once done, is not to be done, and the superior use of the state unused by the action and which, *restored*, produces a purification' (*TD*: 82). In this sense the theatre of cruelty would be the art of difference and of expenditure without economy, without reserve, without return, without history. Pure presence as pure difference. Its act must be forgotten, actively forgotten. Here, one must practise the *aktive Vergesslichkeit*, which is spoken of in the second dissertation of *The Genealogy of Morals*, which also explicates 'festivity' and 'cruelty' (*Grausamkeit*).

Artaud's disgust with non-theatrical writing has the same sense. What inspires this disgust is not, as in the *Phaedrus*, the gesture of the body, the sensory and mnemonic, the hypomnesiac mark exterior to the inscription of truth in the soul, but, on the contrary, writing as the site of the inscription of truth, the other of the living body, writing as ideality, repetition. Plato criticises writing as a body; Artaud criticises it as the erasure of the body, of the living gesture which takes place only once. Writing is space itself and the possibility of repetition in general. This is why 'We should get rid of our superstitious valuation of texts and written poetry. Written poetry is worth reading once, and then should be destroyed' (*TD*: 78).

In thus enumerating the themes of infidelity, one comes to understand very quickly that fidelity is impossible. There is no theatre in the world today which fulfils Artaud's desire. And there would be no exception to be made for the attempts made by Artaud himself. He knew this better than any other: the 'grammar' of the theatre of cruelty, of which he said that it is 'to be found', will always remain the inaccessible limit of a representation which is not repetition, of a *re*-presentation which is full presence, which does not carry its double within itself as its death, of a present which does not repeat itself, that is, of a present outside time, a non-present. The present offers itself as such, appears, presents itself, opens the state of time or the time of the stage only by harbouring its own intestine difference, and only in the interior fold of its original repetition, in representation. [...]

What is tragic is not the impossibility, but the necessity of repetition.

Artaud knew that the theatre of cruelty neither begins nor is completed within the purity of simple presence, but rather is already within representation, in the 'second time of Creation', in the conflict of forces which could not be that of a simple origin. Doubtless, cruelty could begin to be practised within this conflict, but thereby it must also let itself *be penetrated*. The origin is always *penetrated*. Such is the alchemy of the theatre:

> Perhaps before proceeding further I shall be asked to define what I mean by the archetypal, primitive theatre. And we shall thereby approach the very heart of the matter. If in fact we raise the question of the origins and *raison d'être* (or primordial necessity) of the theatre, we find, metaphysically, the materialisation or rather the exteriorisation of a kind of essential drama, already *disposed* and *divided*, not so much as to lose their character as principles, but enough to comprise, in a substantial and active fashion (i.e. resonantly), an infinite perspective of conflicts. To analyse such a drama philosophically is impossible; only poetically . . . And this essential drama, we come to realise, exists, and in the image of something subtler than Creation itself, something which must be represented as the result of one Will alone – and *without conflict*. We must believe that the essential drama, the one at the root of all the Great Mysteries, is associated with the second phase of Creation, that of difficulty and of the Double, that of matter and the materialisation of the idea. It seems indeed that where simplicity and order reign, there can be no theatre nor drama, and the true theatre, like poetry as well, though by other means, is born out of a kind of organised anarchy.
>
> (*TD*: 50–1)

Primitive theatre and cruelty thus also begin by repetition. But if the idea of a theatre without representation, the idea of the impossible, does not help us to regulate theatrical practice, it does, perhaps, permit us to conceive its origin, eve and limit, and the horizon of its death. The energy of Western theatre thus lets itself be encompassed within its own possibility, which is not accidental and serves as a constitutive centre and structuring locus for the entire history of the West. But repetition steals the centre and the locus, and what we have just said of its possibility should prohibit us from speaking both of death as a horizon and of birth as a past *opening*.

Artaud kept himself as close as possible to the limit: the possibility and impossibility of pure theatre. Presence, in order to be presence and self-presence, has always already begun to represent itself, has always already been penetrated. Affirmation itself must be penetrated in repeating itself. Which means that the murder of the father which opens the history of representation and the space of tragedy, the murder of the father that Artaud, in sum, wants to repeat at the greatest proximity to its origin but *only a single time* – this murder is endless and is repeated indefinitely. It begins by penetrating its own commentary and is accompanied by its own representation. In which it erases itself and confirms the transgressed law. To do so, it suffices that there be a sign, that is to say, a repetition.

Underneath this side of the limit, and in the extent to which he wanted to save the purity of a presence without interior difference and without repetition (or, paradoxically amounting to the same thing, the purity of a pure difference),[7] Artaud also desired the impossibility of the theatre, wanted to erase the stage, no longer wanted to see what transpires in a locality always inhabited or haunted by the father and subjected to the repetition of murder. Is it not Artaud who wants to reduce the archi-stage when he writes in the *Here-Lies*: 'I, Antonin Artaud, am my son, my father, my mother, and myself' (*AA*: 238)?

That he thereby kept himself at the limit of theatrical possibility, and that he simultaneously wanted to produce and to annihilate the stage, is what he knew in the most extreme way. December 1946:

> And now I am going to say something which, perhaps,
> is going to stupefy many people.
> I am the enemy
> of theatre.
> I have always been.
> As much as I love the theatre,
> I am, for this very reason, equally its enemy.

We see him immediately afterwards: he cannot resign himself to theatre as repetition, and cannot renounce theatre as non-repetition:

> The theatre is a passionate overflowing
> a frightful transfer of forces
> from body
> to body.
> This transfer cannot be reproduced twice.
> Nothing more impious than the system of the Balinese which consists,
> after having produced this transfer one time,
> instead of seeking another,
> in resorting to a system of particular enchantments
> in order to deprive astral photography of the gestures thus obtained.

Theatre as repetition of that which does not repeat itself, theatre as the original repetition of difference within the conflict of forces in which 'evil is the permanent law, and what is good is an effort and already a cruelty added to the other cruelty' – such is the fatal limit of a cruelty which begins with its own representation.

Because it has always already begun, representation therefore has no end. But one can conceive of the closure of that which is without end. Closure is the circular limit within which the repetition of difference infinitely repeats itself. That is to say, closure is its *playing* space. This movement is the movement of the world as play. 'And for the absolute life itself is a game' (*OC* IV: 282). This play is cruelty as the unity of necessity and chance. 'It is chance that is infinite, not god' (*Fragmentations*). This play of life is artistic.[8]

To think the closure of representation is thus to think the cruel powers of death and play which permit presence to be born to itself, and pleasurably to consume itself through the representation in which it eludes itself in its deferral. To think the closure of representation is to think the tragic: not as the representation of fate, but as the fate of representation. Its gratuitous and baseless necessity.

And it is to think why it is *fatal* that, in its closure, representation continues.

7 Helga Finter

From 'Antonin Artaud and the impossible theatre: the legacy of the theatre of cruelty'*

This is a theoretically sophisticated survey piece on the legacy of the theatre of cruelty with some recent examples from contemporary performance. Finter's article reprises some of her many other publications in the area of voice and the body in contemporary theatre, this time with regard to Artaud's development of an 'aesthetic of the voice'. The importance of this essay lies in its foregrounding of the function of sound and vocal production in Artaud's theatre aesthetics, i.e. that, as with other aspects of his thought generally, these should not serve as illustrations (of a text or concept) but should first of all be experienced directly by the audience, as overpowering and shocking, shutting down the body's system of defences and redistributing its energies. Finter, appropriately, places Artaud's theatre of cruelty 'in the realm of the Real', invoking Lacan's notion of that which resists symbolisation. Finter's argument also makes use of Bataille's related concept of the 'heterogeneous', which she defines as that which 'is excluded by the process of socialisation, on both the individual and the social level' (Finter 1997: 16, fn 2). This aspect of the argument underscores the point made earlier regarding the connection between Artaud's theatre and Bataille's transgression.

[...]

Artaud's public appearances after the war in three radiophonic works and in a soirée at the Théâtre du Vieux-Colombier in Paris focused on the very possibility of articulating in language what is heterogeneous to the subject and to society, while at the same time testing its effect upon the individual. From this moment on Artaud would attempt to speak and write – to inscribe – his own experience with language in texts and theatrical forms. This experience, which he attempted in January 1947 to present to the Parisian audience in the Théâtre du Vieux-Colombier, led him from being in the 1920s the mummy – *momie*, as in his poems '*La Momie attachée*' and '*Invocation à la Momie*' (I*: 263–4) – to a being made of language and words – *Artaud le mômo*, the title of his soirée. This unique experience with language and the languages of the theatre – the boundary experience of a subject – cannot be translated, nor can it be reduced to a theatre aesthetic.

The cruelty of a subject's performance

The evening at the Vieux-Colombier on Monday, 13 January 1947, was announced as a *tête-à-tête* with the author, and the placards promised the *Histoire vécue d'Artaud-Mômo* (Artaud Mômo's Lived History) (see *OC* XXVI, frontispiece). Three poems entitled 'Le retour d'Artaud le mômo' (The Return of Artaud the Mômo), 'Centre-mère et patron-minet' (Centre Mother and Boss-Pussy), and 'La culture indienne' (Indian Culture) were to be read by the author, who later that year published them in book form (*OC* XII: 11–25, 69–74). As witnesses reported, the evening took place according to plan until Artaud, having read the poems, which had duly impressed everyone, began to read his life story from a manuscript, from which he soon deviated into free speech. Finally, after he could no longer find his place among the manuscript pages and began gathering the pages that were scattered across the stage, he broke off, and, confused, was gently escorted away by André Gide after the three-hour performance (Virmaux [and Virmaux] 1976: 79–84; see Finter 1990: 131ff.; and *OC* XXVI: 162–93).

What some, André Breton included, saw as the unbearable exhibition of a mental patient was for Artaud the unprecedented attempt at exploding the boundaries of a theatrical event (see Artaud [1947] 1968: 3–31). The recitation of his poetic texts, which meant a representation of the texts' voices and thereby constituted a theatrical form in *nuce*, had to be followed by a new form that might today be called 'performance', that is, the manifestation of a subject's presence by his doing (see Finter 1994: 153–67) – here attempting to make the causes of suffering audible through the reality of that suffering. On the evening of Artaud's performance at the Vieux-Colombier, this manifestation of the Real – whose impressive cruelty was attested to by all who witnessed it – made it impossible to hear what Artaud had to say about the causes of his suffering. In the context of the symbolic contract implicit in a lecture on a theatre stage, the irruption of the Real in the form of sickness, suffering, and insanity was perceived as sensational exhibitionism and histrionics. Artaud became aware during the course of his 'performance' of the impossibility of making himself heard in a theatre of the Real and later said that only bombs could have achieved the desired effect (Artaud [1947] 1968: 3, 21). Rather than throw bombs, Artaud looked for a new form for articulating the Real with voice and words. With the radio performance 'Pour en finir avec le jugement de dieu' (To Have Done with the Judgement of God), which he recorded late in 1947, he believed that, through a theatre of voices, he had come closer to the 'Théâtre de la cruauté'. And the authorities at Radio France seem to have been of the same mind. The broadcast of the radio work was prohibited, and the first broadcast didn't take place until 25 years later on 5 March 1972 on France-Culture, part of the national broadcast corporation (for the pressbook as well as Artaud's reaction to the ban, see *OC* XIII: 320 ff.).

Artaud's late theatre experience underscores the difficulty of assessing his relevance to contemporary theatre, since Artaud's search proved ultimately to be a search for an 'impossible' theatre, for a theatre of the 'impossible'. This concerns a utopia in that it has to do with a theatre that is not definitely locatable, since its loci can and should only be realised in the minds of its individual spectators and readers. But Artaud's experience with the theatre also implies an 'impossible' theatre because it stems from a subject's boundary experience with language and society, which – if taken seriously – can hardly be thought of as tradition-building, in the sense of an aesthetic. In the period immediately following World War II, Artaud repeatedly pointed out the impossibility of a community-building theatre that could have a therapeutic and cathartic effect. The retreat to the theatricality of radiophonic work makes sense in that the voices appeal directly to the individual subject's imaginary relationship to the body and thereby displace cruelty with a physical attack that puts to the test the relationship of the individual to language.

Could such an analysis of theatre be said to have its successors or imitators? Apparently yes, since several decades of theatre experimentation have been associated with Artaud's name (see Virmaux [and Virmaux] 1979, 1980). Yet, as the diversity of these examples would seem to indicate, it has been the questions Artaud posed rather than the individual answers he offered that have contributed to the development of a tradition around his ideas on the theatre.

What are these questions? Artaud's experience revolves around the relationship between the body, language, and the theatre: How can the inferno of the body, which he felt concretely through his inherited illness – a hereditary syphilis (see Maeder 1978) – but also as a crisis of language, be overcome? And what kind of role can the theatre play in this process? How can the Real of suffering be translated into language without being sublated? How can presence be articulated and rendered in language? How can real cruelty be performed in the theatre as the cruelty of the Real? [. . .]

Grimaces of the Real, or Artaud's 'relevance'

In recent years there has been an increasing number of signs that seem to indicate that a new space is being cultivated onstage for the Real, indeed, that the Real more and more appears to be asserting itself in opposition to the theatre of the 'as if', or the arbitrary signifier. This can be seen, for example, in the perilous presence of living creatures onstage: live tarantulas in Jan Fabre's *Elle était et elle est, même* (1993), poisonous snakes in Jan Lauwers's *Antonius und Cleopatra* (1992), and, most recently, an entire colony of rats in aquariums in Marina Abramovic and Charles Atlas's *Delusional* (1994). Such examples of the use of live creatures, who cannot grasp Diderot's paradox of the actor, illustrate the tendency of trying to make accessible to experience not only the presence of the living, but also the danger and attraction of the Real. The actor, confronted onstage with these animals, works in the face of danger, perhaps even fatal danger, and the actor's performance is perceived as involving real risk. The spectator is liberated in part from the contract of the 'as if' but is with this risk at the mercy of his or her *abjectum* (Kristeva 1980b) – the excluded Other and the heterogeneous, along with their associated unconscious affects. Yet the actor's overexertion and exhaustion onstage are also accompanied by the Real of pain and death. For instance, in Jan Fabre's *Who Shall Speak My Thought . . .* (1993) the body of actor Marc Van Overmeir was attached to electrodes connected to a circuit, which the director, cloaked in Ku Klux Klan robe and hood, operated during the performance in order to influence the actor's speech flow with electric shocks during a monologue concerning the prompted [*souffliert*] character of his discourse. Real physical exhaustion and pain have been used in dance theatre as well, as a form of authentification.[1] And sometimes the announcement of an actor's terminal illness, as in Ron Vawter's last solo performance, evokes the immanent Real, which becomes the theatre's double. Concrete physical violence directed at the audience appears not only in the physical assaults used by the Catalonian group La Fura dels Baus but also in the decibel levels of the music used in, for instance, Reza Abdoh's theatre, which make diaphragms vibrate and eardrums ache.[2]

This theatre does not evoke death through a play of signifiers – as is usually done in theatre – rather, it stages death by means of its real harbingers, that is, through the symptoms of mortality, as if this were the only way that human vulnerability and mortality could penetrate consciousness.

These tendencies have been spoken of as a return of the theatre of the 1960s, a trend we have already been graced with by the fashion world. However, the opening up and unlocking of the boundaries of representation takes place here under different conditions: the attack is no longer on a law that precedes representation and determines its *verisimilitude*, nor are we dealing with a new reality discourse that might be politically motivated. Rather, the absence of a unifying symbolic law, the absence of what Jean-François Lyotard has called the 'grand narratives', calls to our attention the heterogeneous of every symbol – for example, the act or death – which is suggested by means of pain, exhaustion, or danger. Some of today's theatre directors believe that only a discourse of the Real can actually touch the spectator. In the age of simulation and simulacra, being touched appears to be conceivable only as a physical touch; only the provocation of actual danger and actual corporeal pain seems capable of giving meaning or sense, and thereby sensation, to existence – a sense that only makes sense if it touches the spectator physically.

Such an irruption of the Real places the notion of theatre as representation – performance, staging, presentation – in question. And it casts profound doubt on the effectiveness of theatrical staging. Although the aforementioned productions all put into practice a well crafted theatricality, they appear no longer to want to trust it on its own. Because of this lack of faith in the effectiveness of the play, theatre has been replaced by the spectacle of the circus and its sideshows as well as high-risk sports events. Representation, as far as its pact with the theatre goes, has been set free: the nonrepresentable of all that is alive and present, which Artaud had already called for in his theatre, should take its rightful place onstage.

This current situation of experimental theatre differs markedly from that of the performance theatre and art of the late 1970s and 1980s, which had opened up the boundaries of representation through work on the theatre's systems of signification in order to address the personal and cultural memories of each individual spectator. The work, for example, of Robert Wilson or Richard Foreman could be read in this context. For many, however, the possibility of a cultural memory has today again become suspect, if not outright untenable. In order to not just see or hear a production but to experience it requires the active participation of the spectators' imaginations, their Imaginary, their cultural memories. And this is made possible through a participation that proceeds by fixing affects to signifiers – to that which one sees and hears. Yet it is the faith in exactly this capacity for an affective engagement of the theatrical sign that has evaporated. The Real alone is attributed with the capability of setting free affect, resulting in a greater emphasis being placed on bodily affection in the theatre; and the imaginary and sensual dimensions of any and all symbolisation are negated. An unpurifiable *phobos* (terror) becomes the signifier for an absence of signifiers, and physical traces of fear or pain are thus believed to be the sole means of entering the affective memory of the spectator.

The cited examples are representative of an experimental theatre that developed out of performance art toward the end of the 1980s. Since the theatre has always been the site where the crises and the heterogeneous of the discourses that articulate the imaginary relationships of conditions of existence have been played out, it seems important to ask what the recent intrusion of the Real onto the stage might indicate. In the first place, we are faced here with a crisis that has to do with the mutation of modern society into a postmodern society of the spectacle: the point of departure can no longer be designated as the language crisis of a singular subject, as was the case for Artaud; rather, we are dealing with a more general crisis of the subject. The construction of the Imaginary and the projection of the individual subject in language becomes precarious once the grand narratives cease to apply and each subject has to constitute him or herself as a subject in a permanent process, constructing his or her own individual small narratives. The religion of the physical body, which the cited theatre experiments present as their sole certainty, no longer necessarily applies here. The invulnerable body, which the theatre of the 1960s could still celebrate, appears today to be threatened by death, and in the form of the Real this threat becomes the theatre's sole certainty, a nexus of both fascination and terror.

At this point it would seem appropriate to return to Artaud's experience with the theatre. Beginning from a crisis that was based on his experience of rupture of the bond between body and language, Artaud sought a way – following his explorations of poetry, painting, and film (Finter 1990) – to stage the tortured body in his theatre and to make audible the origins of its wounds. [. . .]

Artaud made it possible to aurally experience the constitution of the human being as a speaking and spoken being; and he thereby laid bare the weak spot in the theatre of his day: The integration of the heterogeneous orders of the Imaginary and the Symbolic in the figure of the actor, whose voice and body make the text credible . . . was precisely the social model of the subject that Artaud's unique experience with language had unsettled. The task thus became one of discovering a voice – beyond the prompted rhetoric of the role – that would retain traces of Artaud's corporeal reality, as well as a text capable of reflecting upon and enunciating this reality. The theatre of the 1960s took up Artaud's work, particularly the work regarding the rupture between body and language, and thereby continued the experiments he had begun in the 1930s. But after Artaud there was yet another possible direction for theatre, which explored what in the voice flows from the body and the text and therefore experimented with the represented subject as an effect of audiovisual systems of signification. This took place predominantly in the performance theatre of the 1970s and 1980s. (I will return to this later.) In the theatre experiments that today seek to stage the Real, the despair – motivated by a disastrous, incurable plague and at the same time by an omnipresent, death-denying simulation – seems to repress what the theatre of the past few decades following Artaud had researched: the roles of the voice and of sound, which not only give presence to the body but also make possible the fixing of affect in the spectator. Perhaps for this reason a return to Artaud might be relevant, especially since he had identified what exactly in the theatre makes it vital for the individual as well as for society. Artaud's experience shows how the experience of theatre, the theatrical 'as if', stands at the beginning of a subject's becoming and how, through the voice, theatre can provide a setting for the constitution of a subject.

Subjects onstage

Representation in the theatre is, from the point of view of reception, the product of the audio-vision (see Chion 1990) of each individual spectator and listener. In traditional staging, the *dramatis personae* presents a model for this audio-vision: through use of the voice and the body, the actor renders probable . . . the integration of the heterogeneous orders of perception – hearing and seeing. The actor's representation is a function of the mode in which the text is articulated, which is supported by mime and gesture. Physical presence and the manner of articulating the text thus determine the actor as the representative of a subject. The body's performance and the speech mannerisms of the voice determine which model of the subject it is; for instance: if it is a master of language or a servant to the body, if the accent designates an individualised subject or one whose manner of speech and discourse is dependent on others, or if the subject is shown as precocious or triumphant.

The classical, naturalistic, and psychological theatres have given us such subjects, who although often split, like Phaedra or Ophelia, nonetheless have been bearers and transmitters of texts that spring from the actor's mouth and permit us to identify a type or a character through his or her voice.

In such cases, the voice assumes the role of a *persona*, which in Greek refers to the grammatical 'I' the pronoun; but also means mask. It makes the exhibited body present through vocalised sound images and intonations derived from the national storehouses of rhetoric. But the timbre of the actor's voice also marks that which exceeds pure representation and indicates a momentary presence: the grittiness of the voice – Barthes's *grain de la voix* (1994: 1436–42) – speaks of a reality other than that of the sign and representation. It speaks of the reality of the actor as a desiring being and of the relationship of the actor to his or her own body. When the presence of this reality signal predominates – through a 'beautiful' timbre of the voice, for example, in which the actor is reflected, or through an error-ridden pronunciation, such as lisping, which reveals the all too great pleasure of initial orality – the representation is disturbed by, for example, the identification of the theatre characters with the good, histrionic actor or with the incompetent, bad actor. On the other hand, this vocal mark of a pleasurable body presence fixes the spectator's interest on the voice and makes possible the association of the seen and the heard. The actor's performance, his or her work with the voice, arouses the spectator's interest, as Lacan showed in his seminar on *Hamlet* (1982: 16), precisely because it exhibits this relationship to the body and to the unconscious image of the body, thereby creating a space for the spectator's Imaginary, a space for his or her relationship to the unconscious.

The body of the voice

A theatre of cruelty

Artaud's work with the voice in the theatre and, above all, his late experience with radio reveal this surplus of the actor's play. With his radio work from 1946 and with 'Pour en finir avec le jugement de dieu' from 1947, Artaud succeeded in sketching out a subjective sound space that broke with all existing models. Thus he was able to show that 'the actor lends his presence, his limbs, not only as marionette to the personage', but that he realises the personage 'with his real unconscious, that is, the relationship of his limbs to his own history' (Lacan 1982: 18). In Artaud's works for radio[3] the relationship of his physical body – his limbs – to his own history can be heard in the sonorous projection of a new body in the voice (see Finter 1990: 130–31, 133–8): a *corps sans organes*, a body without organs. The multiple and polyphonous voices of Artaud cannot be attributed to one decisive sexual characteristic, nor can they be assigned one age or background. A polylogous subject sketches out a sound-space in which the semiotic and polymorphic *jouissance* of a decentred subject is inscribed with an ambient range of more than two octaves by prompted voices. Unbearable at its time, the radio work was probably banned because the subject of which it speaks – the abolition and expulsion of language that asserts itself as a thesis (*jugement*) – becomes audible, *physically* attacking the auditor; that is, it no longer reflects but instead shatters the listener's own voice-mediated imaginary body image. The way Artaud made the subject's identification with the French language impossible by acoustically deconstructing his or her relationship to that language and to a vocally mediated first body image in order to reject and expel both as prompted is impressive even today.

Although polyphony can also be observed in the poetry recitations of a few major actors of the time – for example in the recording of Goethe's *Erlkönig* by Alexander Moissi (1927), which is likewise marked by its broad ambient range of one and a half octaves – Artaud's vocal play marks a caesura: a multiplicity of voices and an extremely broad tonal range no longer serve the primary function of realising vocal personae or masks, even if Moissi can be said to have achieved an element of presence through timbre. Rather, the voices Artaud makes heard are the result of a subjective necessity, the product of a unique history, which the text articulates at the level of enunciation. Through its timbre, the voice, as sound, manifests the body as prompted presence and simultaneously doubles and disinforms the intonation of the spoken voice, whose task it is to underscore meaning and mark the identity of a subject of the discursive act. The voice projects a body of the unconscious: the relationship to the imaginary body, to *jouissance*, which is shaped by the desire of the father and mother, becomes audible when the relationship to a first identity, to a first image of the self, resounds as prompted. Thus not only speech, as Derrida has shown, is 'prompted', but the voice itself and therewith the first body image is deconstructed as being indebted to others, to the Other.[4] Artaud shows that the image of the body is a function of the voice. Physical presence becomes the sole function of a vocalisation that is addressed to an identifying listener, who can thus become conscious of the role of the Imaginary in the perception of vocal phenomena.

How did Artaud arrive at this theatre of voices? As I mentioned earlier, his late-1947 radiophonic work came about – after two earlier attempts – following the evening at the Théâtre du Vieux-Colombier, when the physical presence of an Artaud debilitated and marked by illness was too real for the spectators to listen to and hear. The radio performance, on the other hand, allowed for a cruel body presence in the voice, marking his enunciations as real without simultaneously drowning them in another order of perception.

In the context of Artaud's work in the theatre, his occupation with the body of the voice and with the text is in the end a logical development. Only those who still attribute to Artaud's name the myth of a theatre without texts, a purely physical theatre, will have cause to wonder at this turn. Artaud himself understood his last radio play as 'a reduced model of that which I sought to accomplish in the theatre of cruelty' (*OC* XIII: 127), or as the first 'grist for the theatre of cruelty' (*OC* XIII: 139). From the beginning he sought to make the theatre the place 'where thought could find its body' (Sollers 1968: 137). For Artaud's point of departure was, as he noted in the early 1930s, the theatre of the spoken word – *parole* – and also, 'from the necessity of the spoken word more than from a language of words already formed'. And he goes on: 'But finding an impasse in the spoken word, it (the theatre) returns spontaneously to gesture' (*OC* IV: 105–9). This passage from 1932 from his second letter on language, which was printed in *Le Théâtre et son double* (*OC* IV: 105–9), already hints at the field for future experimentation, once the metaphysics of the physical body, the gesture, have been exhausted: it is this 'impasse' of speech that Artaud, following his internment, would seek to break open with his texts and radio works.

What is this impasse? It is blocked by a double wall: not only by the prompted spoken word, but also by the prompted voice. Language, which exposes us to the multiplicity of discourses, not only holds a monopoly on the correct tone – the intonation – it also determines the sound of the voice: the place between body and the word is occupied by verse, and in France in the 1920s still by the Alexandrine, the rhetoric of poetry. But the voices of the mother and father, upon which one's own timbre is modelled, also fill the space between body and word. Thus the human being, as a speaking being, is foremost a product of prompted speech and prompted voices. What psycholinguistics and psychoanalysis have taught us over the past decades about language acquisition and the constitution of the first body image and first identity[5] had for Artaud several years earlier been the object of a painful subjective experience: Artaud rejected the sound-body image mediated by the mother's voice, banished it as prompted, just as he sought to break up the mother tongue, its intonation, and the national vocal model of the subject – the verse. This attack on the mother tongue and on verse implies a cruelty for anyone seeking to anchor identity – the unconscious body image – in a national language. For Artaud in very concrete terms traverses the *jouissance* of the mother and father tongues and their individual and national bodies. And he demonstrates the *jouissance* with which he commits the transgression, which all great theatre has exemplified since its beginnings, namely to give voice to the Other of the Law, be it paternally or maternally determined.

Theatre has always made this Other audible, but it has done so under the protection of a transcendence that ultimately guaranteed a God. Yet for Artaud, this God is no longer the guarantor of the word, but an evil spirit who prompts his body with thoughts, words, and voices, thus usurping the space between body and language. Artaud associates God with excrement; the fact that God is conceivable is for him an indication of a misbegotten creation. Artaud delved into this notion and attempted to make audible the voices that no longer belong to the world of thought – that is, poetic inspiration or the poetic word, prosody, which for Artaud is 'foetus' or 'fly droppings' that the unconscious automatically rhymes (*OC* I*: 9). Artaud, however, was interested – as I already indicated – in screams, in voices that sound like they have been 'bruised by hostile sarcophagi, the seething of burnt flesh' (*OC* I*: 11). Artaud's preface to his collected works, written after Auschwitz in 1946, sheds light on the theatre of cruelty in a manner that rebukes the interpretation of his theatre as foremost a myth-building, socially therapeutic mass spectacle. Artaud sought, on the contrary, to make audible and visible what the seduction exercised by the Nazi-fascistic political theatre first made possible – the denial of the Other, the heterogeneous, and its projection onto others.

'Cruelty', wrote Artaud, is 'massacred bodies'. Artaud experienced first-hand his body as massacred, excoriated, and poisoned. He wanted to give voice to that which had made his body suffer. Through the voices that besieged him, the experience of the Other that impedes the attainment of an integral body should become perceptible. For Artaud this Other was language as Law, the prompted voice and prompted speech, as well as family and society. Yet he also made an Other audible by inscribing in language and modulating in glossolalias the semiotic energies and their *jouissance*. At the end of his life Artaud would represent himself as his own creator in a text entitled with the epitaph *Ci-gît* (here lies): 'I, Antonin Artaud, am my son, my father, my mother, and myself' (*OC* XII: 78). [. . .]

Artaud, our contemporary?

Can such an experience shape theatrical tradition? Even the theatre directors and authors who have expressed their affinity with Artaud have denied this. The work of Pierre Boulez with the voice (1966: 57–62), as well as that of John Cage (Brunel 1982: 71), both of whom have emphasised the importance of Artaud for their work (see Boulez [and Cage] 1991), results not so much from an imitation of Artaud's solutions, but arises from a taking up of the question Artaud posed regarding the sound potential of texts.[6] Robert Wilson, whose *Letter for Queen Victoria* (1975) was produced in Paris just three years after the first radio broadcast of 'Pour en finir avec le jugement de dieu', uses screen arias and duets that recall the glossolalias of Artaud's radio work. Yet the relationship between language and the body, which is the theme of Wilson's opera, is marked by his specific relationship with language and in particular by that of Christopher Knowles; their texts and theatre produce a distinctly individual and at the same time cruel aesthetic. Even Frederico Tiezzi, who together with Sandro Lombardi performed *Artaud* at 1987 *documenta* in Kassel, underscored the singular relation of the Italian Group I Magazzini to Artaud as a mythic figure: in one scene Sandro Lombardi doubled Artaud's recorded voice, duplicating his treatment of the voice with such accuracy that he was able to demonstrate that the imitation of Artaud's voice could be learned like any other theatre rhetoric.

Those for whom the theatre is a necessity must discover for themselves and explore their own relationship to the voice and thereby to their first imaginary sound-body image (*Klangkörperbild*), that is, to a sound image (*Klangbild*) that establishes a relationship between the body and language. That this aspect either is neglected or else retreats into the background to become secondary in the aforementioned examples, perhaps reveals that the horizon of these theatre experiments is still a metaphysics of the body, which Artaud's late theatre experience had overcome by means of a language body, a body projected by voices.

The contemporary theatre of the Real . . . is a reaction to the experimentation of the late 1960s, the 1970s, and the early 1980s, a reaction to their postmodern play with signifiers. During that period, individual artists experimented with the constituent elements of scenic presence and analysed the metaphysics of the body, by deconstructing the constituent elements of its representation (see Finter 1996). Their analysis of the relationship of the individual to verbal language and to that which is heterogeneous to it joins these artists to Artaud, as do their investigations of how language and voice constitute a subject. What sets them apart is the absence of the pressure of suffering in their work; one finds instead a less radical relationship to the body – one not driven to extreme boundaries – as well as an attitude that is more playful and open to compromises [. . .].

Artaud's legacy

The experimentation and experiences that have offered us an aesthetic of the voice in theatre since the end of the 1960s push the self-experience of the performer and the spectator to new limits, in some cases even to the constituent level of subjectivity formation. Their explorations of the Other in the self seldom if ever reach the point at which the lynchpin of aggression – the *jouissance* of violence – can be experienced. It is, however, this experience that connects the theatre to the individual's relation to language and to his or her own body. Thus this experience is a first step towards becoming aware, through one's own excluded Other, of one's potential for violence.

Artaud, however, wanted more. In 'The Theatre and the Plague' he made the demand that the theatrical play 'impel the mind by example to the source of its conflicts' ([1938] 1958: 30). Artaud's spirit suffered, and this suffering affected him physically. In earlier times this suffering was referred to as the 'sufferings of the soul'. Many contemporaries believe that they have surmounted the old-fashioned notion of the soul, even though it was because of this physical suffering that the clinic of the psyche would come into being (see Kristeva 1977: 193). Some . . . explore this soul by means of the vocal and musical manifestations of subjectivity. Others believe . . . that they can heal the body directly, without mediation, even in the theatre – through the Real. However the *phobos* that numbs the body, the affect that erupts wordlessly and briefly brings relief, disappears, cast loose in the meandering of a speechless physical memory; and it is just as meaningless to the self-experience of the spectator as the completed deed is to the self-knowledge of an actual murderer. Artaud compared the murderer to the actor who plays a murderer:

> Once launched upon the fury of his task, an actor requires infinitely more power to keep from committing a crime than a murderer needs courage to

complete his act, and it is here, in its very gratuitousness, that the action and effect of a feeling in the theatre appears infinitely more valid than that of a feeling fulfilled in life.

(*OC* IV: 24–5)

The actor, in contrast to the murderer, is aware of his potential *Mordlust* [the desire to murder], which is why for Artaud the demonstration of this affect in the theatre counted much more than the realised pleasure in an 'acting out'.

That the spectator could become physically aware through theatre of his potential, for instance, for *Mordlust*, not rejecting this sensation but rather letting it permeate into his or her consciousness so that he or she could become aware of the estranged Other *within* – this is the utopian and perhaps impossible task that Artaud's experience bequeaths to us. As Artaud lifts the lid on the inferno of the Real, Kafka's motto, transmitted to us by Gustav Janouch (1951), also seems to hold true for him: to escape the ranks of the murderers . . . through written language, through performance, and through *Sprechsgesang*, which each make their debts to language and to the body audible in the space between language and the body, between language and music.

8 Jerzy Grotowski

'He wasn't entirely himself'*

Grotowski's title is perhaps a little desultory, but the piece it names goes to the heart of the problem of how to perform Artaud's ideas. The description here of the total act is pure Artaud despite its criticism of Artaud's style in *Le Théâtre et son double*. Grotowski returns us to the central challenge that Artaud's theatre writings extend to practitioners, namely how to find the necessity of the gesture, to peel away the strata of fictions and expose the raw impulse, the nervous system of performance. From here, Grotowski suggests, the performer can go anywhere, even ultimately outside the theatrical itself. Just as Artaud could not finally constrain his ideas to the theatrical frame, so Grotowski found his experiments less and less in need of a validating audience. Like Artaud, he would develop his rituals of transformation elsewhere. These parallel trajectories, and an achingly sincere approach to the culture of performance as essential to living and thinking, connect their otherwise divergent views on the actor's task.

Stanislavski was compromised by his disciples. He was the first great creator of a method of acting in the theatre, and all those of us who are involved with theatre problems can do no more than give personal answers to the questions he raised. When, in numerous European theatres, we watch performances inspired by the 'Brecht theory', and are obliged to fight against utter boredom because the lack of conviction of both actors and producers takes the place of the so-called '*Verfremdungseffekt*', we think back to Brecht's own productions. They were perhaps less true to his theory but, on the other hand, very personal and subversive as they were, they showed a deep professional knowledge and never left us in a state of lassitude.

We are entering the age of Artaud. The 'theatre of cruelty' has been canonised, i.e. made trivial, swapped for trinkets, tortured in various ways. When an eminent creator with an achieved style and personality, like Peter Brook, turns to Artaud, it's not to hide his own weaknesses, or to ape the man. It just happens that at a given point of his development he finds himself in agreement with Artaud, feels the need of a confrontation, *tests* Artaud, and retains whatever stands up to this test. He remains himself. But as for the wretched performances one can see in the theatrical avant-garde of many countries, these chaotic, aborted works, full of a so-called cruelty which would not scare a child, when we see all these happenings which only reveal a lack of professional skill, a sense of groping, and a love of easy solutions, performances which are only violent on the surface (they should hurt us but do not manage to) – when we see these sub-products whose authors call Artaud their spiritual father, then we think that perhaps there is cruelty indeed, but only towards Artaud himself.

The paradox of Artaud lies in the fact that it is impossible to carry out his proposals. Does this mean that he was wrong? Certainly not. But Artaud left no concrete technique behind him, indicated no method. He left visions, metaphors. This was surely an expression of Artaud's personality and is partly the result of lack of time and means to put the things he glimpsed into practice. It also comes from what we might call Artaud's mistake, or at least his peculiarity: as he probed subtly, in an a-logical, almost invisible and intangible way, Artaud used a language which was almost as intangible and fleeting. Yet micro-organisms are studied with a precision instrument, the microscope. Whatever is imperceptible demands precision.

Artaud spoke of the magic of the theatre, and the way he conjured it up leaves images which touch us in some way. Perhaps we don't understand them completely, but we realise he was after a theatre transcending discursive reason and psychology. And when, one fine day, we discover that the essence of the theatre is found neither in the narration of an event, nor in the discussion of a hypothesis with an audience, nor in the representation of life as it appears from outside, nor even in a vision – but that the theatre is an act carried out *here and now* in the actors' organisms, in front of other men, when we discover that theatrical reality is instantaneous, not an illustration of life but something linked to life only by analogy, when we realise all this, then we ask ourselves the question: wasn't Artaud talking about just this and nothing else?

For when in the theatre we dispose of the tricks of make-up and costume, stuffed bellies and false noses, and when we propose to the actor that he should transform himself before the spectator's eyes using only his inner impulse, his body, when we state that the magic of the theatre consists in this transformation *as it comes to birth*, we once more raise the question: did Artaud ever suggest any other kind of magic?

Artaud speaks of the 'cosmic trance'. This brings back an echo of the time when the heavens were emptied of their traditional inhabitants and themselves became the object of a cult. Then 'cosmic trance' inevitably leads to the 'magic theatre'. Yet Artaud explains the unknown by the unknown, the magic by the magic. I do not know what is meant by the 'cosmic trance' for, generally speaking, I do not believe that the cosmos can, in a physical sense, become a transcendental point of reference for man. The points of reference are others. Man is one of them.

Artaud opposed the discursive principle in theatre, i.e. the entire French theatre tradition. But we can't accept him as a pioneer in this. Many central European and Eastern theatres have a living tradition of non-discursive theatre. And how do we rate Vakhtangov or Stanislavski?

Artaud refused a theatre which was content to illustrate dramatic texts; he claimed the theatre should be a creative art in itself, and not just duplicate what literature was doing. This was a sign of great courage and consciousness on his part, for he wrote in a language in which the complete works of playwrights were not entitled 'Plays' or 'Comedies' but 'The Theatre of Molière', or 'The Theatre of Montherlant'. Yet the idea of an autonomous theatre came to us much earlier, from Meyerhold in Russia. Artaud intended to suppress the barrier between actors and audience. This seems striking, but note that he neither proposed to abolish the stage separate from the auditorium, nor to seek a different structure adapted to each new production thus creating a real basis for confrontation between the two 'ensembles' formed by the actors and the spectators. He simply proposed to put the audience in the centre and play in all four corners of the room. This is no elimination of the stage/audience barrier, but the replacement of the classical doll's theatre by another rigid structure. And years before all these ideas of Artaud, decisive steps in this direction had already been taken by Reinhardt, Meyerhold in his production of the mystery plays, and again later by Syrkus in Poland with his already elaborated conception of a 'simultaneous theatre'.

Thus we have withdrawn Artaud's supposed merits in order to restore them to their true fathers. It might be thought we are preparing a scene of martyrdom, stripping Artaud of his rags just as he stripped Beatrice Cenci in his production. But there is a difference between stripping someone to torture them, and doing so to find out who they really are. The fact that others have made similar suggestions in other places cannot alter the vital fact that Artaud made his discoveries himself, and that as far as his own country goes, he virtually invented everything.

Must it be repeated yet again that if Artaud had had at his disposal the necessary material, his visions might have developed from the undefined to the defined and he might even have converted them into a form or, better still, a technique? He would then have been in a position to anticipate all the other reformers, for he had the courage and the power to go beyond the current discursive logic. All this could have happened, but never did.

Artaud's secret, above all, is to have made particularly fruitful mistakes and misunderstandings. His description of Balinese theatre, however suggestive it may be for the imagination, is really one big mis-reading. Artaud deciphered as 'cosmic signs' and 'gestures evoking superior powers' elements of the performance which were concrete expressions, specific theatrical letters in an alphabet of signs universally understood by the Balinese.

The Balinese performance for Artaud was like a crystal ball for a fortune-teller. It brought forth a totally different performance which slumbered in his depths, and this work of Artaud's provoked by the Balinese theatre gives us an image of his great creative possibilities. As soon as he moves from description to theory, however, he starts explaining magic by magic, cosmic trance by cosmic trance. It is theory which can mean whatever you require.

But in his description he touches something essential, of which he is not quite aware. It is the true lesson of the sacred theatre; whether we speak of the medieval European drama, the Balinese, or the Indian Kathakali: this knowledge that spontaneity and discipline, far from weakening each other, mutually reinforce themselves: that what is elementary feeds what is constructed and vice versa, to become the real source of a kind of acting that glows. This lesson was neither understood by Stanislavski, who let natural impulses dominate, nor Brecht, who gave too much emphasis to the construction of the role.

Artaud intuitively saw myth as the dynamic centre of the theatre performance. Only Nietzsche was ahead of him in this domain. He also knew that transgression of the myth renewed its essential values and 'became an element of menace which re-established the desired norms'. He did not however take account of the fact that, in our age, when all languages intermingle, the community of the theatre cannot possibly identify itself with myth, because there is no single faith. Only a confrontation is possible.

Artaud dreamed of producing new myths through the theatre, but this beautiful dream was born from his lack of precision. For although the myth forms the basis or framework for the experience of entire generations, it is for the subsequent generations to create it and not the theatre. At the most, the theatre could have contributed to the crystallisation of the myth. But then it would have been too similar to current ideas to be creative.

A confrontation is a 'trying out', a testing of whatever is a traditional value. A performance which, like an electrical transformer, adjusts our experience to those of past generations (and vice versa), a performance conceived as a combat against traditional and contemporary values (whence 'transgression') – this seems to me the only real chance for myth to work in the theatre. An honest renewal can only be found in this double game of values, this attachment and rejection, this revolt and submissiveness.

Nevertheless, Artaud was a prophet. His texts conceal such a special and complex web of forecasts, such impossible allusions, visions which are so suggestive and metaphors which seem, in the long run, to possess a certain soundness. For all this is bound to happen. No one knows how, but it is inevitable. And it does happen.

We shout with triumph when we discover silly misunderstandings in Artaud. The sign which, in oriental theatre, is simply a part of a universally known alphabet, cannot – as Artaud would have it – be transferred to European theatre in which every sign has to be born separately in relation to familiar psychological or cultural associations, before becoming something quite different. All his divisions of breathing into masculine, feminine and neuter are just misinterpretations of oriental texts, and in practice so imperceptible they cannot be distinguished. His study of the 'athletics of feelings' has certain shrewd insights, but in practical work would lead to stereotyped gestures, one for each emotion.

Yet he does touch on something which we may be able to reach by a different route. I mean the very crux of the actor's art, that what the actor achieves should be (let's not be afraid of the name) a total act, that he does whatever he does with his entire being, and not just one mechanical (and therefore rigid) gesture of arm or leg, not any grimace, helped by a logical inflection and a thought. No thought can guide the entire organism of an actor in any living way. It must stimulate him, and that is all it really can do. Without commitment, his organism stops living, his impulses grow superficial. Between a total reaction and a reaction guided by a thought there is the same difference as between a tree and a plant. In the final result we are speaking of the impossibility of separating spiritual and physical. The actor should not use his organism to illustrate a 'movement of the soul', he should accomplish this movement with his organism.

Artaud teaches us a great lesson which none of us can refuse. This lesson is his sickness. Artaud's misfortune is that his sickness, paranoia, differed from the sickness of the times. Civilisation is sick with schizophrenia, which is a rupture between intelligence and feeling, body and soul. Society couldn't allow Artaud to be ill in a different way. They looked after him, tortured him with electro-shock treatment, trying to make him acknowledge discursive and cerebral reason: i.e. to take society's sickness into himself. Artaud defined his illness remarkably in a letter to Jacques Rivière: 'I am not entirely myself'. He was not merely himself, he was someone else. He grasped half of his own dilemma: how to be oneself. He left the other half untouched: how to be whole, how to be complete.

He couldn't bridge the deep gulf between the zone of visions (intuitions) and his conscious mind, for he had given up everything orderly, and made no attempt to achieve precision or mastery of things. Instead he made his chaos and self-division objective. His chaos was an authentic image of the world. It wasn't a therapy but a diagnosis, at least in the eyes of other people. His chaotic outbursts were holy, for they enabled others to reach self-knowledge.

Among his successors, the chaos is in no sense holy, nor sufficiently determined: it has no reason for existing save to conceal something unfinished, to hide an infirmity. Artaud gave this chaos expression, which is quite another matter.

Artaud puts forward the idea of great release, a great transgression of conventions, a purification by violence and cruelty; he affirms that the evocation of blind powers on stage ought to protect us from them in life itself. But how can we ask them to protect us in this way when it's obvious they do nothing of the kind? It's not in the theatre that dark powers can be controlled; more likely that these powers will turn the theatre into their own ends. (Although I don't think they are concerned about the theatre, since they have massive means of domination already at their disposal.) The theatre in the end neither protects us nor leaves us unprotected. I don't believe that the explosive portrayal of Sodom and Gomorrah on a stage calms or sublimates in any way the sinful impulses for which those two towns were punished.

And yet when Artaud speaks of release and cruelty we feel he's touching a truth we can verify in another way. We feel that an actor reaches the essence of his vocation whenever he commits an act of sincerity, when he unveils himself, opens and gives himself in an extreme, solemn gesture, and does not hold back before any obstacle set by custom and behaviours. And further, when this act of extreme sincerity is modelled in a living organism, in impulses, a way of breathing, a rhythm of thought and the circulation of blood, when it is ordered and brought to consciousness, not dissolving into chaos and formal anarchy – in a word, when this act accomplished through the theatre is total, then even if it doesn't protect us from the dark powers, at least it enables us to respond totally, that is, begin to exist. For each day we only react with half our potential.

If I speak of 'a total act', it's because I have the feeling that there is an alternative to 'the theatre of cruelty'. But Artaud stands as a challenge to us at this point: perhaps less because of his work than his idea of salvation through the theatre. This man gave us, in his martyrdom, a shining proof of the theatre as therapy. I have found two expressions in Artaud which deserve attention. The first is a reminder that anarchy and chaos (which he needed as a spur for his own character) should be linked to a sense of order, which he conceived in the mind, and not as a physical technique. Still, it's worth quoting this phrase for the sake of Artaud's so-called disciples: 'Cruelty is rigour'.

The other phrase holds the very foundation of the actor's art of extreme and ultimate action. 'Actors should be like martyrs burnt alive, still signalling to us from their stakes.' Let me add that these signals must be articulated, and they cannot just be gibberish or delirious, calling out to everything and nothing – unless a given work demands precisely that. With such a proviso, we affirm that this quotation contains, in an oracular style, the whole problem of spontaneity and discipline, this *conjunction of opposites* which gives birth to the total act.

Artaud was a great theatre-poet, which means a poet of the possibilities of theatre and not of dramatic literature. Like the mythical prophet Isaiah, he predicts for the theatre something definitive, a new meaning, a new possible incarnation. 'Then Emmanuel was born.' Like Isaiah, Artaud knew of Emmanuel's coming, and what it promised. He saw the image of it through a glass, darkly.

9   Jane Goodall

'The plague and its powers in Artaudian theatre'*

Jane Goodall shows a profound sensitivity to the disjunctions Artaud works in the various protagonists that speak in his texts, aware of the traps he sets for readers in search of the one true voice. In this essay she returns to the topic of Artaud's text on the theatre and the plague and shows how it corresponds to his continuous transformative project, the way he describes theatre as a shape changer which morphs, like the plague, into multiple forms so as to survive and evade capture. Here, Goodall combines a reading of Artaud with Seneca, feasting, sacrificial crisis and taboo to suggest that Artaud's theatre really does require a new form of civilisation to sustain it, but also that this new form is, after all, an old one in disguise, a deep and repressed, irrational mode of being that we only think we've outgrown.

Goodall has also published an important book-length study, *Artaud and the Gnostic Drama* (1994), which tracks the differentials in scope provided by two methodologies used in relation to interpreting Artaud's thought: the philosophical/textual on the one hand, and the dramaturgical/gnostic on the other. Her reading looks at how some of the central tenets of gnosticism appear in his own writings at some of the most crucial moments of his career. The text included here is not extracted from Goodall's book, which operates best as an extended and continuous reading, but is an earlier piece which nonetheless anticipates the later concern with Artaud's assault on civilisation at its most basic levels.

Artaud's essay 'The Theatre and the Plague' begins with an account of a dream vision experienced by Saint-Remys, Viceroy of Sardinia, in 1720:

> . . . he saw himself plague-ridden and he saw the plague ravage his miniature state. Beneath the scourge, the frameworks of society dissolve. Order collapses. He is audience to (*il assiste à*) every moral deviation, to every psychological debacle; he hears in himself the murmuring of his internal fluids, disrupted, in complete derangement, becoming heavy and gradually turning to carbon in a vertiginous shrinkage of matter.
>
> (*TD*: 15)[1]

In 'assisting' at this apocalyptic spectacle, the dreamer is essentially in the position of any audience member in the theatre of cruelty. He knows the dangers to which he is witness cannot kill him, but he realises too 'that the will operates in them to the point of absurdity, to the point of the negation of possibility, to the point of a kind of transmutation of the lie from which you can remake the truth' (*TD*: 5), and this realisation teaches him to act in defiance of destiny and turn the fatal course of events which was set according to his premonition.

His story illustrates that the powers of the plague are powers of revelation, of alchemical transformation, leading through the *nigredo* of dissolution towards a new genesis. Artaud describes how volcanic eruptions on the surface of the flesh violate the inside/outside borders which preserve corporeal integrity, as social, psychological and ethical structures implode. 'Civilised man' disintegrates in an elemental forcefield that seems to be reversing the process of creation, and the more determined his strategies of self-preservation, the more directly they contribute to the process of his destruction. It is as though the logic of causality in which he invests all hope of survival is itself subservient to some more deeply laid design requiring his unwitting co-operation for its fulfilment. So Artaud tells another story, of how Boccaccio and his debauched companions remain unheeding and unscathed in the open countryside whilst

> . . . in a castle nearby, transformed into a fortified citadel with a cordon of armed men to prevent entry, the plague transforms the entire garrison and its occupants into corpses and spares the men at arms who alone have been exposed to contagion.
>
> (*TD*: 22)

Edgar Allan Poe, an acknowledged mentor to the theatre of cruelty enterprise, gives a mesmeric rendition of the story of the garrisoned company in 'The Masque of the Red Death'. The victims of the red death are possessed by a force which manifests itself in a horrific transgression of the inside/outside borders in every sphere – social, biological, territorial, existential:

> No pestilence had ever been so fatal or so hideous. Blood was its Avatar and its seal – the redness and the horror of blood. There were sharp pains, and sudden dizziness, and then profuse bleeding at the pores, with dissolution. The scarlet stains upon the body and especially upon the face of the victim, were the pest ban which shut him out from the aid and from the sympathy of his fellow men.
>
> (Poe 1985: 614)

Prince Prospero, 'happy . . . dauntless . . . sagacious', remains unaided by the occult counsel of the dream vision and thus unable to read the semiotics of the red death, believing that he can evade it by the very strategies of liminality against which its influence is pervasively manifested. He retreats into a fortified castle with a thousand of his retinue, who are instructed to solder the bolts on the iron gates so as 'to leave means neither of ingress nor of egress to the sudden impulses of frenzy from within'. After some months, he proposes to celebrate their privileged sanctuary with a masked ball. Prospero has a fetishistic sense of order and ritual which borders on the pathological, and the appearance of the personified Red Death as the inconceivable climax of his obsessively prescribed ceremony is like the *parousia* of a formless double which has been coming inexorably to meet, possess and devour him in a flamboyant display of the powers of horror.

In Artaudian metaphor, the power base of horror is always inside, a molten core of being which erupts, like the plague, in defiance of all logically calculated defences. This most theatrical of Poe's stories has essential features in common with a number of texts cited by Artaud as exemplary theatre of cruelty: Ford's *'Tis Pity She's a Whore,* Seneca's *Thyestes,* Tourneur's *The Revenger's Tragedy* and his own dramatisation of Shelley's *The Cenci.* All these plays contain scenes in which some extreme act of violence is at once a literal or figurative unmasking, a revelatory confrontation with internally situated forces of destruction and a devastating assault on all forms of order.

This involves systematic taboo-breaking – incest, intrafamilial murder, forbidden feasting – for the truly horrible, as Julia Kristeva demonstrates, is also the vile, the abject, the abhorrent. Carnal contamination and the spoiling of systems are equated in her argument as they are in Artaud's quintessential metaphor of theatre-as-plague. But whence, then, arises his compulsion to seek out what is most repulsive and terrible?

> Apprehensive, desire turns aside; sickened, it rejects. A certainty protects it from the shameful – a certainty of which it is proud holds on to it. But simultaneously, just the same, that impetus, that spasm, that leap is drawn toward an elsewhere as tempting as it is condemned. Unflaggingly, like an inescapable boomerang, a vortex of summons and repulsion places the one haunted by it literally beside himself.
>
> (Kristeva [1980b] 1982: 1)

With the vertiginous displacement of the self envisaged by Kristeva, the distinction between conscious and unconscious is subsumed by 'the fundamental opposition [. . .] between I and Other [. . .] between Inside and Outside' (Kristeva [1980b] 1982: 7). The abject is the pre-objectal Other, the undefined ground against which the self seeks definition. The exteriority of this not-self must be constantly reconfirmed through the drives of fear and loathing, but such perpetual reinforcement of the embargo is prompted by attraction which is the other face of such drives. The abject which threatens to annihilate the ego is also 'magnetic'. Retreat into the fortified castle is a desperate measure to counter its drawing power by those who have failed to ensconce themselves in the security of a symbolic order which enables the construction of objects of desire. Alternatively, the semiotics of abjection may themselves be fetishised as objects:

> The body's inside, in that case, shows up in order to compensate for the collapse of the border between inside and outside. It is as if the skin, a fragile container, no longer guaranteed the integrity of one's 'own and clean' self but, scraped or transparent, invisible or taut, gave way before the dejection of its contents. Urine, blood, sperm, excrement then show up in order to reassure a subject that is lacking its 'own and clean self'. The abjection of those flows from within suddenly become the sole 'object' of sexual desire . . . Abjection then takes the place of the other, to the extent of affording him jouissance, often the only one for the borderline patient who, on that account, transforms the abject into the site of the Other.
>
> (Kristeva [1980b] 1982: 53–4)

But such last ditch attempts to withstand the engulfing morass of abjection have no place in Poe's story or in the theatre of cruelty. Prince Prospero discovers his abhorrent Other as the secret ruling presence in his fortifed castle; Artaud polemically asserts that objectification of the vile, whether it is created as Other through loathing or desire, is a self-cancelling (indeed self-annihilating) delusion:

> And by the same token, if we think negroes smell bad, we don't realise that to anyone who is not European, it's we, the whites who smell bad. And I will even say that the odour we give off is white in the sense that you might speak of a white pustule. As with iron heated to white-heat, you can say that all that is excessive is white; and for an Asiatic, the colour white has become the signifier of the most advanced decomposition.
>
> (*TD*: 11)

As someone who declares repeatedly 'I am nothing' and 'I have no self anymore', Artaud is no desperate frontiersman; he has nothing to lose in making the gesture of abandonment, occupying the forbidden territory. Pitched into the abject sublime of *ego absconditus*, he assaults the fortress of rational, egocentric consciousness from which he is outcast.

In his quest for 'an absolutely pure theatre', he selects works in which the action has its catalyst and catastrophe in the violation of what Freud refers to as 'the two principal ordinances of totemism' (Freud 1985: 192): if the horror of incest and the injunction against parricide constitute the founding principles of social organisation, Artaud's repertoire projects a series of strategic acts of cultural terrorism. There is brother/sister incest in *'Tis Pity She's a Whore,* father/daughter incest in *The Cenci*; brother/sister-in-law incest is an element in the precipitating context of *Thyestes*; stepmother/son incest features in *The Revenger's Tragedy* and is implied in *The Cenci.* Fathers murder sons in *The Cenci* and in the Tantalus myth which forms the prelude to *Thyestes*, brother murders sister in *'Tis Pity She's a Whore*, uncle murders nephews in *Thyestes*, daughter and sons murder father in *The Cenci*, and in *The Revenger's Tragedy* there are examples of both intentional and unwitting fratricide, threatened matricide and execution of a son by unwitting order of his father.

It is as though Freudian insights help to show Artaud the way to the vulnerable core of the social and psychological order he abhors, but his relationship to these insights is itself subversive. Mounting as radical an attack as Freud's upon the sanctity of the family, he offers another version of the nuclear complex that fissures this atomic unit of the social order, an 'Anti-Oedipus' to rupture the tyrannical paradigm which shapes even Kristeva's bold enquiry into the foundations of subjectivity.

In his preface to *The Theatre and its Double,* he announces his commitment to the rediscovery of organic culture through exploration of 'the barbaric and primitive means of totemism, whose savage vitality I would worship' (*TD*: 12). Such a declaration warrants consideration as an explicitly calculated travesty of Freud's theoretical stance in *Totem and Taboo*.[2] Freud repeatedly endorses E.B. Taylor's description of magic as 'mistaking an ideal connection for a real one' (Freud 1985: 136), using it to support his own interpretation of totemic rituals as symptomatic of conceptual immaturity; thus he relegates such practices to the status of 'infantile' or 'neurotic' misprision, equatable with the narcissistic stage in libidinal development. Man in the 'scientific phase' has an unquestionable evolutionary superiority; his is 'the stage at which an individual has reached maturity, has renounced the pleasure principle, adjusted himself to reality and turned to the external world for the object of his desires' (Freud 1985: 148). The hallmark of this superior condition is the ability to discriminate clearly between the relationship of thoughts as it is dominated by the pleasure principle, and the logic of cause and effect as it operates in the external world. An ability to understand the world in terms of scientific logic is therefore prerequisite to the attainment of secure self definition.

Artaud attacks 'civilised man' on both these fronts, privileging magic and derogating science in a diametric reversal of Freud's evaluation and committing himself to the liberation of the anarchic forces of desire which threaten the dominance of the ego. In 'The Theatre and the Plague', he asserts the futility of scientific attempts to establish the cause of the plague or the logic of its dissemination. Microbial research is merely mistaking ideal connections for real ones from an opposite point of view:

> Whatever the aberrations of historians or doctors on the subject of the plague, I think one can subscribe to a notion of the malady as a kind of psychic entity not transmitted by any virus. If you wanted to analyse closely all the facts about pestilential contagion that are presented in historical narratives and memoirs, you would have a hard job to isolate a single verifiable case of infection by contact.
>
> (*TD*: 18)

Freud construes the animistic picture of the external world as the product of an understanding tethered to the object-sign in the absence of a language of abstract thought in which to describe emotional states, and advocates that 'we, with our intensified conscious perception' translate this picture back into psychology (Freud 1985: 121). The opening paragraphs of *The Theatre and its Double* deride civilised man, the man of systems who dissipates the inherent power of his own impulses through conceptual self-scrutiny. Such a man leads his life at one remove and is forever barred from the 'constant magic' of authentic being (*TD*: 10).

The Oedipus Complex – the 'nuclear complex of the neuroses' (Freud 1985: 189), in which the two strongest and most disaster-prone impulses of human nature coalesce – is the lynch-pin of the thesis expounded in *Totem and Taboo*. It is in terms of the Oedipus myth that scientific man must translate the misprisions of animism, for this myth confronts him with the vestiges of taboo still harboured in his own psyche, forcing him to recognise the true causes and consequences of those drives which, unidentified, might undermine his capacity for rational self-government.

In spite of Artaud's emphatic preference for works which deal in incest and intrafamilial violence, he accords Sophocles's *Oedipus Rex* no place in the repertoire which aims to confront man with the dark secrets in his own psyche as they are revealed in dreams, 'his taste for crime, his erotic obsessions, his savagery, his chimeras, his utopian idea of life and affairs, even his cannibalism' (*TD*: 89). The one element in the play which does interest him is its portrayal of errant forces we would do well to guard against, 'manifested in an epidemic of the plague which is the physical incarnation of these forces' (*TD*: 73). To borrow the terminology of Deleuze and Guattari, he opposes a schizophrenic reading of the dynamics of the drama to Freud's paranoic reading. Freud bypasses the plague and its wayward, deterritorialising powers to fix upon the closed triangular dynamic of violence and sexuality within the nucleus of the family where 'everything is preformed, prearranged in advance', where ' . . . in the aggregate of destination, in the end, there is no longer anyone but daddy, mommy, and me, the despotic sign inherited by daddy, the residual territoriality, assumed by mommy, and the divided, split, castrated ego' (Deleuze and Guattari [1972] 1983: 265).

Though the themes of his theatre are not translatable in the reductive terms of Freudian psychoanalysis, or identifiable with any single narrative model, Artaud does go so far as to nominate works in which the 'Great Mysteries' retain an authentic, numinous presence, and he claims that the greatest of all tragic authors, unsurpassed as 'an initiate into the Secrets', is Seneca (Artaud [*OC* III] 1932). The first act of Seneca's *Oedipus* dwells at length on the nature and effects of the plague in a way which corroborates Artaud's assertion that all plagues are psychic entities, transmitted according to principles which have nothing to do with viral behaviour. Besides causing corporeal dissolution, the plague which has attacked Thebes is a violent eliminator of difference amongst the living. Young and old, male and female, rich and poor are alike its potential victims. Anguished fathers and stricken mothers are seen everywhere, without anyone's being minded to look for the cause of their distress in some abominable *personal* tragedy. All creatures lose their distinguishing characteristics: wolves are no longer hungry and stags no longer fearful of them, lions have ceased to roar, bears have ceased to fight, serpents lie shrivelled and venomless upon the ground. (Artaud describes humans similarly denatured – the miser who throws handfuls of gold from his window, the celibate who takes to sodomy, the virtuous son who kills his father.) The Black Death, opening its ravenous mouth to devour all, seems like an inexorable return of the vampire tyrant which in its last metamorphosis took the form of the sphinx; present and future are written in the past. The task of *reading* is central to Seneca's treatment of the drama, and always the text to be deciphered is history.

In a striking departure from Sophocles, he interpolates lurid, extenuated descriptions of the sacrificial rites which accompany Tiresias's attempts to decipher the dark secret of Thebes. Turning the corpses of the victims inside out, this semiotician of the abject reads putrefied livers, shrunken hearts, malformed foetuses, livid veins and swollen, blackened masses of flesh (again, there is a direct parallel here in Artaud's dissertation on the anatomised plague victim, whose exposed entrails are compared with those of a human sacrifice). These somatic emblems prefigure psychic manifestations of the founding spirits of Thebes. A parade of horrific spectres is headed by the Erinys, the Plague and the viper's brood engendered from the teeth of the dragon. The apparition of Laius is the last in a succession of Theban tragic victims, the objects and unwitting perpetrators of violence between parent and child: mad Agave is accompanied by the image of her mangled son Pentheus, whom she tore to pieces in a Bacchic orgy; Niobe, indirectly responsible for the murder of all her children, is reunited with them. The vindictive frenzy of Laius against his son is undercut with silent irony by these attendant visions, in which the murdered and their murderers seem equally wretched pawns of destiny. It is as though the dramatic nucleus of Sophocles's drama were being shifted in a way designed to bring the tragedy of Oedipus closer to that of Thyestes, or Hercules in *Hercules Furens,* or Theseus in *Phaedra;* and in each of these cases it is the *father* who is tricked by fate into the murder of his children.

Georges Devereux, René Girard, and Deleuze and Guattari have all offered influential deconstructions of the Oedipus complex on the basis of a shift in emphasis towards the catalytic role of Laius, but Artaud's quest for the origins of a nuclear complex is bound up with an enquiry into the great religious themes of creation, chaos and becoming. The plague as a process of creation in reverse cycle is neither incidental nor preliminary to Artaudian dramatisations of the nuclear complex: it is their milieu. As he makes explicit in his notes for *The Cenci,* he has no interest in dramas which have their catalyst in personal motivation. Count Cenci is himself presented not as a character but as a forcefield working to destroy subjectivity:

I believe myself to be and I am a force of nature. For me there is neither life nor death, neither god, nor incest, neither repentence nor crime. I am obedient to my law, which gives to me no sensation of vertigo; but so much the worse for whoever is caught and sinks into the abyss which I am become. I seek out and I accomplish evil by destination and by precept.

(*OC* IV: 153)

The Freudian view of the Oedipus myth divorces it from the larger genealogical framework which links it with the myths of creation. Its echoes (ironic and distorted) of atrocities which recur from one generation to the next are taken for prototypical manifestations, the authoritative version of the primal conflict. Artaud chooses not *Oedipus* but *Thyestes* as a definitive text for his theatre and his decision to retitle the play *The Torment of Tantalus* suggests that he is deliberately moving the focus of the tragedy backwards in time (*OC* II: 159–61). Tantalus, like Cenci, is a bad father, and Artaud states explicitly that it is Cenci's role as the father-destroyer which links his story with the 'Great Myths'. Tantalus has killed his son Pelops and served his body as food at a banquet of the gods. This act is a recapitulation of the behaviour of his own forefathers: Tantalus is the son of Zeus, and Zeus was the first of the sons of Chronos to escape being eaten by his father; Chronos was the son of Uranus, who dealt with *his* first offspring by attempting to return them to the womb of their mother, Gaia. The progenitor may be prompted by a savage compensatory impulse to revoke the gift of life he has bestowed, to reverse the birth process literally (as Uranus does) or symbolically, through orally reincorporating the child himself. The son learns quickly that his existence is perpetually threatened by his creator and may be preserved only through treachery and counter-violence: Chronos castrates Uranus; Zeus declares war upon Chronos; Tantalus challenges the divinity of Zeus by attempting to trick him into consuming the murdered body of his grandson. Here the primal conflict enters a new, secondary phase; for the crime of Tantalus is avenged by a father instead of a son and the punishment which is inflicted is a symbolic assertion of the need to overcome the devouring impulse. Tantalus, as we are reminded at the beginning of *Thyestes,* is condemned by Zeus to hunger and thirst in perpetuity. 'Tantalus is mankind and every man alive is a menagerie of vampires' (*OC* XVII: 60).

The Freudian term 'nuclear' could aptly be transferred to describe the first phase of the familial conflict in Hellenistic mythology, for the atomic split between parent and child as Self and Other threatens a holocaust in which all creation may be consumed. When the family is conceived of as a collective self, this establishes an atomic unit which enables the growth of civilisation. In the second phase of the conflict, destruction starts to move in ever-widening circles as the rivalry is staked out diachronically in two dynastic lines, from the initiating enmity between two brothers, as in the case of Atreus and Thyestes. The identification of the threatening Other is removed one stage further with each generation so that enmity between cousins evolves towards the safer model of tribal warfare, but any act of violence within the family (such as Agamemnon's sacrifice of Iphiginia) creates a renewed atomic fissure and a return to the Strindbergian equation 'Eat or be eaten' on the home base.

Whatever compels Atreus to bring about this atomic crisis by murdering his brother's sons and serving them to be eaten by their unwitting father is a psychic force which transcends the logic of personal malice: 'Some greater thing, larger than the common and beyond the bounds of human use is swelling in my soul, and it urges on my sluggish hands – I know not what it is, but 'tis some mighty thing' (Seneca 1953: 57).

His ensuing vision of Thyestes rending and swallowing the limbs of his sons is both atavistic and premonitory. Its realisation is attended by Eucharistic alchemy (the wine turns to blood) and all the signs of Apocalypse. There is darkness at noon, the sun, moon and stars fall to earth as the cosmic structure implodes, and the Chorus anticipate their deaths in the maelstrom. It is understandable that Artaud should have been unable to reconcile Seneca the dramatist with Seneca the moralist (Artaud [*OC* III] 1932: 286), for Stoic monism seems absurdly untenable in the world of Atreus and Thyestes. Atreus is the agent of a Grand Design, that of a devourer god who seeks to reverse the process of creation towards a new Chaos by dissolving differences, transgressing borders, erupting from within.

René Girard's theory of the 'sacrificial crisis' accords in some respects with the mythological patterns Artaud seeks to draw on. Certainly, the metaphor of the sacrificial crisis as a plague which dissolves all differences seems to have a remarkable degree of correlation with the ideas presented in 'The Theatre and the Plague' and Girard's identification of the prototypical conflict as one of enemy brothers invites application to the story of Atreus and Thyestes. As with Freud's exegesis of the Oedipus myth, however, such an application would divorce the story from the larger mythical pattern to which it belongs, and which is radically inconsistent with Girard's thesis. Girard is dogmatic in his assertion that sacrifice *resolves* the crisis of reciprocal violence – that it is 'violence cut short', 'the cure of violence' (Girard 1977: 21, 24). If 'the function of sacrifice is to quell violence within the community and to prevent conflicts from erupting' (Girard 1977: 14), it requires a tortuous logic indeed to account for the cyclic *anathema* that pollutes the House of Atreus. From the murder of Pelops by Tantalus to the sacrifice of Iphiginia by Agamemnon, the trajectory of violence ricochets from one generation to the next. The overwhelming evidence of Seneca's play is that sacrificial murder within the family precipitates and then recharges hostilities. In the opening sequence Tantalus, in an agony of foreknowledge, cries a warning to his sons: 'I warn ye, defile not your hands with accursed slaughter, nor stain your altars with a madman's crime' (Seneca 1953: 98).

For Girard, all mythological and anthropological versions of sacrificial practice have, ultimately, the pragmatic sociological function of restoring or ensuring the peace. He even suggests that the terms 'violence' and 'the sacred' are interchangeable, for 'the theory of generative violence permits us to defend the sacred in simple, concrete terms' (Girard 1977: 258). Such formulaic reductions are alien to Artaud's way of thinking. The Senecan tragedies and their Jacobean descendants are his chosen territory, because they use shock tactics to crack the mould of pragmatic understanding and wrench the preoccupations of the audience away from their moorings in psychological or sociological matters.

In *Totem and Taboo,* Freud dwells at some length upon the pervasive importance of sacrifice in all totemic systems, and observes that 'everywhere a sacrifice involves a feast and a feast cannot be celebrated without a sacrifice' (Freud 1985: 195). However, this phenomenon sits uneasily with his attempt to interpret all rituals associated with totemism and taboo in terms of the Oedipus complex. That the 'sacrificial meal bears no relation to the family' (Freud 1985: 196) – a contention quite bizarre in view of the instances cited above – presents an obstacle to its direct association with the 'nuclear' syndrome of parricide and incest. Secondly, there is the awkwardness of having to explain the dynamics of sacrifice as symbolic parricide when it is performed as a gesture of tribute of a god who is also, irrefutably, a father figure: 'This is the phase in which we find myths showing the god himself killing the animal which is sacred to him and which is in fact himself. Here we have the most extreme denial of the great crime which was the beginning of society and of the sense of guilt' (Freud 1985: 212).

The theatre of cruelty has the gnostic aim 'to give objective expression to secret truths, to bring to the light of day through active gestures that fugitive element of the truth which was lost beneath forms in their encounter with Becoming' (*TD*: 68). Besides being associated with violence and the election of scapegoats, sacrificial feasts are associated with epiphanies or flashes of *gnosis,* and these are far removed indeed from Freudian or Girardian notions of revelation, in which religious belief is explained away as cover for unpalatable truths perfectly consistent with scientific positivism.

The abominable feast scene in *Thyestes* has analogues in *The Cenci, 'Tis Pity She's a Whore* and *The Revenger's Tragedy.* All are scenes of primal taboo-breaking which culminate in pseudo-Eucharistic demonstrations, sacrilegious anti-miracles, epiphanies of horror in which truth erupts as a plague-like force of dissolution. Cenci, Giovanni, and Vindice as celebrants are true Artaudian heroes according to the maxim cryptically included amongst Artaud's notes for *The Torment of Tantalus*: 'heroism, to admit the plague'.

The feast is advertised as a ceremonial reinforcement of communal solidarity, of the strength, security and benevolence of the social order and its leaders, and proceeds with ritual determination. But the semiotics of the ritual are hijacked and instantaneously converted to their opposite by a revelation of violence, the consequence of an alternative premeditation, secret and more deeply purposed:

Revels are toward . . .
The masking suits are fashioning; now comes in
That which must glad us all: we to take pattern

Of all those suits, the colour, trimming, fashion,
E'en to an undistinguished hair almost.
Then entering first, observing the true form,
Within a strain or two we shall find leisure
To steal our swords out handsomely,
And when they think their pleasure sweet and good,
In midst of all their joys they shall sigh blood!
                          (Tourneur 1967: 100)

Thyestes eats the flesh of his murdered sons; Cenci celebrates the announcement of *his* sons' death by purporting to drink their blood from a wine goblet (and forcing the assembled company to do likewise); Giovanni flourishes his sister's bleeding, freshly torn-out heart 'as if to feast upon it' (Artaud's comment); Vindice and his mafiosi kill the guests in their seats, so that they bleed across the banquet table. The Christian God whom Cenci parodies has sent his own son to be sacrificed and then consumed, body and blood, in the Eucharistic feast. The archetypal transforming miracles of good and of evil share an identical semiotic pattern, and the 'alchemical theatre' exploits this insight with the enactment of rituals which may suddenly reveal their powerbase to be the opposite of that which has been assumed.

The association of revelation with abomination in Artaudian theatre is a reassertion of the powerful validity of the religious mysteries which modern Western man is convinced he has decoded and outgrown. Girard, whilst he condemns the 'condescending attitude towards the primitive' (Girard 1977: 236) and asserts that nobody takes *Totem and Taboo* seriously these days, proceeds in the spirit of the Freudian enterprise, for he too wants to create an all-embracing paradigm, 'a true unity and intelligibility' (Girard 1977: 189) which will translate the outlandish phenomena of religious practice into the language of common sense. His sacrificial scapegoat, ubiquitous as Freud's Oedipus, is the ultimate decoding device. Deleuze and Guattari would at least accord the scapegoat its line of flight. They are closer to Artaud (whose most aggressive and provocative assertions they are happy to adopt) in their quest for a return to some kind of *chora* of subjectivity, 'the Body without Organs', and in their fascination with becoming, metamorphosis and contagion as processes which rupture paradigmatic understanding, but they hardly qualify as gnostic revolutionaries. Their campaign against stratification is not the same as the aim of Artaudian theatre: ' . . . to make manifest and to plant in us ineradicably the idea of a perpetual conflict and of a seizure in which life is rent at every moment, in which the whole of creation rises up and sets itself against our condition as constituted beings' (*TD*: 89).

But certain aspects of Kristeva's theory, and in particular her view of the embrace of the abject as the loss of self and therewith the loss of all systems of signification, afford a critical position from which the gnostic purpose of the theatre of cruelty can be explored with new cogency.[3] Gnostic literature describes earthly existence as numbness, sleep, drunkenness or oblivion; Artaud's writings on theatre abound with metaphors of awakening. The theatre-as-plague arouses 'all the conflicts which lie dormant in us' and restores them in full strength to consciousness.

Gnostic 'awakening' is the response to the call from the Alien God (variously inscribed as 'the Other', 'the Unknown', 'the Nameless', 'the Hidden' – all terms used by Kristeva to designate the abject) which produces recognition of the subject's own alien condition in a world created by the nefarious demiurge. In the moment of realisation, Adam cries out against his captivity in 'the stinking body' (Jonas 1963: 88). Kristeva suggests that rituals of purification and dissociation from defilement are the process by which self-definition is reinforced; gnostic anamnesia reverses this process with the revelatory declaration that the embodied self is the *source* of pollution. If the fortress of the ego is the very seat of abjection, in which the contaminating essence of the material universe is incubated, to recognise it as such is to destroy it. Poe's 'Masque of the Red Death' reads effectively as a gnostic admonition.

Kristeva's investigation of the powers of horror takes her through the dietary taboos of Leviticus to an understanding of the Eucharist as 'a way of taming cannibalism', for 'the deathly drive to devour the other', she declares, is a 'primal fantasy if ever there was one' (Kristeva [1980b] 1982: 118). There are moments in Kristeva's argument when she seems to be upon the brink of a gnostic view of abjection, but to cross this threshold would involve a transformation in perspective that she is prepared to contemplate only obliquely and hypothetically:

> Perhaps those that the path of analysis, or scription, or of a painful or ecstatic ordeal has led to tear the veil of the communitarian mystery, on which love of self and others is set up, only to catch a glimpse of the abyss of abjection with which they are underlaid – they perhaps might be able to read this book as something other than an intellectual exercise. For abjection, when all is said and done, is the other facet of religious, moral and ideological codes on which rest the sleep of individuals and the breathing spells of societies. Such codes are abjection's purification and repression. But the return of their repressed make up our 'apocalypse', and that is why we cannot escape the dramatic convulsions of religious crises.
>
> (Kristeva [1980b] 1982: 209)

Artaud and his heroes make more reckless statements. In seeking 'to recover the religious and mystical dimension from which our theatre has become entirely estranged' (*TD*: 45), he is seeking to destroy the safeguards of the ego and precipitate a crisis of social dissolution so that the warring forces of the psyche can surface. 'Let our hid flames break out as fire, as lightning', exhorts Vindice: 'Wind up your souls to their full height again' (Tourneur 1967: 100).

10 Herbert Blau

From 'The dubious spectacle of collective identity'*

In this extract Herbert Blau questions the status of ritual in relation to theatre and culture and Artaud's place in this constellation of topics. Blau is critical of that aspect of Artaud's influence which sees in his writing the deconstruction of the theatrical in the guise of ritual, preferring instead to stare down 'the anxiety of an absence that we glut with representations'. The argument seems to suggest that ritual studies and performance studies tend to reconfigure aesthetic performances in a way which doesn't allow for the ubiquity of representation, i.e. if the world is saturated with images and copies, as Baudrillard suggests, then we are not going to rupture this simulated experience of life and reach an authentic encounter with the real, through an experience of liminal action which is itself already participating and acting out this inauthentic social drama. Blau's point is crucial and goes to the heart of the debate between these disciplines (theatre and performance studies). It is, of course, the case that Artaud felt the in-authenticity of life with a hypersensitivity which made enduring it a torment and that the rituals he devised were inadequate to deal with it. Yet his challenge to the theatre is surely for it to discover its necessity, its own 'life crisis' rituals. Blau's work regularly returns to Artaud to find triggers for re-thinking the theory of the form from scratch, and reinventing the way theatre studies is imagined.

[...]

Far from the 'family shamanism' (Eliade's term) that characterised most ritual theatre experiments in the sixties, like *Dionysus in 69,* Artaud calls for a rigorous intellectuality and 'mathematical meticulousness' in the midst of trance. As Derrida remarks, it is an occult 'theatre of dreams, but of *cruel* dreams, that is to say; absolutely necessary and determined dreams, dreams calculated and given direction, as opposed to what Artaud believed to be the empirical disorder of spontaneous dreams' (Derrida [1967c] 1978: 242). Out of the experimental empiricism of the surrealists Artaud came to believe that 'the ways and figures of dreams can be mastered'. It is not the randomness of the unconscious that he favours but its articulating and linguistic processes, as in recent psychoanalytical theory, though he would have rejected a psychoanalytical theatre in the ordinary sense, as he had rejected the psychological theatre. 'It is the *law* of dreams that must be produced or reproduced' (Derrida [1967c] 1978: 242). Despite the lure of the originary mystery, Artaud refused either a secret interiority or a secret commentary. 'The *subconscious*', he says, 'will not play any true role on stage.' It is possible to conclude, then, that the theatre of cruelty is not intended as a theatre of the unconscious. What Artaud imagines in the notion of cruelty is an intensification of *consciousness* and, in all its naked and emblooded realisation, an 'exposed lucidity' (qtd. by Derrida [1967c] 1978: 242).

Brecht, too, believes that the subconscious will *not* play any true role on stage. And in a remarkably perceptive passage of the essay on Chinese acting he points out – as Artaud does in the cultural analysis of *The Theatre and its Double* – that 'it is becoming increasingly difficult for our actors to bring off the mystery of complete conversion', the sort of conversion we associate with ritual, because the unconscious of our theatre has become so unsuspectingly occupied, colonised, politicised that 'their subconscious's memory is getting weaker and weaker, and it is almost impossible to extract the truth from the uncensored intuitions of any member of our class society even when (as in the case of Marlon Brando) the man is a genius' (Brecht 1964a: 94). As for the mystery of the theatre's origins, memory also falters there. If, for the genius of Artaud, priorities are reversed and, somehow, in the uncensored intuitions of the race, theatre was not born of ritual but ritual born of theatre, Brecht did not worry too much about which came first. As he observes in the 'Short Organum', while theatre may be said to have been derived from ritual, 'that is only to say that it becomes theatre once the two have separated; what it brought over from the mysteries was not its former ritual function, but purely and simply the pleasure which accompanied this'. That pleasure is not, however, simple, so that we can retrace through it the ritual from which it derived. It is rather a pleasure that attains its climaxes 'as cohabitation does through love . . . '. If what we have in ritual is a fixity of signs that can be duplicated and repeated, what we have in theatre is an open scrutiny of signs keeping its distance from ritual in the irreversible rupture of history. For Brecht, the pleasures of theatre are laminated by history, 'more intricate' than ritual, 'richer in communication, more contradictory and more productive of results' (Brecht 1964b: 181).

In the essay on Chinese acting, Brecht addresses the issue central to the ritual concerns of contemporary performance: the transferability of ritual techniques. What is often overlooked in that essay is the distinction he makes between the rational appropriation of a technique and the uncritical acceptance of what often goes along with it by way of cultural oppression. 'Among all the possible signs', he writes, 'certain particular ones are picked out with careful and visible consideration' (Brecht 1964a: 93). Among the signs he does not like in the signifying detachment of the Chinese actor is that the A-effect in his performance is achieved 'by association with magic' (Brecht 1964a: 96). While he could admire the singular performance of Mei Lan-fang, he was put off by the hierarchical structure that preserved in secrecy for the privileged the 'primitive technology' or 'rudimentary science' out of which the performance was made. Brecht had a quick appropriative instinct for 'a transportable piece of technique' (Brecht 1964a: 95–6) but an equally quick aversion to what it might represent. He knew with his friend Walter Benjamin that behind any cultural treasure there is inevitable human cost which is the best-kept secret in art, the anonymity of the labour behind the admired object that does not disclose its barbarous truth. Techniques are also cultural productions. They may require in their historical emergence, as in the case of Chinese acting, a repressive social system for the aesthetic pleasure they give. Carried over through the exchange mechanisms of bourgeois culture, the use value of such techniques is in some measure always already soiled and one would expect that perception to manifest itself in performance, to avoid an obtuse nostalgia, with more or less irony. [. . .]

There is a remarkable passage in 'No More Masterpieces' where the complexity of Artaud's provocative image of theatre merges with his attitude toward ritual repetition in a cathartic function at the virtual limit of thought: 'The theatre teaches precisely the uselessness of the action which, once done, is not to be done, and the superior use of the state unused by the action and which, *restored,* produces a purification' (*TD*: 82). The word *restored* is, of course, peculiar to an idea of theatre that wants to abolish repetition. And Derrida tries to deal with it at the end of his essay by pointing out that Artaud, whose theatre was never achieved, set himself the task of the unachievable, resigning himself 'to theatre as repetition' but unable to 'renounce theatre as nonrepetition' – thus, a theatre of repetition that, at some unimaginable boundary of its tautological form, does *not* repeat itself (Derrida [1967c] 1978: 249–50). As for the act to be forgotten so that the unused state may be restored, that is also implicit in the Brechtian *gestus,* where we are meant to see not only the uselessness of the action that, once done, is not to be done, but also the action not done that should be. Once again, in Brecht, there is nothing sacred about it. The sign includes an absence that, so long as it continues, marks the victim in history, while we think about a violence that will put an end to the violence that, for Artaud, is part of the order of things, a generative violence, ancient and generic, remembered but invisible – like the truth of the victim being signalled through the flames.

If the great myths are dark, it is because they are concealing as they reveal something criminal and evil at their core. However it got there, we know that the drama is obsessed with the sacrificial act or its sublimation and displacements. Artaud does not specify such an act, but he anticipates Girard in the perception of the primordial violence as both 'a *sacred obligation*' and 'a sort of criminal activity' (Girard 1977: 1). What I have been calling ritual desire desires this obligation and is, with more or less romanticism, tempted by such activity, as the outbreak of ritual experiment was preceded in the theatre by fascination with the drama of Genet. But the drama remains another matter, abrading upon the sacred, as Genet demonically knew, in the derisively poignant return of those Allegorical Forms in the Grand Brothel of *The Balcony*. While there are residues of ritual or ritual elements in the drama, drama is by its nature a more open, risible, and fractious thing. It is doubly so in the theatre, if not by virtue of its mysterious Double, then to the degree of its compulsive doubling. The representational mechanisms of the form are further confounded by the dispersive activity of perception. The theatre neither sustains myth by repetition nor discloses deity like ritual. To the extent that the theatre is dramatic, it is both critique and tribunal. (It is perhaps dramatic to that extent.) As far back as the *Oresteia*, it is not ritual practices that are being upheld, but the oldest claims of ritual that are being mediated. I say *mediated* specifically. What is set in motion by Aeschylus in that aetiological drama – which establishes not only the judicial system but the mechanisms of Western drama as they might have been imagined by myth – has passed through the long semiosis of history. Heraclitus said that justice is strife. Now it can be said that it is only mediation. The liabilities of mediation are compounded by the actual omnipresence of the *media* in our time. That not only demoralises judgement and justice – as in the Clinton scandals and the ceaseless spectacle of the O.J. Simpson case – but seems to make, in the proliferation of image and appearance, a mere redundancy of theatre.

Still, there is in the reflexive memory of theatre, a congenital tension with the appearances of ritual order, however alluring or consoling they may seem. Whatever it was in the beginning (and the worst we can say of it now), drama is the subversive impulse that moves the theatre into an open practice that abstracts itself from ritual ends. From Euripides to Ibsen and Genet, it has turned the myths over and over until, as Marx did with Hegel, they seem to be standing on their head. What we have in the canonical drama, and in revisionist productions of the drama – as well as in the refusal or rip-off of the drama in performance art – is the reconstitution of myth by history, and a dissociation from the rigid or static practice and magical purposes of the societies in which ritual prevailed.

There was over the past generation a new incitement to ritual from what appeared to be the signals coming from Artaud. But while he seemed to make a fetish of certain hieratic forms, nowhere does he subscribe to the necessarily repressive fixity of ritual. He calls, rather, for 'states of an acuteness so intense and so absolute that we sense, beyond the tremours of all music and form, the underlying menace of a chaos as decisive as it is dangerous' (*TD*: 51). And when he raises the question of origins, his notion of an 'archetypal, primitive theatre' leads 'metaphysically' (*TD*: 50) to the materialisation of an essential *drama* that implies nothing like the communal unity we associate with ritual. Sexual rupture and carnage are the ontological grounds of an 'essential separation' (*TD*: 30–1). What he is reimagining then is 'the essential principles of all drama, already *disposed and divided,* not so much to lose their character as principles, but enough to comprise, in a substantial and active fashion (i.e. resonantly), an infinite perspective of conflicts' (*TD*: 50). It is certainly nothing like the tribal and psychedelic manifestations of an earthly paradise, the bull-roaring rituals that petered out in the sixties, we thought, until elements of it showed up – multi-mediated but solipsistic – in the mutilations and disenchantments of punk, the parody and taxidermy of video and body art, and the sensory overload of new expressionist forms. What Artaud had in mind, with his insistence on 'a meticulous and unremitting pulverisation of every insufficiently fine, insufficiently matured form until it has passed through all the filters and foundations of existing matter' (*TD*: 51), is far more exacting.

What arises from ritual desire in practice is a sort of pathetic trompe l'oeil of 'collective dramaturgy upon the empty stage of the social' (Baudrillard 1983: 48). Our problem with ritual remains, then, political. Nostalgia keeps eluding that issue. Whatever meaning there may be in a High Mass in Bolivia or a Hasidic Seder in Brooklyn or a pilgrimage to Mecca, there is no way of having anything like the order of ritual in a society predicated on the open competition of overproduced signs mostly divested of value. For a ritual to have efficacious authority it must also assume something as irrevocable in the order of signifiers as in the designation of status, caste, practices of exchange. The clarity of the sign depends on the power of the law or interdiction that preserves it from abrasion or slippage. If the characteristic gesture of postmodern performance is parody, that is because – with ritual elements in the *bricolage* – we make a pretence of revelling in the slippage. We play with signs. But it is like a game of Monopoly in the supply-side economy. The currency is false, as it is, too, in the recycled illusions of performative border crossings, which claim to undermine the game. The ceremony we remember, as Baudrillard says, tolerates no counterfeit, 'unless as black magic and sacrilege, and it is thus that any confusion of signs is punished: as grave infraction of the order of things' (Baudrillard 1983: 84). It is also characteristic of postmodern performance, and the new theoretical discourse that surrounds it, to love in ourselves the image of infraction. What we are playing out, as the signs collapse around us, is a melodrama of subversion and transgression, with talk about cyborgs or bodies that matter.

But who is being subverted, transgressed – or deluded? We deride the logic of late capitalism as if there were other cultures somehow exempt from what Barthes once called 'the tyranny of uncertain signs'. For an uncertain time and a privileged few, perhaps there were. As with the seeming alternatives to the manic aggressiveness of modern life, we are forced to confront an unsettling truth: those alternative or non-aggressive cultures were never what they seemed to be in the *huya iniya* or the flow of the *chi* or the ceremony of *ikebana*. As Brecht observed about Chinese acting, there is the dirty secret of repression in every hallowed gesture. 'If we are starting to dream again, today especially', writes Baudrillard, 'of a world of sure signs, of a strong "symbolic order", make no mistake about it: this order has existed and it was that of a ferocious hierarchy, since transparency and cruelty for signs go together' (Baudrillard 1983: 84). (Baudrillard may bleakly overdo his accounting of the world of simulacra, but he seems to me accurate here.) It was an implication that Artaud could never quite accommodate in his cruel passion for an alphabet of perfect signs, 'the dry, naked, linear gesture all our acts could have if they sought the absolute' (*TD*: 66). His own quest for the absolute was better perceived in 'those strange games of flying hands' of the

Balinese dancers, 'like insects in the green air of the evening', which communicate 'an inexhaustible mental ratiocination, like a mind ceaselessly taking its bearings in the maze of its unconscious' (*TD*: 63). Without the hierarchical ordering of signs, what seems to remain in the maze is the nearly unbearable ferocity of that mind, discovering beyond exhaustion the certitude which escapes it.

Make no mistake about it either, ritual is fascinating. But the struggle now in performance is naively served by the fantasies of ritual desire. We live in a world of broken reciprocity. In our most radical desires we dream like Deleuze, drawing on Artaud, of a 'body without organs'. But our reflexes seem formed by the estrangement of an essential fracture. Whatever ritual has done to heal wounds or seal the divisions of cursive time, it is this fracture that seems ritualised in desire, the anxiety of an absence that we glut with representations. The psychopathology of everyday life is polysaturated with them, as natural as breathing, an overmastering convention, the image of performance as fundamental need. In this context, ritual is myth, another representation. Even when ritual appears to be purely ritual it still depends on representation, a system of exchange in which divinity can be attested to by the power of its signs. What we are dealing with today, however, is not the faintest shadow of a ritual renewal, a virtual impossibility, but rather the incorporation of ritual desire into the mechanisms of a signifying system where signs are no longer, as Eliot said, taken for wonders, nor an approximation of the real. Where signs are still taken for wonders, either tyranny prevails – and not merely the tyranny of signs – or we see the power of divinity on the video screen, where we also see the shadows of our most legible desires. If there is a collective identity there, I am not sure it is the one we want.

Divinity or desire, what we take for reality is a dominion of signs that extends now through our information systems – by satellite transmission through the green air of the evening – to Kinshasa and Bangkok and Kerala, and all those other parts of the world from which we seek the reassuring plenitude of ritual forms. Our addiction to ritual and ritualised performance has intensified just when those symbolic forms are coming out of temple and jungle and suffering the attrition of an exposure they were perhaps never meant to have. Or is it that, in all things of the world, exposure was the first intention? Thus it appears to be with the theatre, never more so than today when, however it resembles ritual, it dissolves with it into the real, which – without sanction or obligation – must live by resembling itself.

11 Susan Sontag

From 'Approaching Artaud'*

This essay, which was also published in Sontag's collection of essays *Under the Sign of Saturn*, is probably the one with which most readers of Artaud in English would be familiar. It stands as one of Sontag's most lyrically analytical texts, as well as a solid introduction to Artaud's work generally. It uses the popular paradigms of the artist as seer and madman to effect a powerfully evocative portrait of the man and his work as an irrecuperable voice which no commentary can grasp, an idea which has enjoyed a peculiar currency in Artaud studies. Given its high profile and significance to a generation of readers, it is especially important to develop a critical reading of this account of Artaud. One such approach follows, in an abbreviated form.

In her concluding pages, not included in this extract, Sontag argues, somewhat ironically, that Artaud is an example of an author who has become a classic precisely because his works are not read, 'being in some intrinsic way unreadable. Sade, Artaud, and Wilhelm Reich belong in this company: authors who were jailed or locked up in insane asylums because they were screaming, because they were out of control; immoderate, obsessed, strident authors who repeat themselves endlessly, who are rewarding to quote and read bits of, but who overpower and exhaust if read in large quantities' (Sontag 1988 [Artaud] 1976: lix). The irony evident here is accentuated by this synthesis of three such disparate figures in a gesture aimed, no doubt, at the countercultural movements in French and American universities of the late 1960s/early 1970s, which appropriated the examples of all three writers for diverse projects of cultural critique. It is doubly ironic that Sontag finishes her own paper on this note, since her implicit critique of the hysterical construction of Artaud as countercultural guru, achieved through substituting the narrative of his life as 'a cultural monument' for a reading of his work, is based on the same logic, if not the same practice. The irony is that the deployment of Artaud's madness has often been effected at the cost of reading the work, yet Sontag's reading invites just this kind of reception.

Her essay attempts to read Artaud's works at the limit and exposes the risk of this in reinscribing them as marginal, unreadable: 'For anyone who reads Artaud through, he remains fiercely out of reach, an unassimilable voice and presence' (Sontag 1988 [Artaud 1976]: lix). In an eloquent and otherwise rigorous argument which attempts to preserve Artaud's uniqueness, Sontag suggests, despite herself, that the cost of this is a non-reading of one complete side of Artaud, the one where he struggles to produce works that will be read. Instead, his mad/metaphysical side is presented as his singular achievement, where he confronts the unsayable end of language, the invisible edge of representation. Nevertheless, Sontag's essay translates the violence of his gestures to presence and their encounter with the aesthetics of pathology in terms which mark out Artaud's place at the core of the modernist project.

[. . .]

Disdaining any detached view of art, any version of that view which regards works of art as objects (to be contemplated, to enchant the senses, to edify, to distract), Artaud assimilates all art to dramatic performance. In Artaud's poetics, art (and thought) is an action – and one that, to be authentic, must be brutal – and also an experience suffered, and charged with extreme emotions. Being both action and passion of this sort, iconoclastic as well as evangelical in its fervour, art seems to require a more daring scene, outside the museums and legitimate show-places, and a new, ruder form of confrontation with its audience. The rhetoric of inner movement which sustains Artaud's notion of art is impressive, but it does not change the way he actually manages to reject the traditional role of the work of art as an object – by an analysis and an experience of the work of art which are an immense tautology. He sees art as an action, and therefore a passion, of the mind. The mind produces art. And the space in which art is consumed is also the mind – viewed as the organic totality of feeling physical sensation, and the ability to attribute meaning. Artaud's poetics is a kind of ultimate, manic Hegelianism in which art is the compendium of consciousness, the reflection by consciousness on itself, and the empty space in which consciousness takes its perilous leap of self-transcendence.

Closing the gap between art and life destroys art and, at the same time, universalises it. In the manifesto that Artaud wrote for the Alfred Jarry Theatre, which he founded in 1926, he welcomes 'the disrepute into which all forms of art are successively falling'. His delight may be posture, but it would be inconsistent for him to regret that state of affairs. Once the leading criterion for an art becomes its merger with life (that is, everything, including other arts) the existence of separate art forms ceases to be defensible. Furthermore, Artaud assumes that one of the existing arts must soon recover from its failure of nerve and become the total art form which will absorb all the others. Artaud's lifetime of work may be described as the sequence of his efforts to formulate and inhabit this master art, heroically following out his conviction that the art he sought could hardly be the one – involving language alone – in which his genius was principally confined.

The parameters of Artaud's work in all the arts are identical with the different critical distances he maintains from the idea of an art that is language only – with the diverse forms of his lifelong 'revolt against poetry' (the title of a prose text he wrote in Rodez in 1944). Poetry was, chronologically, the first of the many arts he practised. There are extant poems from as early as 1913, when he was seventeen and still a student in his native Marseilles; his first book, published in 1923, three years after he moved to Paris, was a collection of poems; and it was the unsuccessful submission of some new poems to the *Nouvelle Revue Française* that same year which gave rise to his celebrated correspondence with Rivière. But Artaud soon began slighting poetry in favour of other arts. The dimensions of the poetry he was capable of writing in the 1920s were too small for what Artaud intuited to be the scale of a master art. In the early poems, his breath is short; the compact lyric form he employs provides no outlet for his discursive and narrative imagination. Not until the great outburst of writing in the period between 1945 and 1948, in the last three years of his life, did Artaud, by then indifferent to the idea of poetry as a closed lyric statement, find a long-breathed voice that was adequate to the range of his imaginative needs – a voice that was free of established forms and open-ended, like the poetry of Pound. Poetry as Artaud conceived it in the 1920s had none of these possibilities or adequacies. It was small, and a total art had to be, to feel, large; it had to be a multi-voiced performance, not a singular lyrical object.

All ventures inspired by the ideal of a total art form – whether in music, painting, sculpture, architecture, or literature – manage in one way or another to theatricalise. Though Artaud need not have been so literal, it makes sense that at an early age he moved into the explicit dramatic arts. Between 1922 and 1924, he acted in plays directed by Charles Dullin and the Pitoeffs, and in 1924 he also began a career as a film actor. That is to say, by the mid-1920s Artaud had two plausible candidates for the role of total art: cinema and theatre. However, because it was not as an actor but as a director that he hoped to advance the candidacy of these arts, he soon had to renounce one of them – cinema. Artaud was never given the means to direct a film of his own, and he saw his intentions betrayed in a film of 1928 that was made with another director from one of his screenplays, *The Seashell and the Clergyman.* His sense of defeat was reinforced in 1929 by the arrival of sound, a turning point in the history of film aesthetics which Artaud wrongly prophesied – as did most of the small number of moviegoers who had taken films seriously throughout the 1920s – would terminate cinema's greatness as an art form. He continued acting in films until 1935, but with little hope of getting a chance to direct his own films and with no further reflection upon the possibilities of cinema (which, regardless of Artaud's discouragement, remains the century's likeliest candidate for the title of master art).

From late 1926 on, Artaud's search for a total art form centred upon the theatre. Unlike poetry, an art made out of one material (words), theatre uses a plurality of materials: words, light, music, bodies, furniture, clothes. Unlike cinema, an art using only a plurality of languages (images, words, music), theatre is carnal, corporeal. Theatre brings together the most diverse means – gesture and verbal language, static objects and movement in three-dimensional space. But theatre does not become a master art merely by the abundance of its means. The prevailing tyranny of some means over others has to be creatively subverted. As Wagner challenged the convention of alternating aria and recitative, which implies a hierarchical relation of speech, song, and orchestral music, Artaud denounced the practice of making every element of the staging serve in some way the words that the actors speak to each other. Assailing as false the priorities of dialogue theatre which have subordinated theatre to 'literature', Artaud implicitly upgrades the means that characterise such other forms of dramatic performance, as dance, oratorio, circus, cabaret, church, gymnasium, hospital operating room, courtroom. But annexing these resources from other arts and from quasi-theatrical forms will not make theatre a total art form. A master art cannot be constructed by a series of additions; Artaud is not urging mainly that the theatre add to its means. Instead, he seeks to purge the theatre of what is extraneous or easy. In calling for a theatre in which the verbally oriented actor of Europe would be retrained as an 'athlete' of the heart, Artaud shows his inveterate taste for spiritual and physical effort – for art as an ordeal.

Artaud's theatre is a strenuous machine for transforming the mind's conceptions into entirely 'material' events, among which are the passions themselves. Against the centuries-old priority that the European theatre has given to words as the means for conveying emotions and ideas, Artaud wants to show the organic basis of emotions and the physicality of ideas in the bodies of the actors. Artaud's theatre is a reaction against the state of underdevelopment in which the bodies (and the voices, apart from talking) of Western actors have remained for generations, as have the arts of spectacle. To redress the imbalance that so favours verbal language, Artaud proposes to bring the training of actors close to the training of dancers, athletes, mimes, and singers, and 'to base the theatre on spectacle before everything else', as he says in his 'Second Manifesto of the Theatre of Cruelty', published in 1933. He is not offering to replace the charms of language with spectacular sets, costumes, music, lighting, and stage effects. Artaud's criterion of spectacle is sensory violence, not sensory enchantment; beauty is a notion he never entertains. Far from considering the spectacular to be in itself desirable, Artaud would commit the stage to an extreme austerity – to the point of excluding anything that stands for something else. 'Objects, accessories, sets on the stage must be apprehended directly . . . not for what they represent but for what they are', he writes in a manifesto of 1926. Later, in *The Theatre and its Double,* he suggests eliminating sets altogether. He calls for a 'pure' theatre, dominated by the 'physics of the absolute gesture, which is itself idea'.

If Artaud's language sounds vaguely Platonic, it is with good reason. Like Plato, Artaud approaches art from the moralist's point of view. He does not really like the theatre – at least, the theatre as it is conceived throughout the West, which he accuses of being insufficiently serious. His theatre would have nothing to do with the aim of providing 'pointless, artificial diversion', mere entertainment.

The contrast at the heart of Artaud's polemics is not between a merely literary theatre and a theatre of strong sensations, but between a hedonistic theatre and a theatre that is morally rigorous. What Artaud proposes is a theatre that Savonarola or Cromwell might well have approved of. Indeed, *The Theatre and its Double* may be read as an indignant attack on the theatre, with an animus reminiscent of the *Letter to d'Alembert* in which Rousseau, enraged by the character of Alceste in *The Misanthrope* – by what he took to be Molière's sophisticated ridiculing of sincerity and moral purity as clumsy fanaticism – ended by arguing that it lay in the nature of theatre to be morally superficial. Like Rousseau, Artaud revolted against the moral cheapness of most art. Like Plato, Artaud felt that art generally lies. Artaud will not banish artists from his Republic, but he will countenance art only insofar as it is a 'true action'. Art must be cognitive. 'No image satisfies me unless it is at the same time *knowledge*', he writes. Art must have a beneficial spiritual effect on its audience – an effect whose power depends, in Artaud's view, on a disavowal of all forms of mediation.

It is the moralist in Artaud that makes him urge that the theatre be pared down, be kept as free from mediating elements as possible – including the mediation of the written text. Plays tell lies. Even if a play doesn't tell a lie, by achieving the status of a 'masterpiece' it *becomes* a lie. Artaud announces in 1926 that he does not want to create a theatre to present plays and so perpetuate or add to culture's list of consecrated masterpieces. He judges the heritage of written plays to be a useless obstacle and the playwright an unnecessary intermediary between the audience and the truth that can be presented, naked, on a stage. Here, though, Artaud's moralism takes a distinct anti-Platonic turn: the naked truth is a truth that is wholly material. Artaud defines the theatre as a place where the obscure facets of 'the spirit' are revealed in 'a real, material projection'.

To incarnate thought, a strictly conceived theatre must dispense with the mediation of an already written script, thereby ending the separation of author from actor. (This removes the most ancient objection to the actor's profession – that it is a form of psychological debauchery, in which people say words that are not their own and pretend to feel emotions that are functionally insincere.) The separation between actor and audience must be reduced (but not ended), by violating the boundary between the stage area and the auditorium's fixed rows of seats. Artaud, with his hieratic sensibility, never envisages a form of theatre in which the audience actively participates in the performance, but he wants to do away with the rules of theatrical decorum which permit the audience to dissociate itself from its own experience. Implicitly answering the moralist's charge that the theatre distracts people from their authentic selfhood by leading them to concern themselves with imaginary problems, Artaud wants the theatre to address itself neither to the spectators' minds nor to their senses but to their 'total existence'. Only the most passionate of moralists would have wanted people to attend the theatre as they visit the surgeon or the dentist. Though guaranteed not to be fatal (unlike the visit to the surgeon), the operation upon the audience is 'serious', and the audience should not leave the theatre 'intact' morally or emotionally. In another medical image, Artaud compares the theatre to the plague. To show the truth means to show archetypes rather than individual psychology; this makes the theatre a place of risk, for the 'archetypal reality' is 'dangerous'. Members of the audience are not supposed to identify themselves with what happens on the stage. For Artaud, the 'true' theatre is a dangerous, intimidating experience – one that excludes placid emotions, playfulness, reassuring intimacy.

The value of emotional violence in art has long been a main tenet of the modernist sensibility. Before Artaud, however, cruelty was exercised mainly in a disinterested spirit, for its aesthetic efficacy. When Baudelaire placed 'the shock experience' (to borrow Walter Benjamin's phrase) at the centre of his verse and his prose poems, it was hardly to improve or edify his readers. But exactly this was the point of Artaud's devotion to the aesthetics of shock. Through the exclusiveness of his commitment to paroxysmic art, Artaud shows himself to be as much of a moralist about art as Plato – but a moralist whose hopes for art deny just those distinctions in which Plato's view is grounded. As Artaud opposes the separation between art and life, he opposes all theatrical forms that imply a difference between reality and representation. He does not deny the existence of such a difference. But this difference can be vaulted, Artaud implies, if the spectacle is sufficiently – that is, excessively – violent. The 'cruelty' of the work of art has not only a directly moral function but a cognitive one. According to Artaud's moralistic criterion for knowledge, an image is true insofar as it is violent.

Plato's view depends on assuming the unbridgeable difference between life and art, reality and representation. In the famous imagery in Book VII of the *Republic,* Plato likens ignorance to living in an ingeniously lit cave, for whose inhabitants life is a spectacle – a spectacle that consists of only the shadows of real events. The cave is a theatre. And truth (reality) lies outside it, in the sun. In the Platonic imagery of *The Theatre and its Double,* Artaud takes a more lenient view of shadows and spectacles. He assumes that there are true as well as false shadows (and spectacles), and that one can learn to distinguish between them. Far from identifying wisdom with an emergence from the cave to gaze at a high noon of reality, Artaud thinks that modern consciousness suffers from a lack of shadows. The remedy is to remain in the cave but devise better spectacles. The theatre that Artaud proposes will serve consciousness by 'naming and directing shadows' and destroying 'false shadows' to 'prepare the way for a new generation of shadows', around which will assemble the 'true spectacle of life'.

Not holding a hierarchical view of the mind, Artaud overrides the superficial distinction, cherished by the surrealists, between the rational and the irrational. Artaud does not speak for the familiar view that praises passion at the expense of reason, the flesh over the mind, the mind exalted by drugs over the prosaic mind, the life of the instincts over deadly cerebration. What he advocates is an alternative relation to the mind. This was the well-advertised attraction that non-Occidental cultures held for Artaud, but it was not what brought him to drugs. (It was to calm the migraines and other neurological pain he suffered from all his life, not to expand his consciousness, that Artaud used opiates and got addicted.)

For a brief time, Artaud took the surrealist state of mind as a model for the unified, non-dualistic consciousness he sought. After rejecting surrealism in 1926, he reproposed art – specifically, theatre – as a more rigorous model. The function that Artaud gives the theatre is to heal the split between language and flesh. It is the theme of his ideas for training actors: a training antithetical to the familiar one that teaches actors neither how to move nor what to do with their voices apart from talk. (They can scream, growl, sing, chant.) It is also the subject of his ideal dramaturgy. Far from espousing a facile irrationalism that polarises reason and feeling, Artaud imagines the theatre as the place where the body would be reborn in thought and thought would be reborn in the body. He diagnoses his own disease as a split *within* his mind ('My conscious aggregate is broken', he writes) that internalises the split between mind and body. Artaud's writings on the theatre may be read as a psychological manual on the reunification of mind and body. Theatre became his supreme metaphor for the self-correcting, spontaneous, carnal, intelligent life of the mind.

Indeed, Artaud's imagery for the theatre in *The Theatre and its Double,* written in the 1930s, echoes images he uses in writings of the early and mid-1920s – such as *The Nerve Metre,* letters to René and Yvonne Allendy, and *Fragments of a Diary from Hell* – to describe his own mental pain. Artaud complains that his consciousness is without boundaries and fixed position; bereft of or in a continual struggle with language: fractured – indeed, plagued – by discontinuities; either without physical location or constantly shifting in location (and extension in time and space); sexually obsessed in a state of violent infestation. Artaud's theatre is characterised by an absence of any fixed spatial positioning of the actors vis-à-vis each other and of the actors in relation to the audience; by a fluidity of motion and soul; by the mutilation of language and the transcendence of language in the actor's scream; by the carnality of the spectacle; by its obsessively violent tone. Artaud was, of course, not simply reproducing his inner agony. Rather, he was giving a systematised, positive version of it. Theatre is a projected image (necessarily an *ideal* dramatisation) of the dangerous, 'inhuman' inner life that possessed him, that he struggled so heroically to transcend and to affirm. It is also a homeopathic technique for treating that mangled, passionate inner life. Being a kind of emotional and moral surgery upon consciousness, it must of necessity, according to Artaud, be 'cruel'.

When Hume expressly likens consciousness to a theatre, the image is morally neutral and entirely ahistorical; he is not thinking of any particular kind of theatre, Western or other, and would have considered irrelevant any reminder that theatre evolves. For Artaud, the decisive part of the analogy is that theatre – and consciousness – can change. For not only does consciousness resemble a theatre but, as Artaud constructs it, theatre resembles consciousness, and therefore lends itself to being turned into a theatre-laboratory in which to conduct research in changing consciousness.

Artaud's writings on the theatre are transformations of his aspirations for his own mind. He wants theatre (like the mind) to be released from confinement 'in language and in forms'. A liberated theatre liberates, he assumes. By giving vent to extreme passions and cultural nightmares, theatre exorcises them. But Artaud's theatre is by no means simply cathartic. At least in its intention (Artaud's practice in the 1920s and 1930s is another matter), his theatre has little in common with the anti-theatre of playful, sadistic assault on the audience which was conceived by Marinetti and the Dada artists just before and after World War I. The aggressiveness that Artaud proposes is controlled and intricately orchestrated, for he assumes that sensory violence can be a form of embodied intelligence. By insisting on theatre's cognitive function (drama, he writes in 1923, in an essay on Maeterlinck, is 'the highest form of mental activity'), he rules out randomness. (Even in his surrealist days, he did not join in the practice of automatic writing.) Theatre, he remarks occasionally, must be 'scientific', by which he means that it must not be random, not be merely expressive or spontaneous or personal or entertaining, but must embrace a wholly serious, ultimately religious purpose.

Artaud's insistence on the seriousness of the theatrical situation also marks his difference from the surrealists, who thought of art and its therapeutic and 'revolutionary' mission with a good deal less than precision. The surrealists, whose moralising impulses were considerably less intransigent than Artaud's, and who brought no sense of moral urgency at all to bear on art-making, were not moved to search out the limits of any single art form. They tended to be tourists, often of genius, in as many of the arts as possible, believing that the art impulse remains the same wherever it turns up. (Thus, Cocteau, who had the ideal surrealist career, called everything he did 'poetry'.) Artaud's greater daring and authority as an aesthetician result partly from the fact that although he, too, practised several arts, refusing, like the surrealists, to be inhibited by the distribution of art into different media, he did not regard the various arts as equivalent forms of the same protean impulse. His own activities, however dispersed they may have been, always reflect Artaud's quest for a total art form, into which the others would merge – as art itself would merge into life.

Paradoxically, it was this very denial of independence to the different territories of art which brought Artaud to do what none of the surrealists had even attempted: completely rethink one art form. Upon that art, theatre, he has had an impact so profound that the course of all recent serious theatre in Western Europe and the Americas can be said to divide into two periods – before Artaud and after Artaud. No one who works in the theatre now is untouched by the impact of Artaud's specific ideas about the actor's body and voice, the use of music, the role of the written text, the interplay between the space occupied by the spectacle and the audience's space. Artaud changed the understanding of what was serious, what was worth doing. Brecht is the century's only other writer on the theatre whose importance and profundity conceivably rival Artaud's. But Artaud did not succeed in affecting the conscience of the modern theatre by himself being, as Brecht was, a great director. His influence derives no support from the evidence of his own productions. His practical work in the theatre between 1926 and 1935 was apparently so unseductive that it has left virtually no trace, whereas the idea of theatre on behalf of which he urged his productions upon an unreceptive public has become ever more potent.

From the mid-1920s on, Artaud's work is animated by the idea of a radical change in culture. His imagery implies a medical rather than a historical view of culture: society is ailing. Like Nietzsche, Artaud conceived of himself as a physician to culture – as well as its most painfully ill patient. The theatre he planned is a commando action against the established culture, an assault on the bourgeois public; it would both show people that they are dead and wake them up from their stupor. The man who was to be devastated by repeated electric-shock treatments during the last three of nine consecutive years in mental hospitals proposed that theatre administer to culture a kind of shock therapy. Artaud, who often complained of feeling paralysed, wanted theatre to renew 'the sense of life'.

Up to a point, Artaud's prescriptions resemble many programmes of cultural renovation that have appeared periodically during the last two centuries of Western culture in the name of simplicity, *élan vital,* naturalness, freedom from artifice. His diagnosis that we live in an inorganic, 'petrified culture' – whose lifelessness he associates with the dominance of the written word – was hardly a fresh idea when he stated it; yet, many decades later, it has not exhausted its authority. Artaud's argument in *The Theatre and its Double* is closely related to that of the Nietzsche who in *The Birth of Tragedy* lamented the shrivelling of the full-blooded archaic theatre of Athens by Socratic philosophy – by the introduction of characters who reason. (Another parallel with Artaud: what made the young Nietzsche an ardent Wagnerian was Wagner's conception of opera as the *Gesamtkunstwerk* – the fullest statement, before Artaud, of the idea of total theatre.)

Just as Nietzsche harked back to the Dionysiac ceremonies that preceded the secularised, rationalised, verbal dramaturgy of Athens, Artaud found his models in non-Western religious or magical theatre. Artaud does not propose the theatre of cruelty as a new idea within Western theatre. It 'assumed . . . another form of civilisation'. He is referring not to any specific civilisation, however, but to an idea of civilisation that has numerous bases in history – a synthesis of elements from past societies and from non-Western and primitive societies of the present. The preference for 'another form of civilization' is essentially eclectic. (That is to say it is a myth generated by certain moral needs.) The inspiration for Artaud's ideas about theatre came from Southeast Asia: from seeing the Cambodian theatre in Marseilles in 1922 and the Balinese theatre in Paris in 1931. But the stimulus could just as well have come from observing the theatre of a Dahomey tribe or the shamanistic ceremonies of the Patagonian Indians. What counts is that the other culture be genuinely other; that is, non-Western and non-contemporary.

At different times, Artaud followed all three of the most frequently travelled imaginative routes from Western high culture to 'another form of civilization'. First came what was known just after World War I, in the writings of Hesse, René

Daumal, and the surrealists, as the Turn to the East. Second came the interest in a suppressed part of the Western past – heterodox spiritual or outright magical traditions. Third came the discovery of the life of so-called primitive peoples. What unites the East, the ancient antinomian and occult traditions in the West, and the exotic communitarianism of pre-literate tribes is that they are elsewhere, not only in space but in time. All three embody the values of the past. Though the Tarahumara Indians in Mexico still exist, their survival in 1936, when Artaud visited them, was already anachronistic; the values that the Tarahumara represent belong as much to the past as do those of the ancient Near Eastern mystery religions that Artaud studied while writing his historical novel *Heliogabalus*, in 1933. The three versions of 'another form of civilization' bear witness to the same search for a society integrated around overtly religious themes, and flight from the secular. What interests Artaud is the Orient of Buddhism (see his 'Letter to the Buddhist Schools', written in 1925) and of Yoga; it would never be the Orient of Mao Tse-tung, however much Artaud talked up revolution. (The Long March was taking place at the very time that Artaud was struggling to mount his productions of the Theatre of Cruelty in Paris.)

This nostalgia for a past often so eclectic as to be quite unlocatable historically is a facet of the modernist sensibility which has seemed increasingly suspect in recent decades. It is an ultimate refinement of the colonialist outlook: an imaginative exploitation of non-white cultures, whose moral life it drastically oversimplifies, whose wisdom it plunders and parodies. To that criticism there is no convincing reply. But to the criticism that the quest for 'another form of civilization' refuses to submit to the disillusionment of accurate historical knowledge, one can make an answer. It never sought such knowledge. The other civilisations are being used as models and are available as stimulants to the imagination precisely because they are *not* accessible. They are both models and mysteries. Nor can this quest be dismissed as fraudulent on the ground that it is insensitive to the political forces that cause human suffering. It consciously opposes such sensitivity. This nostalgia forms part of a view that is deliberately *not* political – however frequently it brandishes the word 'revolution'.

One result of the aspiration to a total art which follows from denying the gap between art and life has been to encourage the notion of art as an instrument of revolution. The other result has been the identification of both art and life with disinterested, pure playfulness. For every Vertov or Breton, there is a Cage or a Duchamp or a Rauschenberg. Although Artaud is close to Vertov and Breton in that he considers his activities to be part of a larger revolution, as a self-proclaimed revolutionary in the arts he actually stands between the two camps – not interested in satisfying either the political or the ludic impulse. Dismayed when Breton attempted to link the surrealist programme with Marxism, Artaud broke with the surrealists for what he considered to be their betrayal into the hands of politics of an essentially 'spiritual' revolution. He was anti-bourgeois almost by reflex (like nearly all artists in the modernist tradition), but the prospect of transferring power from the bourgeoisie to the proletariat never tempted him.

From his avowedly 'absolute' viewpoint, a change in social structure would not change anything. The revolution to which Artaud subscribes has nothing to do with politics, but is conceived explicitly as an effort to redirect culture. Not only does Artaud share the widespread (and mistaken) belief in the possibility of a cultural revolution unconnected with political change, but he implies that the *only* genuine cultural revolution is one that has nothing to do with politics.

Artaud's call to cultural revolution suggests a programme of heroic regression similar to that formulated by every great *anti*-political moralist of our time. The banner of cultural revolution is hardly a monopoly of the Marxist or Maoist left. On the contrary, it appeals particularly to apolitical thinkers and artists (like Nietzsche, Spengler, Pirandello, Marinetti, D.H. Lawrence, Pound) who more commonly become right-wing enthusiasts. On the political left, there are few advocates of cultural revolution. (Tatlin, Gramsci, and Godard are among those who come to mind.) A radicalism that is purely 'cultural' is either illusory or, finally, conservative in its implications. Artaud's plans for subverting and revitalising culture, his longing for a new type of human personality, illustrate the limits of all thinking about revolution which is anti-political.

Cultural revolution that refuses to be political has nowhere to go but toward a theology of culture – and a soteriology. 'I aspire to another life', Artaud declares in 1927. All Artaud's work is about salvation, theatre being the means of saving souls which he meditated upon most deeply. Spiritual transformation is a goal on whose behalf theatre has often been enlisted in this century, at least since Isadora Duncan. In the most recent and solemn example, the Laboratory Theatre of Jerzy Grotowski, the whole activity of building a company and rehearsing and putting on plays serves the spiritual reeducation of the actors; the presence of an audience is required only to witness the feats of self-transcendence that the actors perform. In Artaud's theatre of cruelty, it is the audience that will be twice-born – an untested claim, since Artaud never made his theatre work (as Grotowski did throughout the 1960s in Poland). As a goal, it seems a good deal less feasible than the discipline for which Grotowski aims. Sensitive as Artaud is to the emotional and physical armouring of the conventionally trained actor, he never examines closely how the radical retraining he proposes will affect the actor as a human being. His thought is all for the audience.

As might have been expected, the audience proved to be a disappointment. Artaud's productions in the two theatres he founded, the Alfred Jarry Theatre and the Theatre of Cruelty, created little involvement. Yet, although entirely dissatisfied with the quality of his public, Artaud complained much more about the token support he got from the serious Paris theatre establishment (he had a long, desperate correspondence with Louis Jouvet), about the difficulty of getting his projects produced at all, about the paltriness of their success when they were put on. Artaud was understandably embittered because, despite a number of titled patrons, and friends who were eminent writers, painters, editors, directors – all of whom he constantly badgered for moral support and money – his work, when it was actually produced, enjoyed only a small portion of the acclaim conventionally reserved for properly sponsored, difficult events attended by the regulars of high-culture consumption. Artaud's most ambitious, fully articulated production of the Theatre of Cruelty, his own *The Cenci,* lasted for seventeen days in the spring of 1935. But had it run for a year he would probably have been equally convinced that he had failed.

In modern culture, powerful machinery has been set up whereby dissident work, after gaining an initial semi-official status as 'avant-garde', is gradually absorbed and rendered acceptable. But Artaud's practical activities in the theatre barely qualified for this kind of co-optation. *The Cenci* is not a very good play, even by the standards of convulsive dramaturgy which Artaud sponsored, and the interest of his production of *The Cenci,* by all accounts, lay in ideas it suggested but did not actually embody. What Artaud did on the stage as a director and as a leading actor in his productions was too idiosyncratic, narrow, and hysterical to persuade. He has exerted influence through his ideas about the theatre, a constituent part of the authority of these ideas being precisely his inability to put them into practice.

Fortified by its insatiable appetite for novel commodities, the educated public of great cities has become habituated to the modernist agony and well skilled in outwitting it: any negative can eventually be turned into a positive. Thus, Artaud, who urged that the repertory of masterpieces be thrown on the junk pile, has been extremely influential as the creator of an alternative repertory, an adversary tradition of plays. Artaud's stern cry 'No more masterpieces!' has been heard as the more conciliatory 'No more of *those* masterpieces!' But this positive recasting of his attack on the traditional repertory has not taken place without help from Artaud's practice (as distinct from his rhetoric). Despite his repeated insistence that the theatre should dispense with plays, his own work in the theatre was far from playless. He named his first company after the author of *King Ubu.* Apart from his own projects – *The Conquest of Mexico* and *The Capture of Jerusalem* (unproduced) and *The Cenci* – there were a number of then unfashionable or obscure masterpieces that Artaud wanted to revive. He did get to stage the two great 'dream plays' by Calderon and Strindberg (*Life is a Dream* and *Dream Play*), and over the years he hoped also to direct productions of Euripides (*The Bacchae*), Seneca (*Thyestes*), *Arden of Feversham*, Shakespeare (*Macbeth*, *Richard II, Titus Andronicus*), Tourneur (*The Revenger's Tragedy*), Webster (*The White Devil, The Duchess of Malfi*), Sade (an adaptation of *Eugénie de Franval*), Büchner (*Woyzeck*), and Hölderlin (*The Death of Empedocles*). This selection of plays delineates a now familiar sensibility. Along with the Dadaists, Artaud formulated the taste that was eventually to become standard serious taste – Off-Broadway, Off-Off-Broadway, in university theatres. In terms of the past, it meant dethroning Sophocles and Corneille and Racine in favour of Euripides and the dark Elizabethans; the only dead French writer on Artaud's list is Sade. In the last fifteen years, that taste has been represented in the happenings and the Theatre of the Ridiculous; the plays of Genet, Jean Vauthier, Arrabal, Carmelo Bene, and Sam Shepard; and such celebrated productions as the Living Theatre's

Frankenstein, Eduardo Manet's *The Nuns* (directed by Roger Blin), Michael McClure's *The Beard,* Robert Wilson's *Deafman Glance,* and Heathcote Williams's *ac/dc.* Whatever Artaud did to subvert the theatre, and to segregate his own work from other, merely aesthetic currents in the interests of establishing its spiritual hegemony, could still be assimilated as a new theatrical tradition, and mostly has been.

If Artaud's project does not actually transcend art, it presupposes a goal that art can sustain only temporarily. Each use of art in a secular society for the purposes of spiritual transformation, insofar as it is made *public,* is inevitably robbed of its true adversarial power. Stated in directly, or even indirectly, religious language, the project is notably vulnerable. But atheist projects for spiritual transformation, such as the political art of Brecht, have proved to be equally co-optable. Only a few situations in modern secular society seem sufficiently extreme and uncommunicative to have a chance of evading co-optation. Madness is one. What surpasses the limit of suffering (like the Holocaust) is another. A third is, of course, silence. One way to stop this inexorable process of ingestion is to break off communication (even anti-communication). An exhaustion of the impulse to use art as a medium of spiritual transformation is almost inevitable – as in the temptation felt by every modern author when confronted with the indifference or mediocrity of the public, on the one hand, or the ease of success, on the other, to stop writing altogether. Thus, it was not just for lack of money or support within the profession that, after putting on *The Cenci,* in 1935, Artaud abandoned the theatre. The project of creating in a secular culture an institution that can manifest a dark, hidden reality is a contradiction in terms. Artaud was never able to found his Bayreuth – though he would have liked to – for his ideas are the kind that cannot be institutionalised.

The year after the failure of *The Cenci*, Artaud embarked on a trip to Mexico to witness that demonic reality in a still existing 'primitive' culture. Unsuccessful at embodying this reality in a spectacle to impose on others, he became a spectator of it himself. From 1935 onward, Artaud lost touch with the promise of an ideal art form. His writings, always didactic, now took on a prophetic tone and referred frequently to esoteric magical systems, like the Cabala and tarot. Apparently, Artaud came to believe that he could exercise directly, in his own person, the emotional power (and achieve the spiritual efficacy) he had wanted for the theatre. In the middle of 1937, he travelled to the Aran Islands, with an obscure plan for exploring or confirming his magic powers. The wall between art and life was still down. But instead of everything being assimilated into art, the movement swung the other way; and Artaud moved without mediation into his life – a dangerous, careering object, the vessel of a raging hunger for total transformation which could never find its appropriate nourishment.

12 Leo Bersani

'Artaud, defecation and birth'*

This text poses the question of authenticity in Artaud's theatre writing and shows how fundamental this idea is to his thought and work in general. Leo Bersani treats this idea as a principle of underivedness, of that which has not previously existed in any form. Bersani uses the language of psychoanalysis to indicate the limits of Artaud's anti-psychological project and to demonstrate, for example, the manner in which the need to be authentic and underived could itself derive from an intensification of the anal drives.

For Bersani, Artaud's 'devaluation of the written theatrical text' is part of the larger work of underivedness, but it also suggests a 'subversion of character structures' so radical in its formulation that it becomes 'an attack on the very bases of psychological intelligibility in our culture'. This is a subtle notion, but one which explains the viral quality of Artaud's conception of theatre, that it would infect the culture as a whole with the force of the irrational and 'the truthful precipitates of dreams'.

Nevertheless, there are some questions raised by this reading, especially regarding the priority of physicality in Artaud's theatre writings. For Bersani, cruelty becomes less the necessary and profound task of transformation that Artaud elaborated and instead constructs itself as pure phantasm, which concretises desire and becomes the space of a 'psychic deconstruction'. It is a reading between the lines of Artaud's very physical style, but one which honours the text and largely avoids the biographical tendency which this type of approach might suggest. It is, in short, a highly imaginative text on an important aspect of Artaud's thought by one of the major figures in American literary criticism.

Perhaps the most fundamental aspect of theatrical reform in the twentieth century has been the devaluation of the written theatrical text. And of course the figure most intimately connected with this project is Antonin Artaud. 'We must be done with this superstition of texts and of *written* poetry', Artaud declared in 1933.[1] What is 'this superstition of texts'? The text is the most respectable aspect of theatrical performance; it is, we might say, the strictly mental component of theatre. The literary text qualifies the physical confrontations of theatre (confrontations among actors as well as the spectator's erotic attachment to the actors); it is a reminder that physical presence is not indispensable to the 'essence' of theatre. Significantly, Artaud connects the tyranny of the text with the tyranny of the abstract. To repudiate the domination of theatre by literature is to reaffirm the physical immediacy of the theatre. And the primacy of the physical means that even the language of the theatre must be different from the language of literature.

Balinese theatre was for Artaud the revelation of a theatrical language in which words would be only one element, and not even the most important. In the angular poses of the Balinese actors, in the strange rhythms of their guttural sounds, in their grimaces and calculated muscular spasms, in the mysterious fusions of their voices with the sounds of musical instruments, in the 'dance' of the geometrical robes which transform the Balinese players into 'animated hieroglyphics', Artaud discovers 'the meaning of a new physical language with its basis in signs and no longer in words'. The physical elements of Western theatre are intended to realise a literary text; they sense that text; essentially, they illustrate and decorate it. The secondary importance of actual performance in Western theatre reinforces our traditional sense of the inferiority of the concrete to the abstract: the former carries meaning only to the extent that it reveals the latter. The abstraction is the gold nugget to be removed from the impure ore of concrete reality. What Artaud finds most astonishing in Balinese theatre, on the other hand, 'is this revealing aspect of matter which seems to be suddenly dispersed into signs in order to teach us the metaphysical identity of the concrete and the abstract'. The physical elements of theatre don't need the support of a text in order to be read as meaningful signs. What we must learn to read in the theatre is not the 'parent' text from which each production is derived, but rather the irreducible and immediately perceived language of movement, sounds, shapes and colours.

The devaluation of the literary text is a subversion of character structures. Psychology in the theatre depends on the subordination of theatre to literature or, more fundamentally, to verbal language. Language structures inspire and co-operate intimately with psychological structures. Perhaps the most striking example in all literature of an attempt to bypass both types of structure can be found in Rimbaud. In his effort to reduce or simplify himself to a series of discontinuous, fragmented scenes – scenes of the external world which wholly objectify the desiring imagination – Rimbaud develops a suspicion of language itself. And [. . .] this impatience with language is the sign of Rimbaud's impatience with his own being. His radical negativity involves a continuous self-repudiation; no present moment is to be responsible to any past moment. Rimbaldian freedom implies a chimerical escape from any self-repetitions at all. And if the self is to be entirely without depth or historical references, its mode of expression must be a succession of nonstructurable visual 'illuminations'. Thus, unlike *Une Saison en enfer,* in which language tells a story, and unlike the *Derniers vers,* where complex musical structures both conceal the poet's inner secrets and yet teasingly confirm their reality, the *Illuminations* are Rimbaud's effort to make language transparent to the hallucinated scene. It is as if he had realised that the particular attention which poetic language usually requires of us inevitably becomes a lesson in the strategies by which language constructs a coherent fiction. And coherent fictions undermine the project of constant self-repudiation: they imply duration, stability and repetition. Therefore, in order to escape from the temptation of structured coherence in the self, Rimbaud must also escape from his interest in the principal instrument of all sense-making operations – that is, his interest in language. The *Illuminations* are an attempt to depoeticise language, to deprive it of any poetic opacity and to reduce it to the status of an uninteresting, barely noticeable prosaic vehicle which would never infect the visions it carries with its own (undesirable) orders.

There is a striking parallelism between Artaud's theatrical manifestos and the programme for poetry (and for being) implicit in Rimbaud's *Illuminations*. Far from suggesting that the physical language of theatre should convey the same type of message as the literary text, Artaud emphasises that to end the supremacy of words is to bring about a radical change in the nature of theatrical sense. To be done with literary masterpieces is to be done with psychology in the theatre. 'The domain of the theatre is not psychological, but plastic and physical . . . ' Now theatre is also metaphysical for Artaud, and what he means by a theatrical metaphysic is another question. It's one that his own productions never answered satisfactorily, and in his writings – especially in *Le Théâtre et son double* – the metaphysic of the concrete is often discussed vaguely, and at times it even seems to include notions from the very systems of abstraction which Artaud is apparently rejecting. (I'm thinking especially of his attempt to convince his readers that the violent theatrical gesture is also a 'disinterested' gesture, as well as of his favourable view of spectacles which produce sublimation.) But in the present discussion we can limit ourselves to what I take to be Artaud's more authentic, and also more complexly ambiguous, gesture of rejection. Jacques Derrida has said that Artaud wants to abolish repetition. This is as fundamental a project in Artaud as it is in Rimbaud. First of all, the subordination of theatre to the literary text makes of theatre a mere repetition of literature. Secondly, the supremacy of verbal language is also the supremacy of a code which depends on repetition for its coherence. Finally, Artaud's rejection of psychological theatre is the natural corollary of his attack on logical discourse and on literary textuality. Psychological theatre dramatises self-repetitions which provide the thematic foundations for a coherently structured personality.[2]

But Artaud's hostility to repetition makes him vulnerable to a type of analysis which exposes the thematic continuities of his own life. Part of the inescapable absurdity of the wish to abolish repetition is that the very persistence of that wish, and its various modulations, subvert the content of Artaud's project: he continuously repeats the project of abolishing repetitions. And we can be more psychologically specific about this enterprise. The central theme of Artaud's life, as Derrida has brilliantly shown, is a horror of all derivation. The inferior status of theatrical performance in Europe is the result of theatre being considered as merely derived from literature. It is never entirely present to itself; it is always a reminder of its absent and more prestigious source. But this view, of the relation between performance and text could be thought of as a sublimated version of Artaud's more visceral revolt against his own derivation from his parents. To be born is to be derived, thus Artaud's extraordinary insistence that his birth was a mistake. For example, Artaud wrote to Henri Parisot on 4 September 1945: 'I didn't go to the Tarahumaras to look for Jesus Christ but rather for myself, Mr Antonin Artaud, born September 4, 1896 in Marseille, 4, rue du Jardin des Plantes, from a uterus I had no need of and which I never had any need of even before, because that's no way to be born, when you're copulated and masturbated nine months by the membrane, the shiny membrane which devours without teeth as the Upanishads say, and I know that I was born in a different way, from my works, and not from a mother, but the Mother resolved to take me and you see the result in my life.'

To be born is the most dramatic example of a substance falling away from itself. The common denominator of Artaud's views on theatre, language and psychology, as well as of his rejection of God and his mad claim that he owes his existence to no one but himself, is his revulsion at the phenomenon of dropping. To drop away from a source is to be derived from that source, and derivation is the mode of repetition which Artaud abhors. But it is as if he saw all repetitions as examples of derivation. It is therefore only in doing away with repetition itself that Artaud can hope both to correct the 'mistake' of his birth and (like Rimbaud) to succeed in making the present give birth to itself in freeing it from any responsibility of the past.

In Artaud, the revolutionising of the self implicit in this project is pursued with psychotic panic; and in that panic Artaud makes explicit the terrifying basics about the body which inform both his plans for a theatre of cruelty and his repudiation of birth. These fantasies can be exceptionally useful in helping us to see what is at stake in perhaps all attempts to simplify character to desublimated, discontinuous scenes of the desiring imagination. 'The anus is always terror', Artaud writes in a letter from the asylum at Rodez in which he attacks the 'fecality' in Lewis Carroll's 'Jabberwocky' as being that of 'an English snob, who makes little curls of the obscene in himself as if he were applying curling-tongs to ringlets'. 'Jabberwocky' is soulless because it is without authentic obscenity: '. . . I refuse to admit that one can lose any excrement without acutely suffering from the simultaneous loss of one's soul, and there is no soul in "Jabberwocky".' From his early letters to Jacques Rivière to the hallucinating messages from Rodez, the constant theme of Artaud's anguish is a terrified fantasy of a dropping away of the self. To Rivière, he complains of 'une véritable déperdition', of 'a central caving in of the soul, . . . a kind of erosion . . . of thought'. At Rodez, twenty years later, the connection between this spiritual erosion and loss of the soul through the anus will be made explicit. What is the logic of this connection and why is the anus terror?

We may consider the excremental process and birth as the most appropriate for all ontological reflection about individuality, self-repetition and death. ' . . . Caca is the matter of the soul . . . ', Artaud profoundly writes from Rodez. Given Artaud's terror of the anus and his revulsion with birth, this astonishing formula is, I think, a condensed way of affirming that excremental droppings are inevitably – and, in one sense, rightly – associated with that 'dropping away' from the mother which marks the birth of an individual soul. The connection between the two is by no means only a 'sick' confusion between two fundamentally different biological operations. It's obvious that, in its pathological form, a fantasy equivalence of birth with defecation involves confusing the vagina and the anus and a live infant with fecal matter. But the very real analogies between the two phenomena are perhaps more interesting. Giving birth and moving one's bowels are both concrete illustrations of that 'miracle' – which in fact is a commonplace in the evolutionary scale from the unicellular organism to man – by which one substance becomes two substances. In both processes, being separates from itself.

Now in birth what is separated from the parent organism is new life; in defecation it is of course merely waste, matter which the body can neither destroy nor use. The latter process, while it in fact demonstrates both the living economy of the body and the indestructability of matter, comes nonetheless to be interpreted (especially in the child's fantasies) as a daily manifestation of our bodies' tendency to die. It is as if the body were continuously evacuating part of itself, transforming its living cells into dead waste. Artaud remains faithful to the child's view of fecal matter as a loss of life, as evidence of the mysterious amputation of its own living substance on part of the body. In this fantasy, faeces are the visible, externalised form of the body's death while we are still alive. But to be separated from the mother's body is also a form of death. Birth 'condemns' us to individual life, and therefore to death; the beginning of new life is of course also the promise of a new death. The crude physical analogies between birth and defecation – they are both, as it were, evacuations from below – are therefore reinforced by another, more essential, similarity: both evacuations seem to announce death. It is, very precisely, the 'falling away' from another self which, by giving us individual life, illustrates its affinity with death throughout life. Thus, to the extent that it is the nature of an individual soul to have the awesome privilege of an individual death, the fate of the soul is prefigured in the body's daily 'condemnation' of a part of its own contents as unusable waste. In a sense, the matter of the soul is indeed 'caca', and the anus is, conversely, a principle of spiritual terror: to feel the body's waste pass through the anus and to see that waste is to witness a decomposition (a separation of matter from life) to which another passing through or dropping away originally and irrevocably doomed us.

But of course birth dooms us to death *in time* and the fantasy identification of birth with death implies an indifference to the time *between* the two. Perhaps only a passionate interest in the 'unfolding' of our lives' time can soften the shock of that movement away from the self which is intimately connected with death in both defecation and birth. In effect, we might say that Artaud, in his panic, would abolish all temporal processes, and this has important consequences for his revolutionary vision of the theatre. To understand this, we should look at some other aspects of birth and of the anus as terror. For birth and defecation are instructive not merely about individuality and death: they also throw light on self-repetition and character formation in time. Birth is the fundamental example in human experience of self-repetition as productive of new being. The infant's parents have reproduced themselves in another individual. The unresolvable paradox of birth lies in this equivalence between self-reproduction and absolute difference. Thus birth is the model of all temporal processes which simultaneously establish continuities and discontinuities. It is the major human experience of difference within repetition, of a repetition which does not simply reproduce the same. On the one hand, birth is the model of all recurrences which make it possible for us to see intelligible structures in the world; all sense-making activity depends on the perception of repetition (or of parallelism and analogy). On the other hand, birth initiates us into the world of diversified forms.

Among the latter, we might include the forms of an individual character. The diversified coherence of a particular psychological history consists, precisely, in self-repetitions subverted and enriched by self-betrayals. And there are, of course, possibilities of terror in this process. There is, first of all, the terror of *mere* repetition, of that monotonous, timeless tick-tack of personality which, as we have seen, obsesses Gudrun in Lawrence's *Women in Love*. There is also the potential terror of having to recognise the self in a form alien to the self. In one sense, both the infant and fecal matter defy us to recognise ourselves in a foreign substance. And the history of personality includes numerous shocks of similar (non)recognitions. In literature, *À la Recherche du temps perdu* is the most exhaustive document we have of a man's incredulity in the face of what he himself becomes. The most mysterious crises for Proust's narrator are those moments when he can't find himself in the present, when he perceives no repetitions but only difference. Finally, there is the terror of loss – a terror which can be located both on the side of what has reproduced itself and on the side of what has been reproduced. In birth, defecation and the history of personality, the parent organism dissipates its contents merely by allowing them to be manifested in external forms. The mother literally loses a part of herself in the child; we throw away some of what the body has been containing in the excremental process; and in the time of an individual life, the self is lost (it spends itself) among the multiple alien circumstances in which it enacts and dissipates its history. If we consider loss from the point of view of what has been born, we see that the infant suffers the loss of its origin; and, in the history of personality, each new gesture creates another difference, however minute, which separates us irremediably from the permanently identical self which we might have reserved only by refusing any *performed* repetition at all, by refusing time itself.

It is this terror at the separation of the self from itself which we find in Artaud. The anus and birth are subjects of terror, but, if we accept the logic of what I've just been saying, so is the very time of an individual life. This cruel lesson, which birth, defecation, and an individual history teach us, is that I am never entirely present to myself. As Derrida says, repetition makes a present moment less fully present to itself. Part of what is in the present was already in the past, and therefore the present is, so to speak, partly somewhere (sometime) else. I too am always somewhere else, and all repetition is evidence of my being elsewhere. There are always spaces (physical and temporal) between a present gesture and the gesture it refers to. But there are no gestures from which all the others are derived, every moment in my life sends me to other moments. And, to the extent that I yearn to find an underived origin, I can only suffer from this experience of never being anything but a derived self, one whose differences are inseparable from its repetitions, in short, a self always dropping away from – what?

The answer to this question obviously depends on our views concerning the final term (or the origin . . .) of our myths about origin. It seems likely that the pre-natal experience of living in the mother's body lays the basis for the illusion of perfect presence. The notion of a transcendent being whose nature is wholly concentrated on its unchangeable presence is perhaps the most intellectually rarefied consequence of the pre-natal confusion of our milieu with our being. We never wholly rid ourselves of this confusion; or more precisely we keep a nostalgia for a world in which being would everywhere always be equally present to itself. Instead the self finds that it is at a distance from the world which nonetheless contains it. It is neither identical to the world nor is it clearly distinct from it; rather it is always in the intervals between two fictions: the fiction of a world from which the self is absent and that of the self as a centre without an environment or as a fixed nondisseminated presence. The physical separation of the infant from the parent in birth is the most spectacular evidence we are given of the split between the self and the world as well as between the self and its own history.[3] Artaud's most urgent need is to abolish these spaces to save the self from any extensions or, to use a Derridean term, any dissemination which would scatter and destroy presence. Artaud's ideal in Derrida's striking phrase is a 'Corps-propre-debout-sans-déchet'. Without 'déchet' (waste or residue): nothing must fall away from the body. But since the very shape of the body includes a certain falling away from itself, Artaud lives in terror of the 'articulated body', of anatomical extensions which decentralise our physical being. And we can now see the most profound logic of Artaud's mistrust of verbal language: words articulate the self; they substitute a system of spaced repetitions and differences for pure presence. (Beckett pursues the same chimerical ideal. The 'characters' in the novelistic trilogy move toward silence, immobility and even, in *L'Innommable*, a body reduced to – or perfected in – the shape of a ball with no extensions at all.)

Psychology is the attempt to systematise the self's losses of pure presence. It considers all behaviour from the specific point of view, of other behaviour; the psychological interpretation of repetition and difference assumes the derived nature of all human activity. The antipsychological bias of Artaud's programme for the theatre is therefore a logical and crucial aspect of his passionate antipathy toward all derivation. It's true that Artaud's rebellion, as Derrida has shown, is ambiguous and even self-defeating. Artaud rejects a 'metaphysic of difference' which argues for the ontological inferiority of the phenomenal world by referring that world back to an underived cause which alone enjoys the privilege of full, nonreferential presence. But he keeps the cult of presence. Instead of recognising that to abolish transcendence is also to lose the hope of *any* self contained, 'nondisseminated' presence in the universe, Artaud transfers the locus of perfect presence from a metaphysical reality to the phenomenal world itself, indeed to his own body (the 'Corps-propre-debout-sans-déchet'). And to his thought; in one of the texts of *L'Ombilic des limbes*, Artaud spells out his notions of what thought should be: ' . . . for me thinking is something other than not being completely dead, it means connecting up with oneself at every moment, it means that we never stop feeling ourselves in our inner being, in the unformulated mass of life, in the substance of our reality, it means not feeling any essential hole in ourselves, any vital absence, it means always feeling our thought equal to our thought'. Nevertheless, as far as the consequences for theatrical theory and practice are concerned, this displacement of perfect presence is enormously important. Since in the theatre the dramatic text plays the part of the source from which dramatic performance is derived, to abolish the 'superstition of texts' is the first requirement of the theatre of cruelty. To do away with psychological theatre is just as necessary: the presence of the theatre's multiple physical realities has been violated by our habit of translating dramatic performance into the psychology from which it presumably derives. Theatrical shapes and movements have been the mere 'déchet', the 'droppings' of abstract psychological and moral truths.

To shift the emphasis in theatre from the textual to the scenic implies a redefinition of character and desire which would be as radical as that proposed by the *Illuminations*. Although Artaud never discusses his ideas in the terms I'm now using, his theatrical programme is nonetheless an attack on the very bases of psychological intelligibility in our culture. The notion of a structured unified character is inseparable from the phenomenon of derivation (and from a willingness to accept that phenomenon). In any coherent psychological portrait the unity of personality depends on interrelated traits which are stabilised by their positions in a hierarchical structure. There are dominant traits and there are subordinate traits; certain aspects of personality are derived from other aspects; the self's 'extensions' into various activities both diversify and repeat character. This unifying, hierarchical logic of personality is easy enough to see in early psychologies of the humours or of dominant faculties. It is also present in more sophisticated forms, in the psychoanalytic classifications of character traits as derived from fixations on different bodily pleasures; and the same unifying logic governs the judgemental discriminations about behaviour in, for example, the Freudian use of such labels as 'symptoms' and 'sublimations'.

Now Artaud himself is not very instructive about the consequences of a rejection of psychological drama. This is partly because his theatrical practice (what there was of it) was less original than his speculations about theatre, and perhaps also because his own entrapment in the ideology of presence would in any case have condemned him to a static, monumental type of theatrical event. In his tortured struggle with the presence–absence duality, Artaud seems to have been incapable of imagining a theatrical scene which would neither refer us to pre-existent texts (or to an implicit psychological unity) *nor* merely transfer the cult of total presence from abstract sources behind the scenes to the physical elements of theatre themselves. As we shall see in a moment in looking at some contemporary examples, it's possible to conceive of a nonpsychological and a nontextual theatre in terms of a certain inadequacy between dramatic presence and dramatic significance. The significance, however, would be literally nowhere, neither in the theatre nor out of it; its nature would be more a question of positioning than of content. That is, nothing would ever be designed to centralise (and conceptualise) dramatic meaning for us. All the physical elements of theatre would be both excessive and inadequate: either charged with energies untranslatable into sense, or de-emphasised in ways designed to make us look elsewhere. And this decentralisation of theatrical presence forces the spectator to abandon a fixed, fetishistic attention to actors' bodies which, it could be argued, has provided the principal erotic pleasure of traditional theatre.

Repetition has various modes, but it is inconceivable that repetition itself be abolished. The mode which haunts Artaud, and which he tries so desperately to eliminate, both in theatre and in his own being, might be thought of as vertical or transcendental repetition. Phenomena repeat the course from which they derive, and, ontologically, the phenomenal world is inferior to its origins and causes. Performance is subordinate to texts; behaviour merely illustrates character. There are viable alternatives to this sort of repetition, but it would be difficult to overemphasise its powerful (if frightening) appeal. As I suggested earlier, the connection between individuality, death and character formation would seem to be a biologically authenticated connection. Artaud profoundly saw that to reject derivation implies a 'refusal' of birth (and of defecation). We *are* dropping away from an origin which we relive, in fantasy, as wholly adequate to itself; and in the body's wastes, death seems to be produced and made immediately visible to the living. The psychology most natural to us undoubtedly involves us in thinking of visible behaviour as proceeding from and illustrating profound character structures.

And the successful throwing off of this psychology involves a kind of murder. Birth is a 'falling' from above, and so, in a sense, is vertical derivation (the play is a 'déchet' from the text, behaviour a 'déchet' from our nature). Vertical derivation is therefore biologically linked to having parents. For Artaud to escape from being a 'dropping', he must deny his birth, 'kill' his parents. A murder, Derrida writes, is always at the origin of cruelty – murder of the parent, of the all-powerful Logos behind the theatrical scene, and, of course, murder of God ultimately; only deocide restores the dignity of concreteness to the theatre (and to all human experience), for 'God's history is . . . the history of excrement'.

Artaud, like Rimbaud, forces us to see the unavoidable connection: between the deconstruction of character and violence. Theatre is intrinsically cruel – although for reasons which have little to do with the vague notions of 'necessity', 'difficulty' and 'appetite for life' with which Artaud watered down his intuitions about theatrical cruelty. The particular power of theatre lies in its immediately scenic nature. While Rimbaud had always to struggle against the conceptualising tendencies of language, a theatrical performance can return us at once to visual modes of self-definition. Theatre is the ideal space in which a regression from the structured sublimations of character can be enacted. No human performance eliminates psychology; but theatrical performance can return us to a psychology of the concrete. In what sense is this return violent or cruel?

First of all, theatre allows us momentarily to forget the distinction between the self and the world – a distinction based on the infant's painful recognition that the scenes of his desiring imagination are internal scenes. Desire is mental, and therefore abstract, and our capacity for abstraction depends on our having been forced to discriminate between fantasies of desire. We can see the complicity of language with this learning process. The most elementary verbal grammar helps us to systematise these discriminations (I'm thinking, for example, of the distinctions among pronouns, as well as of the implicit opposition between concrete and abstract in the difference between the present tense and past and future tenses), and we of course use words to represent – to present once again – realities no longer or not yet present. Thus a non-verbal coincidence of the self with the world is replaced by verbal descriptions of both what we perceive and what we feel, by the transposition of pictorial desire into narrative fictions. Our fictions express, elaborate and disguise our desires; they sublimate desire.[4] Finally, we reflect on the nature of our fictive scenes and stories, and finding patterns, analogies, themes (in short, repetitions) in the history of our imagination, we are naturally led to view that history as the display of a coherent character. Desire, blocked in its naive confusions with the world, repeats itself at different levels of mental activity. A single desire runs through various preferences (preferences for certain sexual activities, for certain styles in other people, for particular rhythms of behaviour, for particular systems of thought). Repeated and sublimated, desire thus creates personality.

Theatre can offer us the extraordinary luxury of briefly destroying this entire process. We can now see that the violence of the theatre which Artaud proposes to us is not only a question of patricide (or matricide) and deocide. The theatrical scene that is not subordinated to a literary text can also brush aside the hard-earned knowledge of the world as more than a performing space for my own identity. Theatre reobjectifies desire, and when its scenes coincide with those of the spectator's own desiring imagination, it is as if, for a moment, he had recovered the happy illusion that his desires literally possess the world. Furthermore, in an essentially nonverbal theatre no longer retelling stories already told in literature, we may also enjoy a loss of the continuities which our verbal fictions have discovered in (or imposed on) our desires. Psychological continuity thrives on the frustration of desire; desire, duplicated and sublimated in ideals and mental faculties, organises a self. The victims of this process are the fragmentary, the accidental, the peripheral, the discontinuous. The scenic finality of theatre allows for the reinstatement of a heterogeneous multiplicity of desire. A mass of memories and fantasies no longer has to be sacrificed to the structural harmony of character. Theatre is the privileged aesthetic space for structurally unassimilable desires.

But the indulgence of those desires obviously entails certain brutalities. To re-emphasise the fragmentary and the discontinuous is to fracture, to wound, the self. We undermine a psychological unity which we no longer think of as an inescapable psychic fate, but which has performed the far from negligible service of providing us with an identity in the world. Representations of discontinuous impulses express partial selves; the person is dismembered by the very fertility of its resources. And in our exuberant fusion with those scenes which offer themselves, literally, as the theatre of our desires, we may also become more readily disposed to violate *any* otherness in the external world. Consciousness liberated from the restrictive continuities of character may also be consciousness abandoned to the brutal if illusory omnipotence of masturbatory fantasies. The deconstruction of character in contemporary theatrical experiments is a complex adventure. Desiring impulses no longer contained by conscience or by a sense of responsibility toward one's own coherence are perhaps even more ferocious than the vengeful desires sanctioned by conscience. Some of these experiments (I'm thinking especially of Robert Wilson, Joe Chaikin, Peter Brook and Charles Ludlam) have in fact found strategies to tame a desiring imagination which they also encourage us to cultivate. Our discussion of contemporary theatres of desire will have to include a close look at the consequences of all serious enterprises of psychic deconstruction. For among those consequences, we inevitably find, to some degree, the pornographic tyrannies intrinsic to all desire.

Part III
On writing and fine arts

This section assembles four readings of Artaud's texts: one (by Blanchot) in terms of a poetics, and another (by Kristeva) a psycholinguistic treatment. The two other essays relate to Artaud's conception of the image. The first of these is by Derrida (he has devoted four essays to Artaud) and concerns the notion of force in visual production. The final piece, by Umberto Artioli, examines Artaud's writing on Van Gogh.

13 Maurice Blanchot
'Artaud'*

This piece was first reprinted in Blanchot's *Le Livre à venir* (Paris: Gallimard, 1959, pp. 51–62). It focuses on Artaud as a poet and examines one of Artaud's earliest publications, 'The correspondence with Jacques Rivière'. It is an influential piece and arguably established a paradigm for an entire generation of critics in France, reading Artaud as a writer who refused to confide in conventional literary and artistic forms and who made this protest the subject of an entire oeuvre. Derrida's essay 'La Parole soufflée' and Foucault's discussion of Artaud in *Histoire de la folie à l'âge classique*, as well as many other less celebrated examples of scholarship on or around Artaud, for example some of the essays in Roger Laporte's *Quinze Variations sur un thème biographique*, are written in the wake of these few pages.

It problematises the biographical approach of a number of Anglophone critics (see Greene 1970, Knapp 1971, Esslin 1976, Sontag in Artaud 1976, Hayman 1977) in interesting ways since, for Blanchot, Artaud's writing poses the question as to why 'the work is at times realised, at times sacrificed, for the sake of the very movement from which it comes' (Blanchot 1959: 51). Blanchot avoids the confusion engendered by collapsing this movement into the work itself; i.e. the experience of the generation of the work should not be seen as the work's constitutive achievement. He looks at how its fate (as letter or poem, etc.) was determined, even at the very start of his career, by the consideration of its founding trace.

Blanchot, after Jacques Rivière, observes the contrast between Artaud's awkward and tentative verse and the conceptual and figurative power of the letters. Yet Blanchot proceeds from this to make a kind of defence of poetry in general. He does this by revisiting the same gesture which he witnesses in Rivière's reception of the poems, arguing that their value lies in the fact that they were produced 'from the absence of mind' which Artaud suffered and which later came to mark one of the distinctive features of his written work. But it is 'only the poems' that expose Artaud 'to the central loss of thought from which he is suffering' (Blanchot 1959: 52). For Blanchot, the significance of the poems consists in the fact that only the confrontation with such conventionally determined forms of literature produces in Artaud the experience of loss and lack that becomes both the driving force behind the letters and their dominant theme.

At this point in the essay, Artaud's experience is deployed to exemplify the link between poetry and thought, with thought considered as 'that impossibility of thinking' (Blanchot 1959: 53). Blanchot's argument, which here seems curiously defensive of those literary considerations which Artaud, in the course of this correspondence, gradually repudiates, then turns to a discussion of Artaud's new works, the letters, a form which would in the course of his career constitute the bulk of his oeuvre. Blanchot has written another piece on Artaud's poetry entitled 'La Cruelle raison poétique', in *L'Entretien infini*, which is interesting for comparisons with this earlier seminal essay.

At the age of twenty-seven, Artaud sends some poems to a journal. The editor of the journal politely turns them down. Artaud then tries to explain his attachment to these flawed poems; he is suffering from such a dereliction of thought that he cannot simply disregard the forms, however inadequate, which he has wrought from this central non-existence. What is the worth of the resulting poems? An exchange of letters follows, and Jacques Rivière, the journal's editor, suddenly suggests publishing the letters written about these unpublishable poems, some of which will now, however, appear in an illustrative, documentary capacity. Artaud accepts on condition that the truth should not be disguised. This is the famous correspondence with Jacques Rivière, an event of great significance.

Was Jacques Rivière aware of the anomaly here? Poems which he considered inadequate and unworthy of publication cease to be so when supplemented by the account of the experience of their inadequacy. As if what they lacked, their failing, became plenitude and consummation by virtue of the overt expression of that lack and the exploration of its necessity. Rather than the work itself, what interests Jacques Rivière is clearly the experience of the work, the movement which leads up to it, and the obscure, anonymous trace which, clumsily, it represents. More than that, this failure, which does not in fact attract him as much as it will subsequently attract those who write and who read, becomes the tangible sign of a central event of the mind, on which Artaud's explanations shed a surprising light. We are coming close, therefore, to a phenomenon to which literature and indeed art are often linked: namely, that there is no poem which does not have its own accomplishment as a poem as its implicit or explicit 'subject', and that the work is at times realised, at times sacrificed, for the sake of the very movement from which it comes.

We may recall here Rilke's letter, written some fifteen years earlier:

The further one goes, the more personal and unique life becomes. The work of art is the necessary, irrefutable, and forever definitive expression of that unique reality . . . It is in this respect that the work affords extraordinary help to whoever is compelled to produce it . . . This gives us a sure explanation of the need to submit ourselves to the most extreme ordeals, but also, it seems, to say nothing of them until we immerse ourselves in our work, not to diminish them by talking about them: what is unique – what no one else could understand or would have the right to understand, that particular derangement which is our own – can only acquire any worth by taking its place in our work (travail), there to reveal its law, an original figure which the transparency of art alone makes visible.

Rilke intends, therefore, never to communicate directly the experience from which the work comes, the extreme ordeal whose value and truth only arise from its immersion in the work in which it appears – visible, invisible – in the distant light of art. But did Rilke himself always maintain this discretion? And did he not articulate this discretion precisely to break it even as he safeguarded it, knowing moreover that he did not have the power to break it, no more than anyone has, but could only keep in contact with it? That particular derangement which is our own . . .

The impossibility of thinking which is thought

Jacques Rivière is impeccably understanding, attentive and sensitive. But, in their dialogue, there is a clear degree of misunderstanding which none the less remains difficult to define. Still very patient at this time, Artaud keeps a constant watch over this misunderstanding. He sees that his correspondent is seeking to reassure him by promising that the future will bring the coherence which he lacks, or else by showing him that the mind's frailty is necessary to it. But Artaud does not want to be reassured. He is in contact with something so serious that he cannot bear it to be assuaged. This is because he is also aware of the extraordinary, and for him almost unbelievable, relationship between the ruination of his thought and the poems which he is able to write despite this 'veritable decay'. On the one hand, Jacques Rivière fails to perceive the exceptional nature of the event, and, on the other, he fails to see what is extreme about these works of the mind which are produced on the basis of a mental absence.

When he writes to Rivière with a calm penetration which impresses his correspondent, it is no surprise to Artaud to be in command of what he wants to say. It is only his poems which lay him open to the central loss of thought from which he is suffering, an anxiety which he later evokes in trenchant terms and, for instance, in the following form: 'What I am speaking of is the absence of any mental lapse, a sort of imageless, feelingless, cold suffering, which is like an indescribable collision of abject failures.' Why then does he write poems? Why does he not content himself with being a man using language for everyday ends? Everything suggests that poetry, linked for him 'to this sort of erosion, at once essential and ephemeral, of thought', thus essentially involved in this central loss, at the same time gives him the certainty that it alone can be the expression of this loss, and promises, to a certain extent, to save this loss itself, to save his thought in so far as it is lost. So it is that he comes to say, in a fit of impatience and arrogance: 'I am he who has most keenly felt the bewildering disarray of his language in its relation to thought . . . I become lost in my thought exactly as one dreams, as one suddenly drifts off in thought. I am he who knows the innermost recesses of loss.'

He is not concerned with 'thinking clearly, seeing clearly', with having coherent, appropriate, well-expressed thoughts, all of which aptitudes he knows he possesses. And he is annoyed when friends say to him, you think very well, it's a common experience to be lost for words. ('I am sometimes thought to be too brilliant in the expression of my inadequacies, my fundamental failings, and my professed helplessness for this expression to be anything but a fiction, a complete fabrication.') He knows, with the profundity afforded by the experience of suffering, that thinking is not simply having thoughts, and that the thoughts he has only make him feel that he has not 'yet *begun* to think'. This is the dire torment with which he is struggling. It is as if, despite himself and through a woeful error at which he cries out, he has reached the point where thinking is always already not being able to think yet – an 'im-power', as he puts it, which is, as it were, essential to thought, but which makes thought a most painful lack, a debility which immediately radiates out from this centre and, consuming the physical substance of whatever it thinks, at every level divides into so many individual impossibilities.

That poetry is linked to the impossibility of thinking which is thought, this is the truth which cannot disclose itself, because it always turns away, requiring that he experience it beneath the point at which he would really experience it. This is not only a metaphysical difficulty, it is the ravishment of suffering, and poetry is this perpetual suffering, it is 'darkness' and 'the night of the soul', 'the absence of a voice to cry out'.

In a letter written some twenty years later, when he has undergone ordeals which have made him a difficult, fiery being, he says with the utmost simplicity: 'I started out in literature by writing books in order to say that I could not write anything at all. My thought, when I had something to write, was what was most denied me.' And again: 'I have only ever written to say that I have never done anything, never could do anything, and that, when doing something, in reality I was doing nothing. All my work has been and can only ever be built on nothingness.' Common sense immediately poses the question why, if he has nothing to say, does he not in fact say nothing? We may reply that one can content oneself with saying nothing when nothing is merely almost nothing; here, however, we are apparently confronted with such a radical nullity that, in the exorbitance it represents, the danger of which it is the approach, the tension it provokes, it demands, as if it were the price to be freed from it, the formulation of an initial word which would banish all the words which say something. How could someone who has nothing to say not endeavour to begin to speak, to express himself? 'Well, my particular weakness and my absurdity consist in wishing at all costs to write and to express myself. I am a man who has endured great mental suffering and, as such, I have the right to speak.'

Description of a struggle

In a movement which bears his own particular authority, Artaud approaches this void which his work – of course, it is not in fact a work – will exalt and denounce, span and safeguard, fill as it is filled by it. At the outset, before this void, he still seeks to recapture some plenitude of which he thinks he is sure, and which would put him in touch with his rich instinctive capacities, the integrity of his feeling and an adherence to the continuity of things which is so consummate that, within him, it is already crystallising into poetry. He has, he believes he has, this 'deep seated aptitude', as well as a wealth of forms and words with which to express it. But 'at the point where the soul is preparing to organise its treasures, its discoveries, this revelation, at that unconscious moment when the thing is about to emerge, a superior, malevolent will attacks the soul like an acid, attacks the mass of word and image, attacks the mass of feeling, and, as for me, it leaves me gasping for breath, as if at the very gates of life'.

It is easy to say that Artaud is the victim here of the illusion of the immediate, but everything begins with the way in which he is banished from the immediate which he calls 'life'; this comes about, not through some nostalgic swoon nor through the sensory oblivion of a dream, but rather through a rupture so conspicuous as to introduce into its very core the affirmation of a perpetual deviation which becomes what is most distinctively his own and, so to speak, the shocking revelation of his true nature.

Through an unerring and painful exploration, then, he comes to reverse the terms of this movement, according that place to dispossession instead of the 'immediate totality', whose simple lack this dispossession had at first seemed to be. What comes first is not the plenitude of being, but the breach and the fissure, erosion and laceration, intermittence and gnawing deprivation: being is not being, it is this lack of being, a living lack which makes life faltering, elusive and inexpressible, except through the howl of savage abstinence.

When he thought he had the plenitude of 'indivisible reality', perhaps Artaud was only sensing the shadowy depths projected behind him by this void, since the only evidence within himself of this complete plenitude is the awesome power which denies it, an immense negation which is always at work and capable of an infinite proliferation of emptiness. This is so dreadful a pressure that it expresses him, even as it demands that he devote himself entirely to producing and to sustaining its own expression.

However, at the time of the correspondence with Jacques Rivière, when he is still writing poems, he clearly nourishes the hope of becoming a match for himself, an ambition which the poems are destined at once to accomplish and to thwart. At this time, he says that he is 'thinking at a lower level'; 'I am beneath myself, I know – it grieves me.' Later, he remarks: 'It is the contradiction between my deep-seated aptitude and my external difficulties which causes the torment which is killing me.' At this point, his anxiety and guilt stem from thinking beneath his thought, which he therefore keeps behind him, assured of its ideal integrity, so that, in expressing it, if only in a single word, he would reveal himself in his true stature, his own incontrovertible witness. His torment comes from being unable to acquit himself of his thought and, within him, poetry remains the hope, so to speak, of annulling this debt which, however, it can only extend far beyond the limits of his existence. One sometimes has the impression that the correspondence with Jacques Rivière, the latter's disregard for his poetry and his interest in the central turmoil which Artaud is only too inclined to describe, that these displace the centre of his writing. Artaud had been writing against the void, endeavouring to evade it. Now he is writing so as to expose himself to it, to try to express it and draw expression from it.

This displacement of the centre of gravity – which *The Umbilicus of Limbo* and *The Nerve Metre* represent – is the painful constraint (*exigence*) which compels him, forsaking any illusion, to pay heed henceforth to one point alone: the 'point of absence and inanity' around which he wanders with a sort of sarcastic lucidity, a sly good sense, to then be driven by movements of suffering in which one can hear wretchedness cry out, as only Sade before him could cry out, and yet, like Sade again, without any compliance, and with a power to fight which is at all times the equal of the void he is embracing. 'I want to get beyond this point of absence and futility – this stagnation which is debilitating me, making me inferior to everything and everyone. I have no life, I have no life! My inner spark is dead . . . I cannot manage to think. Can you understand this emptiness, this intense, lasting nothingness? . . . I can go neither forward nor backwards. I am fixated, confined around a single point which is always the same and which all my books convey.'

We must not make the mistake of reading as analysts of a psychological state the precise, unflinching and detailed descriptions of this which Artaud offers us. Descriptions they are, but of a struggle. This struggle is in part imposed on him. The 'void' is an 'active void'. The 'I cannot think, I cannot manage to think' is an appeal to a deeper thought, a constant pressure, a forgetting which, unable to bear being forgotten, none the less demands a more complete forgetting. Thinking now becomes this step back which is always to be taken. The struggle in which he is always defeated is always engaged again at a lower level. The powerlessness is never powerless enough, the impossible not the impossible. But at the same time, this struggle is also what Artaud wants to pursue, for in this fight he always clings to what he calls 'life' – this explosion, this blazing vitality – which he cannot bear to lose, which he wants to unite with his thought, and which, with a magnificent and dreadful obstinacy, he categorically refuses to distinguish from thought, whereas the latter is nothing other than the 'erosion' of this life, its 'emaciation', the depths of rupture and decay where there is neither life nor thought, but only the torture of a fundamental lack in which the demand issuing from a more decisive negation already asserts itself. And it begins all over again. For Artaud will never accept the scandal of a thought separated from life, even when he is subjected to the most direct, savage experience ever known of the essence of thought understood as separation, of this impossibility which thought asserts against itself at the limit of its infinite power.

Suffering, thinking

It would be tempting to draw a parallel between what Artaud says and what Hölderlin or Mallarmé tell us, namely that inspiration is first of all that pure point where inspiration is lacking. But we must resist the temptation of these too general affirmations. Each poet says the same, and yet it is not the same, it is, we feel, unique. Artaud's contribution is distinctively his own. What he says is of an intensity which we should be unable to bear. There speaks here a suffering which refuses any depth, any illusion and any hope, but which, by that refusal, offers thought 'the ether of a new space'. When we read these pages, we learn what we never succeed in knowing: that the fact of thinking cannot be anything other than devastating; that what is to be thought is that which, in thought, turns away from thought and inexhaustibly exhausts itself in it; that suffering and thinking are secretly bound together for, if suffering, when it becomes extreme, is such that it destroys the power to suffer, thus, in time, always destroying, ahead of itself, the time in which it might be grasped and accomplished as suffering, then this same is perhaps true of thought. Strange relations. Could it be that extreme thought and extreme suffering open the same horizon? Could suffering, in the end, be thinking?

14 Julia Kristeva

From 'The subject in process'*

In this book-length essay on Artaud, written in 1972, Kristeva places Artaud at the centre of her thesis on the dynamics of subjectivity in its volatile relations with language, a topic which fed into much of her later work. This piece is the foundation text to Kristeva's important early work in psycholinguistics and shows how writing places the author's subjectivity in process/on trial. This notion is often quoted, but rarely sourced to this early piece on Artaud. It is generally considered more important as an example of Kristeva's work than an essay for Artaud scholarship, but in certain places Kristeva's reading of Artaud is extremely powerful and astute.

The concept of semiotic *chora*, an instinctual state prior to language, is explained here in the context of Artaud's writing, which always sought a language prior to language. Kristeva enables an understanding of the process of Artaud's writing as a performance in language, but also the aims of such a stratagem: a more fundamental principle for communication than language but which would also be significative. Both Kristeva and Artaud are interested in reactivating the energetic states prior to language and maintaining this energy as a mode of creativity.

Artaud also appears in her work on abjection in *Powers of Horror* and in *Desire in Language* as a figure who returns language to its source outside the symbolic order. For Foucault in *The Order of Things*, Artaud had a similar function, restoring to language its being, 'that formless mute unsignifying region where language finds its freedom' (Foucault 1966: 395). For an earlier Foucault, Artaud was also an exemplary figure of the mad artist whose work is always at the limit of the intelligible, of the representable, just before it disappears into the silence of madness.

Kristeva's writings around Artaud mirror these concerns but her focus here is poetic language, not in the sense of an aesthetic object, but rather a process by which language calls forth its other, the place from where it set out and to which it will return. Kristeva's work in naming these places and defining their attributes and functions, semiotic *chora*, expulsion and negativity, constitutes perhaps her most significant achievement in the field of psycholinguistics/literary analysis. In putting poetic language on trial, her best witness may prove to have been Artaud.

A theoretical discourse can only attempt to 'take account' of a signifying function refused by our culture by consigning it to the domain of art, that is, to libraries or conferences. At the very most it can try to intervene in the accepted and operating conceptual systems on the basis of the experience that the subject of theory might herself have of this functioning. The following is thus concerned, on the one hand, with an intra-theoretical attempt with ideological consequences (which in no sense provides a comprehensive account of Artaud's experience), and, on the other hand, with an invasion of the positivist neutrality of theory by the subjective experience of the theorist, by her capacity to put herself 'on trial', to move out of the enclosure of her individuality, be it split, to then return to the fragile site of metalanguage so as to utter the logic of this process, suffered if not understood. [. . .]

In its most audacious moments current (Lacanian) psychoanalytic theory proposes a theory of the subject as a divided unity which arises from and is determined by lack (void, nothingness, zero, according to the context) and engages in an unsatisfied quest for the impossible, represented by metonymic desire. This subject, which we will call the 'unitary subject', under the law of One, which turns out to be the Name of the Father, this subject of filiation or subject-son, is in fact the unvoiced part, or if you like the truth, of the subject of science, but also of the subject of the social organism (of the family, the clan, the state, the group). Psychoanalysis teaches us this: that any subject, inasmuch as he or she is social, supposes this unitary and split instance, initially proposed by Freud with the Unconscious/Conscious schema, while it also points to the role of originary repression in the constitution of the subject. If originary repression institutes the subject at the same time as the symbolic function, it also institutes the distinction between signifier and signified in which Lacan sees the determination of 'any censorship of a social nature' (Lacan 1966: 372). The unitary subject is the subject instituted by this social censoring.

However, despite being constitutive, this censoring and the subject which it installs do not behave according to a universal law. We cannot yet undertake the history of the subject or of the development of the forces of production and the modes of production which correspond to them across human history, although Deleuze and Guattari's *Anti-Oedipus* (1972) is a first step in this direction. We can only recognise, empirically for the moment, the existence of signifying practices which seem to point to the existence of *another economy*. To take only a few examples: pre-Socratic Greece (Heraclitus, Anaxagoras, Empedocles), the China of the 'Asiatic mode of production', and, particularly, capitalist society since the end of the nineteenth century; all propose texts remarkable for a practice in which the unitary subject, as an indispensable pole assuring the capacity to verbalise, is annihilated, liquefied, exceeded by what we will call the 'process of *signifiance*', that is, by pre-verbal drives and semiotic operations logically if not chronologically anterior to the phenomenon of language. In this process, the unitary subject discovered by psychoanalysis is only one moment, a time of arrest, a stasis, exceeded and threatened by this movement. The process [. . .]

goes as far as rejecting even the Unconscious/Conscious division, the Signifier/Signified division, that is, even the very censoring through which the subject and the social order are constituted.

The process dissolves the linguistic sign and its system (word, syntax), dissolves, that is, even the earliest and most solid guarantee of the unitary subject: Artaud's glossolalia and 'eructations' reject the symbolic function and mobilise the drives which this function represses in order to constitute itself. [. . .] This pulsional network, which is readable, for example, in the pulsional roots of the non-semanticised phonemes of Artaud's texts, represents (for theory) the *mobile-receptacle site of the process*, which takes the place of the unitary subject. Such a site, which we will call the *chora*,[1] can suffice as a representation of the subject in process [. . .].

The practices we are interested in here, those of modern texts, realise a subtle, fragile and mobile equilibrium between the two aspects of heterogeneous contradiction. The passage of 'free energies' is ensured against the fragility of their marking and of the *representamen* which are generated by them and which bind them. But the latter, under the violent assault of heterogeneous contradiction, do not manage to enclose it in the symbolic stereotype of a linguistic structure or an ideology established according to the dominant social mould (family or state), or constructed locally (the analyst–analysand relation). [. . .]

Consequently, Artaud, while referring to it as 'the toxic state', distinguishes his practice through a 'will to meaning': he searches for a language, speaks to others. The function of 'art' as a signifying practice appears in this light: the reintroduction in society and under the appearance of a pleasing difference, acceptable for the community, of a fundamental expulsion, of divided matter.

A 'language' without exteriority

What happens to language in this process of expulsion and its resistant stases? Artaud refuses the assimilation of his practice to any abstraction of meaning or of spirit, but also any assimilation of it to a purely linguistic function: 'Now I don't operate but by breaths, not by fluids . . . but on the reality which you get into after the explosion of the compacted maché box' (Artaud 1971: 30–1).

If the tissue of language is this 'compacted maché box', if it is indispensable to set up a resistance to expulsion (*le rejet*), expulsion explodes it and it is at this point that it is possible to see the text as a *practice*: 'The question for me was not to know what would ensue if you insinuated yourself into the structures of written language. But into the weft of my living soul' (*OC* I: 9).

The word is subordinated to a function: to translate the drives of the body, and in this sense it ceases to be a word and is paragrammatised, even to the extent of becoming simply noise: 'through what words could I enter into the thread of this scowling meat (I say SCOWLING, which means squinting, but in Greek, there is *tatavuri* and *tatavuri* means noise etc.)' (*OC* I: 9). Language will seek out this proximity with the drives, with the heterogeneous contradiction where death is profiled, and with it *jouissance*:

> This flux, this nausea, this language, here is where the fire starts. The fire of languages, the fire woven into the twists of language, in the brilliance of the earth which opens like a pregnant belly with entrails of honey and sugar . . . I look in my throat for names and the vibrative filament of things. The stench of nothingness, a must of absurdity, the dung of total death . . .
>
> *(OC* I: 141–4)

A language of expulsion, murderous for the subject and his readers:

> I left because I realised that the only language I could have used with a public audience would have been to take some bombs out of my pockets and throw them in its face with a characteristically aggressive gesture. Because I don't think conscience can be educated or that it's worth bothering to try to educate it. And violence is the only language I feel capable of speaking . . .
>
> These are not just words, ideas, or any other kind of phantasmatic bullshit, these truly are real bombs, physical bombs, but it is so naïve and childish of me, isn't it, to say these kind of things so innocently, so pretentiously.
>
> (Artaud 1996: 33–4)

At the most violent moment of this rupture, where the drive invades and imprints itself on the binding of language, humour acts as intermediary, as the passage from meaning to non-sense: 'the dung of total death . . . light and rarefied humour . . . ' (*OC* I: 144).

From the perspective of language, expulsion is principally a passage outside meaning, the shadow of non-sense through sense, which releases laughter. [. . .]

Language and rhetoric are illusions (gestures of thought) to be penetrated so that in spite of them the process which crystallises and exceeds them can pass:

> And art is to bring this rhetoric to the necessary point of civilisation, so that it becomes one with certain real ways of being, of feeling and of thought. In a word, the only writer to survive will be the one who knows how to manage this rhetoric as if it were already thought, and not thought's gesture.
>
> (*OC* I: 193)

Artaud is aiming for what metaphysics would call an exteriority of language, of the mark, that is, a deviated, signified operation; he is looking for a language susceptible to exteriority, in conflict and thus in dialectic with himself. This exteriority is fundamentally different from that specific to the Hegelian force (*Kraft*) which suppresses itself if it is not invested in the concept. But, as is apparent in the brief text 'Rimbaud and the Moderns', the 'exteriority' Artaud wants to introduce into language is the process of things itself, and in this sense it is interior to them, and this is precisely what the 'moderns' miss, preoccupied as they are with logical and syntactic relations, with 'folds' and 'slopes' and with a 'poetry of invented relations'. Artaud therefore reproaches Mallarmé, for example, perhaps underestimating the conflict which the Mallarméan text bears witness to, but doing so correctly as concerns the formalist and ornamentalist interpretations of Mallarméan enterprise – he therefore reproaches the classificatory, purely semantic exteriority of Mallarmé's writings:

> In his eagerness to give each word its full burden of meaning [Mallarmé] classified his words as if they were values existing outside the thought that conditions them, and performed those strange inversions in which each syllable seems to be objectified and to become preponderant.[2]

This material heterogeneity (and not exteriority) passes through language in order to shift it towards the process which produces and exceeds it; it is itself subject to laws; it is precise, 'logical', but of a logic other than that of repressive rationality. Artaud emphasises this:

> In the realm of the affective imponderable, the image provided by my nerves takes the form of the highest intellectuality, which I refuse to strip of its quality of intellectuality. And so it is that I watch the formation of a concept which carries within it the actual fulguration of things, a concept which arrives upon me with the sound of creation. No image satisfies me unless it is at the same time Knowledge, unless it carries with it its substance as well as its lucidity. My mind, exhausted by discursive reason, wants to be caught up in the wheels of a new, an absolute gravitation. For me it is like a supreme reorganisation in which only the laws of illogic participate, and in which there triumphs the discovery of a new Meaning . . . But it does not accept this chaos as such, it interprets it, and because it interprets it, it loses it. It is the logic of Illogic. And this is all one can say. My lucid unreason is not afraid of Chaos.
>
> (*SW*: 108)

This passage, which echoes quite closely Hegel's reflection on force (*Kraft*), the logification of force and the loss of the reality of this force in the logification (Hegel 1971: 179–213), not only suggests a theoretical postulation, that the movement of the signifying matter obeys laws which are yet to be discovered, obeys an objective regulation which functions without being thought, an asymbolic pulsation whose tremors are recorded on the body. It also suggests the working of the impossible stakes of the text: if material heterogeneity were enounced, denounced, it would no longer be heterogeneous; only the 'noises of creation', cries, the diction or otherwise the dislocation of syntax, evoke, according to the new laws, the 'formation of concept'. The aim, then, is to produce 'concept-texts' from the formation of concepts in the dialectic of matter, and in doing so allowing the 'impulsiveness of matter' to appear in these concepts, so as never to give the subject the impression of status and calm, that is, ultimately, to find concepts which correspond precisely to a real madness: 'The truth of life lies in the impulsiveness of matter. The mind of man has been poisoned by concepts. Do not ask him to be content, ask him only to be calm, to believe that he has found his place. But only the Madman is really calm' (*SW*: 109).

A certain logical mastery, through the return of the drive within language, is the way to overcome dementia. In this sense, the paragrammatic, syntactic or pulsional explosion of language is the condition of the maintenance of the heterogeneous as well as the condition of the overcoming of madness: 'But he is the Great Consciousness. But he is the pedestal of a breath which turns your bad demented brain, for at least it has won this – to have overcome dementia' (*OC* I: 280).

In clinical schizophrenia, in order to reintroduce the signifying instance in the movement of the drive, pluralising or immobilising the body, one tends to attempt to include the subject in a relation to the other, to create a relation of transference which operates along the path of communication. This is never completely possible with so-called psychotic patients: the transference in this case is a 'grafted transference' (to use Gisele Pankow's term) (Pankow 1969: 26). This graft is intended to provoke the subject's *desire*, through including him or her in an affective participation in relation to the body of the analyst. In transferring the violence of exclusion into a demand in which desire signifies itself, this 'graft' displaces the motility of expulsion from the body proper, language and the ideological system it clothes, into the sphere of interpersonal relations in which expulsion is not only deferred but retained, to end up enmeshed in the mechanics of social functioning (the work of modelling, manipulation, encounter with the other, etc.). Such a restriction of expulsion through 'grafted transference' significantly uses a non-verbal, kinetic or graphic functioning; the 'sick' are made to make models, drawings, and so on. These exercises seize the body and its *signifiance* at a pre-verbal level, thus at a level prefatory to the sign and representation, sites where exclusion fixes itself, and which are so far only marks, an absent object not yet having transformed them into *representamen*.

Expulsion has not yet dissociated subject and object, but runs across the body and the immediate environment in a logically a-representative rhythm. It binds, links, arranges and organises, but does not attain a representation of the object opposite the coagulated presence of the subject. This pre-verbal logic structures the space in which the subject–object sensation will be set up. But before this occurs, expulsion runs through the totalising receptacle, the *chora* (Artaud's 'gyrations of fire'), fragmenting it, cutting it up, rearranging it, and traversing the subject who is present only in an 'absent point', a 'dead kernel', with 'total lucidity'. Gestural motility, fixed in marks or in modelled spaces, can then function as the relay which translates expulsion into the verbal signifying system or into the system of its pictural representation. However, the constraints of these signifying systems through the injection of expulsion into them are modified and made more supple. The rules of pertinence, of logical coherence, and so on, which are necessary in normative or scientific signifying systems, are thrown into disarray. It is as if expulsion excepts a compromise with representative stases and with the logic of information and its destructive destinatees, but only to deploy itself there with violence, displacing these stases and conserving only the marks and articulations of the *chora* determined by the logic of expulsion and objectively determined by the experience of the subject within the natural and social configuration. The mobile receptacle of all the objective determinations of expulsion, of its own workings, and its specific character relative to objective constraints can be considered as the trans-verbal mode of the process. This is what we call *signifiance*. It can also be called the topology of practical experience, since the trans-verbal mode is realised through a practice of transformation of matter, within the dynamic of expulsion, without there being a solid differentiation between subject and object.

'Grafted transference' tends to transplant this topology into the domain of representation, first of all to ensure its subjective and semiotic binding, and then to establish social and inter-subjective submission. However, the psychiatrist often doubts the success of this ruse: 'It is difficult to know if the structure of the illness is affected by this therapeutic intervention' (Pankow 1969: 29).

As textual practice is a struggle with language, and thus with communication, it does not choose the relay of 'grafted transference'. That such a graft might occur in the biography of the subject and ensure him or her the ephemeral moment of unity indispensable to the process is a question outside the realm of artistic practice. [. . .]

The fragmented and reorganised *chora* is best realised in dance, gestural theatre or painting, rather than in words. Artaud's theatrical practice, and perhaps especially the Rodez paintings, or those which accompany the last texts, bear witness to this non-verbal but logical (in the sense of 'binding') organisation of expulsion.

It is thus on the stage of a revolutionised theatre that the mobile *chora* of language is most completely liberated: the word becomes a drive which is thrown out in enunciation, and the text has no other justification than to give rise to this music of pulsions:

> For the purposes of this definition that we are trying to give of the theatre, only one thing seems to us unassailable, only one thing seems real: the text. But the text as a distinct reality, existing in itself, sufficient unto itself, not in terms of its spirit, for which we have very little respect, but simply in terms of the displacement of air created by its enunciation. This is all we care about.
>
> (*SW*: 159)

The above is a formulation *avant la lettre* of the attempts in which we are presently engaged to define the text not according to its signified, nor its signifier, Artaud would say its *idea* (spirit), but according to the organisation of expulsion within it, the oralisation of expulsion, or, for Artaud, 'the displacement of air created by its enunciation'.

Representations are the *substance* (in the Hjelmslevian sense) of this *chora*: however, if the *chora* moves and functions it is because expulsion returns to dissolve substance, to renew representation and thus to prevent it from closing up, immobilising itself in fantasy. *In the mobile* chora *of the text there are no fantasies*: 'My lucidity is total, keener than ever, what I lack is an object to which to apply it, an inner substance' (*SW*: 169). This renewal is produced in the topological mode through the logic of marks and of kinesis, or, in relation to language, through isolated, non-lexicalised, non-semanticised phonemes, or phonemes susceptible of a fluid semanticisation through linguistic multiplicity. It is this expulsion and its mobile *chora* that Artaud's practice presents in all its purity; assigning representation and fantasy their subordinate place as guardians of a unity which is exceeded, as a cell of pleasure to be expelled in a movement towards *jouissance.*

The only use of language possible will thus be as a ridge between binding reason and the heterogeneity which produces it, which wedges itself into thought and splits it: the proximity of death renders this language sibylline, that is, receptive to pulsional shocks and splits.

Our attitude of absurdity and death is the attitude of greatest receptivity. Through the fissures of a reality that is henceforth non-viable, there speaks a deliberately sibylline world. 'Yes, this now is the only use to which language can be put, a way of madness, of the elimination of thought, of rupture, a maze of madness and not a Dictionary into which the college scores of the banks of the Seine channel their spiritual strictures' (*SW*: 103).

The same search for an extra-linguistic logic of the heterogeneous inspires the 'Letter to the Chancellors of European Universities': 'Enough playing on words, syntactic stratagems and formula juggling. We must now discover the Heart's great Law, the Law which is not a Law (a prison), but a guide for the Mind lost in its own labyrinth' (*CW* I: 179).

There is therefore what Artaud calls a 'will for meaning' (*OC* I: 271) binding the ruptures of an intensely separated body and constituting, indirectly, a formula for it, which is itself separated, broken, 'badly put' and 'confused'. Language is a detour, a displacement of the drive and its topology: language is a substitute for expulsion, but one in which 'the mind lets its limbs show', a substitute (Logos) which perpetuates itself through chaining and binding expulsion.

The process, insofar as it is maintained, reaches a point where the signifier disappears under the attack of the death drive, which is not recuperable by any sign. But through a detour, the process blocks this loss, and, faced with lack, formulates and speaks. Expulsion in this instance is characterised by the tension of language: 'a perpetual erection of language, tension after lack, the knowledge of the detour, the acceptance of the badly put' (*OC* I: 270). Language, always and already a detour of expulsion, under the pressure of a renewed expulsion, becomes divided, fragmented, discredited; it is no longer language as such, and can only be understood by 'aphasiacs, and in general all the rejects of words and speech, the pariahs of Thought' (*OC* I: 271). But it is only in this way that it can take on the possibility of presenting matter in discourse: 'All matter begins with a spiritual disturbance' (*OC* I: 287). Spiritual can be read as 'of meaning' in this instance. For in the disturbance of meaning it is expulsion which returns, through the unconscious where it is supposed to remain repressed: 'The invisible treasures of the unconscious become palpable, directly leading language in a single thrust' (*AA*: 118).

The body, having become mobile *chora*, cosmic and social mutation and essential site of natural and social operations, invalidates the contemplative mentalism which appears when writing shuts itself up in a purely linguistic state, or if it is thought solely in relation to linguistics. Linguistic structures are the blockages of the process. They intercept and immobilise it, subordinating it to semantic and institutional unities which are in deep solidarity with each other. The whole series of unities – linguistic, perceptive, conceptual and institutional (the ideological, political and economic apparatuses) – oppose this process, enclose it and aim to sublimate it, to 'put it under a spell, to destroy it through magic'. 'Magic' and 'spell-casting' are the effects of the unitary enclosures of the process, and are executed through social apparatuses but also, and to the same effect, through the structure of meaning, itself conceived as a simple, disincarnate sign, a Word beyond experience.

> It is by magic that the abominable institutions which enclose us: country, family, society, mind, concept, perception, sensation, affect, heart, soul, science, law, justice, right, religion, notions, verb, language, don't correspond to anything real.
>
> (Artaud 1969: 50)

15 Jacques Derrida

From 'To unsense the subjectile'*

The reason for the inclusion of this piece[1] by Derrida in addition to one of the earlier and more famous essays on Artaud from *Writing and Difference* (1967c) may need some brief discussion. It is because the present essay does two important things. First, Derrida reads Artaud's drawings as 'pictographs', writings which are also drawings and vice versa, and as such these pictographs problematise the laws of Western language, in particular those of the structuralist sign. While doing this, he also shows how all forms of art were ineluctably hybrid for Artaud and therefore that any appropriation of Artaud by particular disciplines, including theatre studies, is based, in part, on a misunderstanding of Artaud's ideas about forms. Second, this piece provides a basis for understanding Artaud's insistence on the value of force rather than form, which is a fundamental principle for Artaud.

Here the focus is the cluster of images and texts, portraits and sketches which Artaud produced at the end of his time at the asylum of Rodez and after his return to Paris in 1946. Derrida reads them as a direct continuation of Artaud's concerns with the limits of signifying practices. As does Kristeva, Derrida identifies these as the attempt to reconnect with and deploy the states prior to the subject's symbolic orientation in the world, before the attribution of form, the art anterior to art. Derrida theorises this as the dementing of the subjectile to describe how Artaud works directly on the material he is using in order to release the repressed (conceptual?) energy hidden within it. He stabs holes in his pages not just to foreground the material, but to reveal what it has hidden about its own active role in artistic production. Derrida's account is by no means exhaustive, but his arguments concerning Artaud's deliberate technical clumsiness open on to several crucial areas in Artaud: dispossession and its objects (the theft of true work, language, body, etc.), that the visible is no more 'ineluctable' than any other faculty, and how Artaud strives to render a more intensive response from the viewer or reader, to reconstruct the missed encounter. The other of the work is always there somewhere in Artaud's work, folded into it as its destination and its hidden resource.

I would call this a scene, 'the scene of the subjectile', if there were not already a force at work prepared to diminish the scenic elements: the visibility, the element of representation, the presence of a subject, even an object. Subjectile, the word or the thing, can take the place of the subject or of the object – being neither one nor the other.

Three times at least, to my knowledge, Antonin Artaud names what is called the subjectile. He says exactly that: 'what is called . . . '. Indirect naming, invisible quotation marks, an allusion to the discourse of the other. He uses the word of the others but perhaps he will have it say something else, perhaps he will tell it to do something else.

All three times, he is speaking of his own drawings, in 1932, 1946, and 1947.

Nevertheless, is it likely that he really ever *spoke* about his drawings? And above all, that we can or are able to? We won't tell the story of the subjectile, rather some record of its *coming-to-be.*

The first time (later we will pay attention to what only happened *once* for Artaud), on 23 September 1932, he concludes a letter to André Rolland de Renéville like this: 'Herewith a bad drawing in which what is called the subjectile betrayed me.' Wait a minute: a subjectile can betray?

And wait a minute: when Artaud evaluates his painting or his drawings, when he badmouths them ('a bad drawing'), a whole interpretation of what is bad is behind this. Already, in 1932, it is not simple to figure out what he is indicting here: it is not only a question of technique, of art, or of skill. The indictment is already levelled at god, is denouncing some treason. What must a subjectile do to commit treason?

In 1932, the word could seem to have been recently created. The current dictionaries then had not yet admitted it to the spoken tongue. So the legitimacy of a 'subjectile' remains in doubt. Paule Thévenin (who has said everything that has to be known about Artaud's drawings and whose work I am presuming everyone knows)[2] judges it necessary to be more precise in a note: 'Perhaps it's in the part torn from this letter that the drawing was to be found. Antonin Artaud, having considered it too revealing, must have removed it, tearing off the bottom of the page. He certainly wrote "subjectile"' (*OC* V: 274).

This note tells us at least two things. First, a drawing can *be a part of* a letter, which is completely different from just accompanying it. It joins with it physically because it is only separate by dint of being 'the part ripped off'. And then to betray can be understood in a very particular sense: to fail in one's promise, belittle the project, remove oneself from its control, but in so doing to *reveal* the project as it is thus betrayed. Translating it and dragging it out to broad daylight. Betraying the subjectile would have made the drawing 'too revelatory', and of a truth sufficiently unbearable for Artaud to destroy its support. This latter was stronger than him, and because he had not mastered the rebel, Artaud is said to have snatched it away.

'He really wrote "subjectile".' Paule Thévenin warns those who, because they do not know this rare word, might be tempted to confuse it with another.

With what other word could we have confused the drawing itself, that is, the graphic form of the 'subjectile'? With 'subjective', perhaps, the nearest possible treason. But so many other words, a great family of bits and snatches of words, and Artaud's words are haunting this word, drawing it toward the dynamic potential of all its meanings. Beginning by subjective, subtle, sublime, also pulling the *il* into the *li*, and ending with projectile. This is Artaud's *thought*. The body of his thought working itself out in the graphic treatment of the subjectile is a dramaturgy through and through, often a surgery of the *projectile*. Between the beginning and the end of the word (*sub/tile*), all these persecuting evils emerging from the depths to haunt the supports, the substrata, and the substances: Artaud never stopped naming, denouncing, exorcising, conjuring, often through the operation of drawing, the fiends and the succubi, that is the women or sorcerers who change their sex to get in *bed* with man, or then the vampires who come to suck your very substance, to subjugate you to steal what is most truly yours.

Through the two extremities of his body, such a word, itself subjectile, can, like the drawing of a chimera, mingle with everything that it is not. Although it seems so close to them, it lures them toward the illusion of an entire resemblance: the *sub*jective and the pro*jectile*.

What is a subjectile? Let's go slowly, not rushing things, learning the patience of what is developing, and make it precise: what is 'called the subjectile'? For Antonin Artaud doesn't speak of the subjectile, only of what 'is called' by this name. To take account of the calling, and what is called. A subjectile first of all is something to be called. That the subjectile is *something* is not yet a given. Perhaps it comes across as being *someone* instead, and preferably something *else*: it can betray. But the other can be called something without being, without being a being, and above all not a subject, not the subjectivity of a subject. Perhaps we don't know yet what 'is called' like this 'the subjectile', the subjectility of the subjectile, both because it does not constitute an object of any knowing and because it can betray, not come when it is called, or call before even being called, before even receiving its name. At the very moment when it is born, when it is not yet, and the drawing of Artaud situates this *coup de force*, a subjectile calls and sometimes betrays. That's what I can say about it to begin with.

At least in this language. In French, we think we have just found out recently what the word 'subjectile' means currently. We believe it to be contemporaneous with Artaud. Contemporary dictionaries date it from the middle of the twentieth century. But they are wrong, they are really reactivating an old word, French or Italian.[3] The notion belongs to the code of painting and designates what is in some way lying below (*subjectum*) as a substance, a subject, or a succubus. Between the beneath and the above, it is at once a support and a surface, sometimes also the matter of a painting or a sculpture, everything distinct from form, as well as from meaning and representation, not representable. Its presumed depth or thickness can only be seen as a surface, that of the wall or of wood, but already also that of paper, of textiles, and of the panel. A sort of skin with pores. We can distinguish two classes of subjectile, by a criterion that will decide everything in Artaud's way of operating: in this apparently manual operation that is a drawing, how does the subjectile permit itself to be traversed? For we oppose just those subjectiles that let themselves be *traversed* (we call them permeable or *porous*, like plasters, mortar, wood, cardboard, textiles, paper) to the other impermeable ones (metals or their alloys) that permit no passage.

About the subjectile we would have to – yes – write what is untranslatable. To write according to the new phrasing, but discretely, for resistance to translation when it is deliberate, noisy, spectacular, we already know it has been repatriated. In truth its secret should only be shared with the translator.

A subjectile appears untranslatable, that is axiomatic, it sets up the struggle with Artaud. This can mean at least two things. First, the word 'subjectile' is not to be translated. With all its semantic or formal kinship, from the subjective to the tactile, of support, succubus or fiends with a projectile, etc., it will never cross the border of the French language. Besides, a subjectile, that is to say the support, the surface or the material, the unique body of the work in its first event, *at its moment of birth*, which cannot be repeated, which is as distinct from the form as from the meaning and the representation, here again defies translation. It will never be transported into another language. Unless it is taken over bodily and intact, like a foreign substance. So we shall be able to conclude: (1) What exceeds translation really belongs to language. (2) What so drastically exceeds linguistic transfer remains on the contrary foreign to language as an element of the discourse. (3) The word 'subjectile' is itself a subjectile.

How to measure the consequences of this paradox? I will dare to claim that we have to embroil ourselves in the paradox in order to get anywhere near the painted or drawn work of Artaud. This spatial work would be first of all a corporeal struggle with the question of language – and at the limit, of music.

No way of passing over this fact: what I am writing here in French, in a language that was up to a certain point and most often that of Artaud, is first appearing in a language said to be foreign. You are reading in German here[4] what was first intended to offer a subtle resistance to translation. But since you are reading me in German, it means that this text has nevertheless been translated, whereas at no moment would one have thought of translating the drawings or the paintings, nor indeed the words or phrases contained in them – in Artaud's own hand. Incorporated, that is to say, inscribed in the graphic corpus *in the very substance* of the subjectile.

To challenge the foreigner, not in order to write in good old French, but on the contrary to perform an *experiment,* to *translate* the crossing of my language, to the point of forcing the French, my natural language, the only mother tongue able to serve as an ultimate support to what I am calling upon first. The French language is the one in which I was *born*, if you can put it like that, and in which *I find myself* even as I debate with it or against it. I am writing *from within the substance* of the French language. (How will they translate that?)

Now at the moment of speaking the language said to be maternal, I remember the last stop of the subjectile, the ultimate occurrence of the word *in the hand* of

Artaud. Father and mother are not far off: 'The figures on the inert page said nothing under my hand. They offered themselves to me like millstones which would not inspire the drawing and which I could probe, cut, scrape, file, sew, unsew, shred, slash, and stitch without the subjectile ever complaining through father or through mother' (1947).

How can an untranslatable subjectile betray, we were wondering just a moment ago? What must it have become now, in the return of the word fifteen years later, in order never to complain 'through father or through mother', at the moment when I am attacking its unresisting body with so many *coups de force* and in so many ways, giving myself up to him in order to give him so many operations, when the surgeon that I am demands to probe, cut, scrape, file, sew, unsew, shred, slash, and stitch?

What had happened in the interval (1932–1947)? Something? An event, once, on such and such a date? 'And since a certain day in October 1939 I have never again written without drawing. Now what I am drawing . . . These are no longer themes of Art transposed from . . . ' (Artaud 1947: 8).

No longer to have to transpose, to translate. Must we write against our mother tongue to do that? Precisely in order to *render* what is untranslatable?

But no one can say calmly that French was Artaud's only mother tongue, nor that language is just a support, as you might say of a paper or a textile, of a wall or a panel. Unless you treat it in its turn as a subjectile, this sort of subject without a subject, with this manner or this manoeuvre betraying the whole story in an instant, in fact the story of a betrayal. Being and god would be implicated in this trial of the subjectile: perversion and malfeasance, subterfuge or swindle.

So it would be necessary, while drawing by hand, to write against this language, and have it out with the so-called mother tongue as with any other, making oneself scarcely translatable, starting from it but also within it (I am speaking of *Auseinandersetzung*, of *Übersetzung*, and, why not, of *Untersetzung*), in it where I am supposed to have been *born*: but where I was still, Artaud would say, in the twist it imposes on the syntax of this word innate. This supposed natural tongue, this tongue you are born with, it will be necessary to force it, to render it completely mad, and in it again the subjectile, this word that is scarcely even French, in order to describe the support of the pictogram that is still resonating with the trace left in it by a projectile. This came to perforate its sensitive but sometimes resistant surface, the surface of a subjectivity appeased and reassured: the precarious outcome of the work.

The Germans don't have any word *subjectile,* although they were the first to project this great corpus of Antonin Artaud's pictograms, and to publish it separately, even though it is inseparable. As certain dictionaries tell us, we didn't have this word in French either a short while ago, but at least it suits our Latinity. The Germans – think of Fichte or Heidegger – have always tried to take back their language from Rome. Artaud too, and this isn't the only thing they have in common, however horrifying this seems to some. In other conditions, with time enough and taking the necessary precautions, I would be tempted to insist on the possible encounters which did not take place between Heidegger and Artaud. Among many other themes the one of the *innate* and the *Ungeborene* in Heidegger's reading of Trakl, and the question of being, quite simply, and of *throwing* (*jeter*) and of *giving* (*donner*).

Artaud, then, against a certain Latinity. What he says on this subject about the *mise-en-scène* is also valid, as is always true, for the pictogram and for what doesn't necessarily happen or does so only through words:

> In opposition to this point of view, which strikes me as altogether Western or rather Latin, that is, obstinate, I maintain that insofar as this language is born on the stage, draws its power and its spontaneous creation from the stage, and struggles directly with the stage without resorting to words . . . it is *mise-en-scène* that is theatre, much more than the written and spoken play. No doubt I shall be asked to state what is Latin about this point of view opposed to my own. What is Latin is the need to use words in order to express ideas that are clear. Because for me clear ideas, in the theatre as in everything else, are ideas that are dead and finished.
>
> (*OC* IV: 39)[5]

The Germans have no subjectile, but how would we know that without Artaud, who doesn't only use it but attacks it, quarrels with it openly, seduces it, undertakes to pierce it through, puts it through the wringer, and, first of all, names it? Not so much in order to dominate it but to deliver from a domination, to deliver someone or something else that isn't yet born. He attacks it like a Latin word. Without having any fear of the word: like a Latin thing, like this historical sedimentation of a thing and a word consolidated near subject and substance, from Descartes' 'clear ideas'.[6]

I don't know if I am writing in an intelligible French. 'Forcener le subjectile', is that still French?

Forcené, this word that I wanted to decompose surreptitiously, subjectilely, in *for, fort, force, fors,* and *né,* letting all the words in *or, hors, sort* incubate in it, I thought it was limited to its *adjectival* usage as a past participle. The infinitive seemed to me excluded, foreclosed in fact, and I thought it was limiting it for a cause requiring some forcing of language. But that isn't it at all, for *forcener* exists, even if its use is rare and outmoded. But only in an intransitive form. You can't *forcener un subjectile* in French without forcing the grammar of the word at the same time. *La forcènerie* or *forcènement,* the act or the state of the *forcené,* consists simply, and intransitively, in *forcener* or in *se forcener,* that is to say, losing your reason, more exactly, your *sense,* in finding yourself *hors sens,* without sense (*fors* and *sen*). The etymology the Littré dictionary gives seems reliable in this case: 'Provençal *forcenat;* Italian *forcennato;* from the Latin *foris, hors* [outside], and the German *Sinn, sens* [sense]: outside of your senses. The spelling *forcené* with a *c* is contrary to the etymology and incorrect; it isn't even borne out by traditional use, and only comes from an unfortunate confusion with the word *force,* and it would be far better to write *forsené.'* The word would then correspond with the German *Wahnsinnige* about which Heidegger reminds us that it doesn't initially indicate the state of a madman (*Geisteskrank*), of someone mentally sick, but what is without (*ohne*) any *sense,* without what is sense for others: 'Wahn belongs to Old High German and means *ohne*: without. The demented person [der Wahnsinnige, which we could translate in French as *forsené*] dreams [*sinnt*] and he dreams as no one else could . . . He is gifted with another sense [with another meaning *anderen Sinnes*]. *Sinnan* originally means: to travel, to stretch toward . . . , to take a direction. The Indo-European root *sent* and *set* mean path' (Heidegger 1959: 53).[7]

I am sure that what I am writing will not be translatable into German. Nor into Artaud's language. Should I be writing like Artaud? I am incapable of it, and, besides, anyone who would try to write like him, under the pretext of writing toward him, would be even surer of missing him, would lose the slightest chance ever of meeting him in the ridiculous attempt of this mimetic distortion. But we should not give in either to the kind of judgement *about* Artaud that will not be, any more than his name, the subject or the object, still less the subjectile of some learned diagnosis. All the more because it is a matter of his drawing and his paintings, not only his speech. Moreover, and we can verify this, he himself never writes *about* his drawings and paintings, rather *in* them. The relation is different, one of imprecation and argument, and first of all one that relates to a subjectile, which is available for a support.

We cannot and should not write *like* Artaud *about* Artaud who himself never wrote *about* his drawings and paintings. So who could ever claim to write *like* Artaud *about* his drawings or paintings? . . . We have to invent a way of speaking, and sign it differently. [. . .]

But if a subjectile is never identified with the subject or the object even when it occupies their place and being, is it the same as what Artaud so often likes to call a *motif*? No, it would prevent the motif, but the very counterforce of this prevention sets up an extreme tension. What exactly is a motif, then? 'For what is the motif?', Artaud asks in 'Van Gogh, ou le suicidé de la société' (Van Gogh the Man Suicided by Society), implying by the question that a motif is nothing but so singularly nothing that it never lets itself be constituted in the stasis of a being. This word *motif* (how will they translate that?) has the certain advantage of substituting the dynamics and the energy of a motion (movement, mobility, emotion) for the stability of a *-ject* [jet] which would set itself up in the inertia of a subject or object. When he gives up describing one of Van Gogh's canvases, Artaud inscribes the *motif* in the centre of the 'forces' and the *writing* forces ('apostrophes', 'streaks', 'commas', 'bars', etc.) with these acts of 'blocking', 'repression', 'the canvas', and so on as protagonists. Here we have to quote, starting with 'How easy it seems to write like this', the whole page that prepares the question: 'For what is the motif?'

So I shall not describe a painting of Van Gogh after Van Gogh, but I shall say that Van Gogh is a painter because he recollected nature, because he re-perspired it and made it sweat, because he squeezed onto his canvases in clusters, in monumental sheaves of color, the grinding of elements that occurs once in a hundred years, the awful elementary pressure of apostrophes, scratches, commas, and dashes which, after him, one can no longer believe that natural appearances are not made of.

And what an onslaught of repressed jostlings, ocular collisions taken from life, blinkings taken from nature, have the luminous currents of the forms which work on reality had to reverse before being finally driven together and, as it were, hoisted onto the canvas, and accepted?

There are no ghosts in the paintings of Van Gogh, no visions, no hallucinations . . . But the suffering of the pre-natal is there.

(*OC* XIII: 42–3)[8]

The fact that later on Van Gogh is credited with having had 'the audacity to attack a subject' doesn't mean that there was any subject for him, no matter how simple, even if it happened to be 'of such disarming simplicity'. In the flow of this way of speaking, it can be understood that the subject precisely attacked was no longer going to be one, or shouldn't be one any longer. And this is the following paragraph: 'No, there are no ghosts in Van Gogh's painting, no drama, no subject, and I would even say no object for what is the motif? If not something like the iron shadow of the motet of an ancient indescribable music, the leitmotiv of a theme that has despaired of its own subject. It is nature, naked and pure, seen . . .' (*OC* XIII: 43–4).[9]

We don't know what this motif is – neither this nor that – it doubtless no longer even belongs to being, nor to being as a subject. If it is 'of nature' we shall have to think of nature completely differently, and the history of nature, the genealogy of its concept, in other words of its birth and conception: up to the innate [*inné*], this neologism of Artaud where nature collides with its contrary, what is not born in what seems to be innate, the 'suffering of the pre-natal' which appears as a monstrosity.

Under the surface of the word, and under the sense, *hor sens*, the passage from *motif* to *motet* doesn't obey only the formal attraction of the words, the *mots*, *motifs*, and *motets*, although when you let the attraction play under the meaning, you draw or sing rather than speaking, you write the unwritable. No, this passage also convokes the multiplicity of the voices in a motet in painting. It promises something essential in what Artaud still understands by painting: an affair of sonority, of tone, of intonation, of thunder and detonation, of rhythm, of vibration, the extreme tension of a polyphony.

This should be read like a book about music, according to Artaud. The 'ancient indescribable music' tears apart the veil of a birth, revealing 'naked nature', the origin whose access has been forbidden by this 'nature', concealing even the source of this interdiction. The leitmotiv, this really musical motif of painting, its guiding force and its major aesthetic passion, must not be confused with a theme, the meaning of an object or a subject, such as it could be *posed* there. A theme is always posed or supposed. The leitmotiv for its part doesn't always answer in itself like a stable support: no more a subjectile, this last is carried away by the motif. The property of a theme is what an expropriation has deprived us of, and it is as if we had been deprived of our own memory, distanced from our own birth. Across the 'pre-natal suffering', we cannot meet back up with innate nature (*in-né*) except by forcing the subjectile, rendering it *unsensed from birth*. You have to make it frenetically desire this birth, and to unsense it from the outset in making it come out of itself to announce this next proximity: 'It is nature, naked and pure, seen as she reveals herself when one knows how to approach her closely enough'. Music, nature, seeing: the same: seen [*vue*]. Such a proximity confines you to madness, but the one that snatches you from the other madness, the madness of stagnation, of stabilisation in the inert when sense becomes a subjectivised theme, introjected or objectivised, and the subjectile a tomb. But you can force the tomb. You can unsense the subjectile until – unsensed from birth – it gives way to the innate which was assassinated there one day. A violent obstetrics gives passage to the words through which, however, it passes. With all the music, painting, drawing it is operating with a forceps.

Of course, Artaud was speaking of Van Gogh here. But without giving in to a cliché such as 'speaking of Van Gogh he is speaking of himself', and so on, we still have to recognise that Antonin Artaud couldn't have entered into that *relationship,* into the realm of the relation with Van Gogh, except in giving *himself* over to the experiment that he is describing just at the moment when he is refusing to describe the stability of a painting.

And this experiment is the traversal of this *jetée*, its trajectory. I am calling spurt or *jetée* the movement that, without ever being *itself* at the origin, is *modalised* and disperses itself in the trajectories of the *objective*, the *subjective*, the *projectile*, *introjection*, *objection*, *dejection*, and *abjection*, and so on. The subjectile remains *between* these different *jetées*, whether it constitutes its underlying element, the place and the context of birth, or interposes itself, like a canvas, a veil, a paper 'support', the hymen between the inside and the outside, the upper and the lower, the over here or the over there, or whether it becomes in its turn the *jetée*, not this time like the motion of something thrown but like the hard fall of a mass of inert stone in the port, the limit of an *'arrested* storm', a dam. Giving himself over entirely to this, hurling himself into the experience of this throwing [*jetée*], Artaud could enter the realm of relationship with Van Gogh. And all the questions we will listen to from now on will continue to resound: what is a port, a *portée*, a *rapport* if the subjectile is announced as the support of the drawing and painting? What does the carrying, the carrying over [*porter*] mean in this case? And throwing, hurling, sending? Is spurting [*la jetée*] a mode of sending or of giving? Might it be rather the inverse. Must we choose? What is it? Is it the same thing? *Is it*? Is it still possible to submit that to the question *what is it*? The way Artaud treats the question of being [*être*] and of beingness [*êtreté*] (his word) will occasionally be open to doubt. Being begins, starting with the *jetée*, not the inverse. We don't even have to speak of pulsion or compulsive interest in the direction of the spurt. The thought of the throwing is the thought of pulsion itself, of the jet of pulsional *force,* of compulsion and expulsion.

Force before form. And I shall try to show that it is Antonin Artaud's *thought* itself. Before any thematics of the spurt, it is *at work* in the corpus of his writings, his painting, his drawings. And from the beginning, indissociable from cruel thought, in other words, a thought of *blood.* The first *cruelty* is a spurt of blood. In 1922, 'Les Oeuvres et les hommes' (Works and Men): 'We have to wash literature off ourselves. We want to be humans before anything else. There are no forms or any form. There is only the gushing forth of life. Life like a spurt of blood, as Claudel puts it so well, speaking of Rimbaud. The mode now is anti-Claudel, and Claudel among us is perhaps the only one who in his good moments doesn't make literature' (*OC* II: 204).

The subjectile: itself between two places. It has two situations. As the support of a representation, it's the subject which has become a *gisant,* spread out, stretched out, inert, neutral (*ci-gît*). But if it doesn't fall out like this, if it is not abandoned to this downfall or this dejection, it can still be of interest for itself and not for its representation, for *what* it represents or for the representation it bears. It is then treated otherwise: as that which participates in the forceful throwing or casting but also as what has to be traversed, pierced, penetrated in order to have done with the screen, that is, the inert support of representation. The subjectile, for example the paper or the canvas, then becomes a membrane; and the trajectory of what is thrown upon it should dynamise this skin by perforating it, traversing it, passing through to the other side: 'after having exploded the wall of the problem', as he says in *Suppôts et suppliciations* (Fiends and Torturings) (*OC* XIV: 135). [. . .]

Neither object nor subject, neither screen nor projectile, the subjectile can *become* all that, stabilising itself in a certain form or moving about in another. But the drama of its own becoming always oscillates *between* the intransitivity of *jacere* and the transitivity of *jacere*, in what I will call the *conjecture* of both. In the first case, *jaceo*, I am stretched out, lying down, *gisant*, in my bed, brought down, brought low, without life, I am where I have been thrown. This is the situation of the subject or the subjectile: they are thrown beneath. In the second case, *jacio*, I throw something, a projectile, thus, stones, a firebrand, seed (ejaculated). Or dice – or I cast a line. At the same time, and because I have thrown *something*, I can have lifted it or founded it. *Jacio* can also have this sense: I lay down foundations, I institute by throwing out something. The subjectile does not throw anything, but it has been laid down, even founded. A foundation in its turn, it can thus found, sustain a construction, serve as a support.

Between the two verbs, the intransitivity of *being-thrown* and the transitivity of *throwing*, the difference seems from then on to be as decisive as temporary, that is to say, transitory. The being-thrown or the being-founded founds in its turn.

And I cannot throw [*jeter*] or project [*projeter*], if I have not been thrown myself, at birth.

Everything will play itself out from now on in the critical but precarious difference, unstable and reversible, between these two. Such at least would be our working hypothesis. But what we will surely verify is that, hypothetically, the subjectile always has the function of a hypothesis, it exasperates and keeps you in suspense, it makes you get out of breath by always being *posed beneath.* The hypothesis has the form here of a conjecture, with *two* contradictory motifs in one. Thrown throwing, the subjectile is nothing, however, nothing but a solidified interval *between* above and below, visible and invisible, before and behind, this side and that.

Between laying down and throwing, the subjectile is a figure of the other toward which we should give up projecting anything at all. . . . The other or a figure of the other? . . . What does Artaud's drawing or painting *have to do* with such a figuration of the other?

Will this figuration accept limits? Painting and drawing only, in opposition to the discursive text, even in the theatre? Yes and no, yes in fact and up to a certain point, whose arbitrary nature covers over precisely a whole history of a dissociation that Artaud wants to *traverse* like a limit or a wall. But not by rights and rigorously, and this is why I shall propose to give another sense to the word *pictogram* in order to designate this work in which painting – the colour, even if it is black – drawing, and writing do not tolerate the wall of any division, neither that of different arts nor that of genres, nor that of supports or substances. The choice of this word pictogram may seem odd. It does not lead back to any supposed primitivity of some immediately representative writing. Certainly, through the magical force sometimes ascribed to a proto-writing upon which we project all the myths of origin, through the efficacity of spells cast or exorcised, the incantatory or conjuring virtues, alchemy, magnetism, such a pictography would have some affinity with Artaud's drawings, paintings, *and* writings. But I shall take it to mean especially the trajectory of what *is literally* understood to cross the border between painting and drawing, drawing, and verbal writing, and, still more generally, the arts of space and the others, between space and time. And through the subjectile, the motion of the motif assures the synergy of the visible and the invisible, in other words theatrical painting, literature, poetry, and music. Without any totalisation and taking due account of the subjectilian wall, of this dissociation in the body of which the singularity of the event made into work will always be marked.

We can only speak of this whole pictographic work by insertion and precipitation, by the acceleration of a rhythmical projection and the inscription of a projectile, beyond what we calmly call words and images. Artaud: 'These are written drawings, with sentences inserted in the forms so as to precipitate them. I think that here I may have managed something special, as in my books or in the theatre' (*OC* XI: 20). This was at Rodez in 1945, and we will have to take account of a trajectory, in fact that of the subjectile. But as if we were at the end of this trajectory, and in the past ('I think . . . I may have managed'), a sort of destination seems to prevail after the fact. There is 'here', on this side [*de ce côté*], that is, drawing which will be distinguished on *one* hand from literature, from the theatre (that is, from sentences). *But on the other* hand these drawings are written drawings that cannot just be put on one side any longer and which – here is 'something special' – contain phrases and, even better, sentences that are not only taken in, *stuck*, *inserted*, but where the insertion itself precipitates the forms. From then on, the analogy sweeps away the limits. What I have managed is certainly special, unique, irreplaceable, inimitable, but singular like what I 'managed' 'in my books or in the theatre'. Just as in the interior of the 'written drawing' the limit has been crossed, the breaking down of the barrier in the other 'arts' abolishes the border between *all* these 'arts'. Everything is singular each time and each time analogical: a figuration of the other.

If in the pictogram the relationship between the verbal writing, the phonogram, the silent line, and colour is analogous to what it will have been in literature or in the theatre *according* to Artaud, no body, no corpus is entirely separable. The phrase inserted remains at once quivering. It works the charter, the frame of a stubborn spatiality that locks it in [*cadre/carcan*]. The phrase is not *softened*, it no more lets itself be domesticated than it masters the map. It does not lay down the law, it does not enunciate the charter of a constitution. But its protest accelerates a rhythm, imprints intonations, pulls the forms along in choreographic motion. Without this mobility, the figures once more, like the 'clear ideas' of the Latin world, 'dead and finished'. Even if we recognise some of the workings of words, the inserted phrases rise up like enticing themes, trajectories of sound and writing, and not only like propositions. Once they are put forth, they destabilise proposition, that is, a certain historical relation between the subject, the object, and the subjectile. A relationship of representation. From now on, pictogram will indicate this destabilisation made into work.

16 Umberto Artioli

From 'Production of reality or hunger for the impossible?'*

This essay concerns Artaud's 'Van Gogh, ou le suicidé de la société' (*OC* XIII: 9–64), a significant text not least because it is the only one of his ever to win a literary award (the Prix Sainte-Beuve, 1948). The value of this particular reading lies in its use of alchemical language to explain Artaud's thinking about transformation in art and in its polemic about the relations between Artaud and recent continental philosophy, particularly Deleuze's collaborative work with Felix Guattari in *L'Anti-oedipe*, a work which Artioli argues would be unthinkable without Artaud. The influence of Artaud on continental philosophy is often unremarked but, in this essay, some of the important connections, as well as the disjunctions, are made apparent, while Artaud's esoteric connections are also examined. Here it is argued that Artaud's conception of art is fundamentally alchemical, as it is not a simple question of constructing representations, but a vision of artistic creation as the invention of new matter. Van Gogh is characterised as Artaud's alter ego in this project, described variously as the 'Grand Oeuvre' or the '*opus*'.

Fundamental to the structure of Artaud's piece on Van Gogh is the movement of *solve* and *coagula*, of liquefaction and condensation which, during Artaud's last years, was the starting point for his incessant reflexions on the process of rebirth. If, in contrast with the 'metaphysical' period,[1] the mind is no longer the great invalid, the mind whose sulphurous power has become impure; if it is matter that is now the dismembered body, the 'real' incapable of life because of the proliferation of 'asphyxiating gases', the shadow of the alchemical code continues to underlie the dynamic of forces Artaud puts into operation. [. . .]

A central issue in Artaud's intervention is the complex relation between representation and drive, the double movement by which the paintings of Van Gogh are at once a submission to the codes of painting and an explosion of them, the acceptance of restraint and its subversion. The wall of representation constitutes the extreme limit of Artaud's own poetics: to represent is to present again, to double that which is extant, to fix the movements of force in a single point and render them as an inert copy. So, in this sense, representation is the phantasm, the sterile effigy. So why, therefore, did Artaud trust the theatre? Is there, however refracted, any positive aspect of representation or does the post-Rodezian turnabout in Artaud's thinking mean an irreconcilable division between theatricality and spectacle? [. . .]

Let's pick up a leitmotif in the text:

> Van Gogh has reached that state of illumination where thought flees in disorder before its invading discharges . . . and where to think is no longer to be used up *and is no longer* . . . and where you have to start *gathering up* bodies, I mean *piling up bodies* . . . it's no longer the astral world that is recaptured in this way, beyond the realms of the conscious mind and the brain, but the world of creation.
>
> (*OC* XIII: 34–5)

[. . .] In the depths of his delirium Van Gogh is working on 'the forces of dementia', he knows that to get out of 'hell', 'the world has to . . . be returned to the furnace of the crucible' (*OC* XIII: 38). So the alchemical theme is established, but, in accordance with the phase of 'materialism', is turned toward anti-metaphorical concerns. The rhythm of *solve* and *coagula* corresponds to destruction and reconstruction, but it's no longer a 'virtual' operation for decanting the impurities of the mind. In its manifestation as a parasite and incubus, the mind is responsible for the repudiation of the body. This radically anti-representative affirmation establishes a decided correlation between the theatre and the *opus* (they are associated by their capacity to change inert matter into a higher composition, no longer reducible to a kind of Jungian self, but pushing beyond bounds of the real).

A consequence of the inversion (from metaphysics to materialism) is that terms with positive connotations begin to secrete, in a kind of systematic counter sequence, the dance of their dematerialised, demonic doubles. Like the theatre in its spectacular mode, alchemy, in its weak and ancillary formulations, is still a form of dupery: a ruse for relegating to the vanity of the symbol what can only be realised through the tearing apart of exposed organs, cruelty and blood.

Vestiges of this debased lesson are present here and there in Van Gogh, who in his later works also engaged in the positivist employment of occult propositions (formulae). It is this sanguine aspect to Van Gogh, viewed by Artaud with reference to the operating table, and not by accident, as 'the red butcher' (*OC* XIII: 59), which assumes something of an alternative polarity – for instance, when sunflowers are defined as 'more dangerous than the will of the ancient alchemist' (*OC* XIII: 178); or compared to Breughel and Bosch, whose work, says Artaud, 'offers nothing more than can be deduced from going through a heap of alchemical manuals. With Van Gogh the opposite is the case, the more you seek the less you find, he offers nothing that can be deduced from this order of knowing' (*OC* XIII: 197).

The antithesis made between magic writing and living body, between a book of spells and cutting into open flesh, is eloquent. The book removes the body, interlinking symbols replace, for Artaud, the reality of the *opus*, the raw evidence from which the non-given of creation is constructed. Van Gogh, 'the quiet epileptic' (*OC* XIII: 38), is opposed to the Flemish masters who are, in contrast to him, mere artists. He shows enduring contempt for finished form, for tissues of lines and colours refined to the point of presuming, not the drama of being-as-lack, but the sense of a complacent and precise knowledge: 'No-one has ever written or painted, sculpted, modelled, constructed, invented, except in order to get out of hell' (*OC* XIII: 38).

Taking account of these principles, it isn't hard to understand the opposition between alchemy, with its dynamic, operative, material signs, and the exhausted gestures of representation, with its doubling of pre-existent forms and its recourse to preformulated knowledge. Taking another essential passage: 'In the depths of those plucked butcher's eyes Van Gogh devoted himself relentlessly to one of those dark alchemical operations that took nature for its object and the human body as its vessel or crucible' (*OC* XIII: 34). What emerges in this passage is the stress on the term 'dark'. Beyond any idealised interpretation of desire as motivator of regenerative process, the activity of the *opus* evokes images of flaying, of tearing apart.

This is not contingent, but is an authentic and essential theme of the text. The same vocabulary recurs every time the painting of Van Gogh – 'the "Grand Oeuvre" of a perpetual and timeless transformation' (*OC* XIII: 26) – is brought back to its ultimate purpose:

> These crows painted two days before his death did not, any more than his other paintings, open the door for him to a certain posthumous glory, but they open to painted painting, or rather to unpainted nature, the occult gate of a possible beyond, to a possible permanent reality, through the door opened by Van Gogh to an enigmatic and sinister beyond.
>
> (*OC* XIII: 26, 27)

The passage through the doorway is 'sinister': so the operation of forces (drives), which produces a new reality, is quite other than the joyful abandon to the currents of desire; rather, it evokes the 'sufferings of imminent birth' (*OC* XIII: 43), the shadow of 'torments and pains resolutely endured, systematically applied' (*OC* XIII: 186); just as its product, the series of paintings exhibited at the Orangerie, continue 'their sombre reverberations' (*OC* XIII: 47) after the spectators have ceased to look at them.

Form becomes sound, amplifying a murmur which spreads, speaks to the soul of the spectator and incites them to the act of genesis. Again, the same notion obstinately returns in the subject of Van Gogh's ceremony of self-mutilation – the act of giving his ear to a prostitute is a gesture which translates the theme of sacrifice and invitation: 'The soul gives to the body its ear, Van Gogh has given it back to the soul of his soul, a woman, so as to intensify the sinister illusion' (*OC* XIII: 51). Here one rediscovers one of the great topoi of Artaud's later work: the glorious body, which is equally a body without organs, a glowing and absolute mass, demanding the sacrifice, the operating table, the 'sinister' work of butchery. The bad ear, accomplice of the actual or 'miserable body called Van Gogh' (*OC* XIII: 178), is severed in the name of the body to come, but the sacrificial gesture is also a secret prayer for 'the soul of his soul', the beloved woman and fellow traveller. [. . .]

Although Van Gogh is 'the truest painter of all the painters' (*OC* XIII: 46), the figurative arts in comparison with the theatre will constitute a demi-art, as though Artaud were confirming the celebrated 30's definition according to which painting is 'silent theatre', an incomplete form despite its extraordinary efficacity.

Let's take a decisive passage:

> Van Gogh couldn't shake off in time that vampirism of a family with a vested interest in what the genius of Van Gogh painted, and restricted him to painting, without at the same time proclaiming the revolution essential to the corporeal and physical blossoming of his visionary personality.
>
> (*OC* XIII: 36)

When the act of painting, here pushed to its extreme limits, passes beyond the wall of representation, something in the grandeur of this gesture speaks the language of loss. Van Gogh's power is what Artaud calls the 'motif', which he, Van Gogh, stoically maintains without any concession to the anecdote, to drama, to the bloodless appeal of the literary incident. This power is brought to a point at which nature shakes off its own inertia, splits its molecules and returns to the crucible. But all the same, the 'motif' wasn't Van Gogh's own choice of medium; it was imposed on him in order to divert him 'from a certain path which was for him eminently liberatory' (*OC* XIII: 180); he who instead of painting would have preferred the 'delirium at the end of a paintbrush or a tree, haystack, sown meadow etc. etc.' (*OC* XIII: 180).

What's the significance of 'delirium' here? The term assumes another meaning in passages of the text where the obligation to paint (so assiduously reinforced by Dr Gachet) disappears, significantly, at the moment when Van Gogh 'would have done better to take himself to bed . . . to incubate the next out break of his health' (*OC* XIII: 53, 62). Pictorial delirium, applied to the transformation of natural objects, is analogous with another delirium that operates directly on the body, rending it apart in order to effect its regeneration. Of these two forms of the Dionysian, the first is undoubtedly venomous: to paint is to die, or at least approach the moment of one's own death. Painting to Van Gogh isn't an exhibition of mastery or the unfolding of a display of knowledge. In the process of dissociating objects and landscapes, pacifying them, but with a convulsive peace, unleashing forces, saturated with a sonorous frisson which makes of form something mobile and incredibly intense, there is a 'music' and a 'nerve' plucked 'straight out of the heart' (*OC* XIII: 46). Van Gogh's heart is offered as a sacrifice in witnessing the instant of its resurrection. Painting is alchemy and it is no accident that the painter, possessing the power of transformation, should also be a 'sorcerer' (*OC* XIII: 208); but this can be an enervated form of alchemy, where the subject and object of transformation fail to merge and instead reopen the circuit of expropriation, the tragedy of sacrifice: 'the water is blue but not the blue of water, it has the blue of liquid paint: the suicided madman has been there and has restored the painted image of water to nature, but who is going to effect this restoration in reverse'? (*OC* XIII: 58, 59).

But Van Gogh's painting provides the model of 'another world, another state of living, another breath of liberation, of absolute freedom' (*OC* XIII: 221) and awaits, in the depths of his burning landscapes, the wind of 'primitive apocalypses' (*OC* XIII: 51). There is a recurring sense of finality in the text, a reference to ends as the achievement of the *opus* [. . .]:

> For there is more than light in Van Gogh's landscapes and flowers, more than an atmosphere painted as though it came from the most unspeakably isolated depth . . . there is something of ground earth, pulverised and reconstituted and which Van Gogh has returned to life and to which Van Gogh will one day return to give reality to his own true life.
>
> (*OC* XIII: 189)

Van Gogh's paintings are dependent on a linguistic code, of which he accepts the limits, but nevertheless they're capable of discharging a sound which breathes with the moving life of matter. In the sense they constitute, in their authenticity, a form of true theatre. This is not a linguistic event, much less a place where you can reconstruct a reality from stolen breath, but an act of 'true genesis', through which all that is rotten in the body is returned to the depths in order to be revitalised. [. . .]

The difference between theatre and painting as Artaud understood it in his later works is situated at the level of a mortal void: the exact space left empty by the theatre is occupied by the tormented gaze of poor Van Gogh, 'suspended, glued and glassy behind his raw pupils' (*OC* XIII: 59). These disturbing images of suspension and vitrification recall Artaud's juvenilia and relaunch the theme of lack of being: 'Even Van Gogh could never resurrect himself, not even for ten years, not even for one, not for anything at all' (*OC* XIII: 222) and 'I believe that there is always someone else there at the point of our death, stealing away our own proper life' (*OC* XIII: 61).

Death is the Other, the intruder which insinuates itself like a bad organ or a psychic phantasm and diverts the vital force; it's the Difference that deprives the body of its cohesion in preventing it from 'glowing and shining'. Rot, decomposition, loss are the consequences of a furtive presence, which turns existence into the contrary of real life. Van Gogh couldn't tolerate this blank 'tombstone' existence like a 'buried boneyard' (*OC* XIII: 48) and launched his glowing suns against it like bloody meteors.

Yet again the dynamic is opposed to the inert, active to passive, force to form. An axiological reversal of principles is going on, but the irresolvable conflict of principles between the bestiality of the majority and the heroism of the elite is maintained and intensified: 'Now Van Gogh, who cooked one of his hands, never shirked the struggle of life, that is, as distinct from the idea of existence . . . and anyone who does not smell of cooked bomb and compressed vertigo is not worthy of being alive' (*OC* XIII: 52, 53).

In this universe of passion, where only those who can charge themselves with the energies of suffering and the risk of being torn apart have the capacity for regeneration (the distinction between the titanic individual and 'normal consciousness'), there is no place for happy spontaneity. Words like 'sinister' and 'sombre' have been underlined because Artaud constantly uses them to describe the dynamic of the *opus* and because in his cosmos the flows of innocence can't just be sheltered from voracious energies. Everything is already poisoned, shot through with impurities, 'cooked tumour' and 'chafed bedsores' (*OC* XIII: 52) and to purge them you have to apply yourself unstintingly to the task.

This is characteristic of Van Gogh, 'a terrible workman' (*OC* XIII: 212), a term which contains the notion of the worker and evokes activity and concentration with none of the connotations attributed by Deleuze and Guattari: i.e. this is not a decentred subject always beside the desiring machines, yielding his own activity to them and parasitically enjoying their productions.

Artaud's conception of the subject in his later work, whilst in no way assimilable to the fiction of the 'I', is something quite other than the identity 'homo-natura' postulated in *Anti-Oedipus*. The author of Van Gogh, moreover, insistently repeats this: 'It is not nature but myself who acts in the depths of everything, myself who captures the wandering impersonal energies and through the bilious pain of hepatitis restores them to my own will, after which I push my way forward' (Artaud 1971: 20); 'What is "body" but the emaciation of the material of the self; regained by the self, whatever is not won through the suffering of the self falls at the hour of death to become pure spirit' (Artaud '*Suppôts et suppliciations*', *OC* XIV**: 49); 'The body does not come [is not produced] through temporal evolution, but through will in the milieu of time' (*OC* XIV**: 73).

It's not the unconscious that constitutes the 'real in itself' in a happy conjunction of desire and the object; so that it's enough to just give oneself up to the flow of desires, which circulate outside any territoriality and codification, to produce a new reality; this is the *will* of a subject, with the unconscious as its instrument. If, to designate this genesis in reverse (palingenese), Artaud sometimes evokes a mythical anteriority represented by the image of the body aflame, composed only of bones and blood, the theme of the return is for him indissociable from the idea of conflict: in an 'anarchic creation', the tragedy of poisoning, the presence of evil, is a given that one can't be rid of but can be counteracted without being effaced.

Forces of gravitation are always on the look-out, energy is repossessed, the body takes fright, the molecules of the void suck the breath out of the 'real' life. This is why regeneration, the gesture by which a body is remade in an appeal to a deep reserve of being, does not arrive by 'merit' or 'quality'. It demands the heroism of the one who, engaged in the dissociation of the extant, feels flooding over him the shudders of conflicts which bind him there, yet forces them to yield to his own power: 'Van Gogh seemed to know the exact amount of cross-hatching he had to do to recompose his subjects beyond the reach of danger' (*OC* XIII: 212, 213). [. . .]

Van Gogh's works are simultaneously convulsive and placid, bearers of form and the means of dissolution, fixed yet always on the point of 'disappearing' (*OC* XIII: 55) – they are the luminous, though fainter, equivalent of Artaud's later conception of theatre:

> The Theatre is the arena, the state, the point where the human anatomy can be seized, cured and revivified . . . Yes, universal gravitation is a seismic force, appalling and impassioned, which can be diverted through the limbs of the actor . . . layer upon layer, the actor develops, he opens out or closes in the walls, the impassioned and invigorated facets inscribed with the theory of life. Muscle by muscle in the body of the methodically traumatised actor, one can grasp the development of universal impulses and divert them.
>
> (Artaud 1948a)

In this passage a significant jump is made: concern with the revolt against an intolerable society gives way to a questioning of life itself. Set it against the passage in Van Gogh, where it's said of Van Gogh's landscapes that they 'have a nature and an atmosphere far truer than that of nature itself' (*OC* XIII: 46). It's a sick state of being which collects powers in order to destroy them, in which all pathos condenses and spreads out and which, whilst presented as 'good health', is 'gnawed by a plethora of evils and powerful fevers for life while festering with a hundred wounds' (*OC* XIII: 53).

Far from identifying man and nature as united against a predatory society, Artaud associates nature and society as a state of bewitchment, which is why the shadow of the gnostic demiurge, author of a marred creation, appears again on the scene. In according every individual a constructed ego and a role, in diverting sexual energy through the grid of eroticism, society endorses the status quo, but its crime is only the reflection of a more ancient crime.

It all started at the point of origin, when the double took the place of the single being, the flaming body lost its cohesion and now, infested with repulsive larvae, it has become the nest of intolerable vapours. Contemporary society, preoccupied by self-preservation, can't take the condition of sulphurous anarchy through which one makes new worlds and remains, in Artaud's vision, a false order based on 'a primitive injustice' (*OC* XIII: 13). [. . .] This society, which does not want a renewed existence, mistrusts 'true' theatre with its capacity to 'channel stage, screen and microphone' as instruments for 'detecting the explosive possibilities too dangerous for the present state of life' (*OC* XIII: 259).

For Artaud the materialist, the centre of gravity lies not in his detestation of social institutions, but in his gnostic conception of existence, which construes the world as an eternal conflict between the forces of Good and Evil, to be concluded only in the Apocalypse. A conflict where the remains of the divine, those martyrs in which the memory of pre-existent being continues to rise, are referred to as *uncreated* or *imperishable*: 'And it's not a matter of hallucination or delirium, it's a matter of this dubious and verified rubbing shoulders with an abominable world of spirits where every imperishable actor and uncreated poet senses his purest impulses polluted by the parties of shame' (Artaud 1948b).

Misery, the inevitability of evil and suffering, in which good takes the form of superimposed cruelty, means that the effort of renewal is an incessant process: the great myth of the glorious body, far from representing a happy epiphany of desire, puts in motion a relentless tragic machinery. Tragic not in Deleuze's sense, when in his reading of Nietzsche in *Anti-Oedipus* he situates the term within the sphere of *jouissance* and joy, as opposed to that of sad passions and the labour and suffering of the negative.

In Artaud's case there is never *jouissance* – rather he denounces it, from his first essays, and furiously reproaches the surrealist orthodoxy for it, in contesting their edenic, tranquillised vision of the unconscious. For him, on the contrary, there is suffering and work and if, in Van Gogh, he recalls the 'unhappy Nietzsche' (*OC* XIII: 59), it's perhaps because he remembers the passage from *Beyond Good and Evil* where the formative discipline of suffering is achieved by tormenting the human all-too-human:

> Do you know what it is, this discipline of suffering that has led man to the summits of being? In man, creator and creature are united – man is at once creator, sculptor, the hard hammer, the divine spectator who on the seventh day contemplates his work. Do you understand this contradiction? Do you understand that your own pity addresses the creature in man, the one who must be paralysed, broken, forged, engraved, burned, dissolved, purified of all his excrescence; it addresses all that, of necessity, *will suffer and must suffer*?

> (Nietzsche 1963: 273)

Man as subject and object of transformation, the productive value of suffering, the rhythm of destroying and reforging: doesn't this passage contain a theme that one finds incessantly in Artaud, even if the author of Zarathustra insists on the 'pessimism of power', on suffering in the cause 'of superabundance itself', while Artaud is obsessed with expropriation and lack which does not cease to consume him?

Is Artaud dialectical? Is his vision eschatological? If the term 'dialectical', of which Artaud was so suspicious, is purged of its associations with idealism, it serves to describe the rhythm of the *opus*, the drama of alienation transformed through reappropriation. 'A corpse that no tempest can assail' (*OC* XIII: 2). In Artaud's cry there is the presentiment of a threshold dreamed of and never attained, an irreducible sign of failure. His fury stopped him on the threshold, because all he had to put forward were the dispersed shreds of his miserable body. To remember, as it is said in *Anti-Oedipus*, that 'no one ever died of contradictions. And the more this deranges, schizophrenises, the better it works, in the American way' (Deleuze and Guattari 1972: 178) is to invert the entire axis of Artaud's thought and to deny the suffering involved in the work of the true theatre of 'ineluctable necessity'. [. . .]

Is the 'small joy' of schizophrenisation, really the free play of deterritorialised flows, an eternal return of intensity? Or isn't it rather a tragic rift between the omnipotence of desire and the misery of limitation, an experience exacerbated by lack, the lack which is life itself? If we've been harping on about *Anti-Oedipus*, it's because this book, which is masterly in so many respects, would be unthinkable without Artaud's oeuvre. It's irrelevant to point out that nominally he occupies a minor place in it, smaller than Miller, Lawrence or Reich, and certainly less than Freud or Lacan.

Whether you like it or not, the motifs which constitute the framework of Deleuze and Guattari's thesis are Artaudian, even if in their wild proliferation of schizos it's not always possible to hear Artaud's voice: the body without organs (BwO); desire as 'an overheated factory'; alchemical incest and its possibilities for infinite regeneration; the anti-oedipal refusal of pseudo-being or stasis; the refusal of lack; the production of a 'new reality', in the form of an insurrection by the repressed unconscious; the process characterised as eternal renewal; the breath and the cry as indices of desire; the apocalypse as a desert where non-codified flows can be made to stream; the distinction between the catatonic regression and breakthrough, etc.

The schizo has become the antidote to the 'malaise of civilisation', the source of the liberating wind which emanates from the book and has inspired some of the alternative political practices in Italy in recent years. While the persistent dualism of Artaud, attributable to his 'matrix' of gnosticism, is dissolved in the positivity of a desire, which, having evaded the oedipal trap and pierced 'the wall of the signifier', rediscovers the breakthrough point, the objective proof of 'pure reality', of 'the reality of oneself'.

Established at the outset, the identity of homo and natura becomes an excuse for explosive desire and wild productivity, ipso facto defined as revolutionary, whilst the active, 'necessary' and 'purifying' role of suffering is denied, suppressed or attributed to the operation of mechanisms of constraint. The result is that breakdown, death, the effects of gravity are seen, not as the intervention of hostile influence, but as the propelling impulses of the creative process, precipitating happy transitions from one phase to another, from one strip of intensity to the one that replaces it.

The obsession with personal immortality (around which revolve the Artaudian motifs of 'labour', 'deserving', 'quality' and, above all, 'mastery' of 'the impersonal errant drives') is broken down in the identity of the subject and life: a subject on the margins, without stable identity, forever decentred; an immortality consequent upon desire 'instinctive and sacred', free and unceasingly reborn.

But the real Gordian knot appears in the opening pages of their work, when Deleuze and Guattari confront something that presents itself as an inescapable aporia: how can you reconcile Artaud's aversion for the organ, the partial object, for any interruption of the flow (and the metaphysics of subject as self which results from that), with the fact that the authors of *Anti-Oedipus* bring the dynamics of productivity back to disjunction and separation? How can you reconcile the BwO and its diffuse, undifferentiated energies, its luminosity, with the 'paranoia' machine that is 'molar' and totalising, or with the fragmentary and partial nature of desiring production? [. . .]

How does Artaud's repulsion of the machine become attraction to it in solidarity with Deleuze and Guattari's attraction towards it? [. . .] And, again, how can you connect the totality of production with the BwO, unless you regalvanise it as cohesive tissue, as cosmos, if you don't resurrect the phantom of unification that Deleuze and Guattari so arrogantly denounce in their polemics against Tansk and Klein?

This is one danger that Deleuze and Guattari acknowledge, when, with a curious triadic manoeuvre that can only recall their antagonist Hegel, they consider it opportune to introduce a third type of machine with the precise and declared aim of making 'an effective reconciliation' (Deleuze and Guattari 1972: 23). What is this 'celibate' machine, if not an attempt to safeguard both the repulsive state of the BwO and the attractive state of the 'miraculous' machine by reconciling them in such a way as to make from the glorious body something compatible with the essential thesis of the book, i.e. a place where 'the opposed forces of attraction and repulsion produce an open series of intensities, all positive, which never constitute the final equilibrium of a system, but rather an unlimited number of metastable stations through which a subject passes' (Deleuze and Guattari 1972: 26)? After such a great polemic against the oedipal trinity, this evocation of a new, ternary element that is 'machinic' is very odd – a recourse to an old dialectical ruse in order to effect the refutation of dialectic itself.

In spite of this, *Anti-Oedipus* remains a great book. It retains one dimension of the Artaudian experience – that which associates lack with social fault and pushes the implication of that dimension (of lack) to extremes in creating from 'non human sex' a paradise regained. Without denying the value of *Anti-Oedipus*, stress needs to be laid on how the myth of liberation, obsessive for Artaud, continues to be linked with the gnostic 'matrix' of his thought and on how for the author of Van Gogh the crime of society is nothing but the infinite repetition of a metaphysical crime. If you put the two projects back together, Artaud's revolt, far from attaining the miracle of the *breakthrough*, resonates with the devastating cry of setback. But the hunger for the impossible has a tragic grandeur, a paroxysmal fury, which makes Artaud one of the most stirring voices of the modern era.

Part IV

Beyond words

On film and radio

In this section Allen S. Weiss, the scholar primarily responsible for the development of the study of Artaud's radio work, and Denis Hollier take the ideas in the radio works beyond conventional media and even conventional systems of language. Mikhail Yampolsky's piece comes from a larger work detailing connections with Borges and deals with the concept of dubbing, something which fascinated Artaud. Francis Vanoye's 'Cinemas of cruelty?' is the most recently published text in this collection and assesses the key notion of cruelty in terms of cinema.

17   Allen S. Weiss

'K'*

Allen S. Weiss is a prolific writer and scholar, author of some twenty-five books in English and French on everything from avant-garde radio, e.g. *Breathless: Sound Recording, Disembodiment, and the Transformation of Lyrical Nostalgia* (Middletown, CT: Wesleyan, 2002); to French gardens and gastronomy, e.g. *Feast and Folly: Cuisine, Intoxication, and the Poetics of the Sublime* (Albany: SUNY Press, 2000); and the pioneering study of Artaud's radio work, which he has developed in a number of different contexts and written about extensively. One significant aspect of this is how Weiss restores the specificity of the radiophonic dimension of Artaud's opus, while resituating it, as a distinct cultural form, in the midst of current theoretical debates on the linkages between the physical and the technological, the psychological and the musicological, as well as the more familiar themes of textuality and subjectivity. Weiss is particularly skilful at reading Artaud's invented language (glossolalia) as a kind of material poetics, in which the violence and pleasure of the experience of a physicalised sound assume precedence over the phatic, communicative aspects of linguistic production. An extended version of this text can found in Weiss's *Phantasmic Radio* (1995: 9–34).

'Nobody in Europe knows how to scream anymore' (*OC* IV: 163)

What does it really mean, 'To hear death in his voice'? How can one attain the impossible narrative position established from the point of view of one's own death? In 1933 Antonin Artaud gave a lecture at the Sorbonne entitled 'Le théâtre et la peste' ('The Theatre and the Plague'), which was to become a chapter of his masterpiece, *Le Théâtre et son double* (The Theatre and its Double). His presentation is described by Anaïs Nin:

> But then, imperceptibly almost, he let go of the thread we were following and began to act out dying by plague. No one quite knew when it began. To illustrate his conference, he was acting out an agony. 'La Peste' in French is

so much more terrible than 'The Plague' in English. But no word could describe what Artaud acted on the platform of the Sorbonne. [. . .] His face was contorted with anguish. One could see the perspiration dampening his hair. His eyes dilated, his muscles became cramped, his lunges struggled to retain their flexibility. He made one feel the parched and burning throat, the pains, the fever, the fire in the gut. He was in agony. He was screaming. He was delirious. He was enacting his own death, his own crucifixion.

(Nin 1966: 191–2)

This extremely disturbing scene may serve as the prolegomena to a consideration of a later disruption of our aesthetic field, Artaud's 'Pour en finir avec le jugement de dieu' (To have done with the judgement of god), his final work and major radiophonic creation.[1]

'The century no longer understands the fecal poetry, the intestinal ills, of that one, Madam Death . . . ' (OC IX: 191)

The written project for 'Pour en finir avec le jugement de dieu' begins with a short text containing glossolalia typical of Artaud's writing at Rodez and after:

kre	Everything must	puc te
kre	be arranged	puk te
pek	to a hair	li le
kre	in a fulminating	pek ti le
e	order	kruk
pte		

Glossolalia is a type of speech or babble characteristic of certain discourses of infants, poets, schizophrenics, mediums, charismatics.[2] It is the manifestation of language at the level of its pure materiality, the realm of pure sound, where there obtains a total disjunction of signifier and signified. As such, the relation between sound and meaning breaks down through the glossolalic utterances; it is the image of language inscribed in its excess, at the threshold of nonsense. Thus, as a pure manifestation of expression, the meaning of glossolalia depends upon the performative, dramatic, contextual aspects of such utterances within discourse and action; meaning becomes a function of the enthusiastic expression of the body, of kinetic, gestural behaviour.

In *Le Théâtre et son double* Artaud already provides the rationale for the utilisation of such enunciations in his theatre of cruelty:

To make metaphysics out of a spoken language is to make language express what it usually does not express: this is to make use of it in a new, exceptional and unaccustomed fashion; to reveal its possibilities of physical shock; to actively divide and distribute it in space; to handle intonations in an absolutely concrete manner, restoring their power to tear asunder and to really manifest something; to turn against language and its basely utilitarian – one could even say, alimentary – sources, against its hunted-beast origins; this is finally to consider language in its form as Incantation.

(OC IV: 58)

Updating these remarks upon his return to Paris after Rodez, he writes:

And shit on psalmody,
bomba fulta
enough seeking the true poetic psalmody,
caca futra
ça suffira
mai danba
debi davida
imai davidu
eve vidu
by repeating I annul . . .

(OC XXIII: 16)

And in another text (also punctuated by glossolalia, or rather, glossographia – omitted here) that may serve as an explanation of the use of glossolalia in 'Pour en finir avec le jugement de dieu', 'To be rid of the idiotic and perishable stamp of baptism [. . .] it does not suffice to say it, but I said it and I say it again, I repeat: I renounce my baptism. And the incomprehensible words that precede this are at most imprecations against the fact of having been baptised' *(OC* XXII: 377–8). Artaud proposes the religious, magical use of glossolalia as catharsis, as a mode of exorcism: to rid himself of God's influence and judgement.

'Is God a being? If so, he's shit.' (OC XIII: 86)

The phonetic structures of glossolalia generally parallel those of the speaker's mother tongue (one rarely, if ever, creates a truly new language), though such enunciations are often marked by features idiosyncratic to the speaker. In Artaud's case, there is an extremely high frequency of the letter /k/ in his glossolalia/glossographia, as well as of the phonetic equivalents of this sound, the hard /c/, /ck/, and /ch/. (We should note that the letter /k/ is one of the least frequent in the French language, yet one of the most frequent consonants in Artaud's glossolalia: it is thus transformed into a highly pertinent feature of this language, and its significance must be sought.) [3]

The scatological signification of the instance of the letter/sound /k/ in Artaud's glossolalia is apparent.[4] Once again in terms of an incantatory exorcism, he writes from Rodez:

The expulsion of the spirits had been effected one day, not in order to protect the body, for it is spirit, but to save the soul.
cou cou la ni le ri
ca ca lo lo lo lo
cou cou roti moza

(*OC* XVIII: 190)

And from the same period he explains that the soul is cacophony while the text is stylistics. But such scatological pronouncements are far more than sheer expletives; they bear an ontological signification, which Artaud explains in a letter written from Rodez dating from the same month as the previous citation:

The name of this matter is caca, and caca is the matter of the soul, which I have seen so many coffins spill out in puddles before me. The breath of bones has a centre, and this centre is the abyss Kah-Kah, Kah the corporeal breath of shit, which is the opium of eternal survival.

(*OC* IX: 192)

Excrement, as a sign of death, is formless matter excluded from the organisation of the symbolic order. It poses a threat to cultural formations, both because it signifies a wasteful expenditure that circumvents societal modes of production and because it is an originary sign of autonomous production, of sovereign creativity bypassing societal structures of exchange. Excrement marks the body, and not the socius, as the centre of production, whence the necessity, in the process of socialising the infant, of controlling the anal functions and establishing the anus as the place of possession and exclusion. This exclusion entails, in the major irony of human ontogenesis, the rejection of one's own body, a rejection which is the very origin of sublimation. Any desublimated return to anality in adult life marks a return of the repressed, and serves as a contestation of the symbolic law.[5]

Artaud pits his own creativity against that of God, where the two are nevertheless mediated by death: '. . . the Word is not made flesh, the flesh will be made shit and this will henceforth be the only word of imprecation . . .' (*OC* XVII: 214). In restating the Johannine myth of creation, Artaud specifies the corporeal origins, the 'latrines of sublimity' (*OC* XII: 41), the chaotic magma of existence, where life and death are in constant struggle, and where the soul is torn between angelic purity and diabolic filth and corruption. In a moment of hyperbolic hubris and blasphemy, Artaud proclaims that,

When I say caca, prison, poison, penal servitude, sodomisation, assassination, urgency, thirst, a quick piss, scurvy of thirst, Sodom, Gomorrha, assassination, urgency, thirst, a quick piss, God responds inflamed logos . . .

(*OC* XIV: 178)

Yet Artaud wishes to preclude even this response, to finally end God's judgement altogether. The diatribe becomes even more vicious, more blasphemous, in 'Pour en finir avec le jugement de dieu', where in the text of 'La Recherche de la fécalité' he poses the question: 'Is God a being? If so, he's shit' (*OC* XIII: 86). (We might note that, perhaps not coincidentally, this work was published by the publisher K.) Struggling against the return of the repressed, trying to resist and scorn the judgement of God and the judgement of man (which was perhaps even harsher), this final work would become a sort of epitaph, destined (in its very absence) to mark an unfulfilled possibility of radiophonic art and an unclaimed moment in the history of poetry.

'... the limbo of a nightmare of bones and muscle ...' (*OC* I*: 177)

All expression is informed by language and the body, bounded by signs and libido. The figuration of force – in what might be termed the 'visceral imagination' – always attempts to escape the hermeneutic circle within which force is transformed into form, into meaning. This significative evasion, beneath the threshold of sense, is precisely the level at which Artaud's texts must be read. Given the paranoid, theological deliria specific to Artaud's condition, these corporeal/semiotic restraints must be interpreted in a very specific manner. In an early text entitled 'Sur le suicide' ('On Suicide' 1925), Artaud explains:

> If I kill myself, it will not be in order to destroy myself, but in order to reconstitute myself; suicide will be for me only a means of violently regaining myself, of brutally bursting into my own being, of forestalling the uncertain advances of God. By means of suicide, I reintroduce my own plan into nature, and install for the first time the form of my volition into things.
>
> (*OC* I** : 26)

Thus the force/form distinction is a matter of life and death, and the corporeal/semiotic restraint is transformed into a classic double-bind, expressed on the cosmic level:

> Even to be able to arrive at the point of suicide, I must await the return of myself. I need the free play of all the articulations of my being. God placed me within hopelessness as within a constellation of impasses whose radiation ended in myself. I can neither live nor die, neither not wish to die nor to live. And all men are like me.
>
> (*OC* I**: 28)

The existence of God creates a double-bind for Artaud: the negation at the core of the self, that which separates the self from itself, is God. Whence the need to kill God, to be done with his judgement, in order to gain one's own autonomy, in order to conquer the work of the negative by means of life's creative forces.

The torment of my flesh, the dispossession of myself, the bewitching of my soul, the theft of my voice, all must be overcome; the task is to reduce the difference between force and form, and thus transform the stigmata of God's judgement into the expression – and not the betrayal – of life. This is to be the goal of the theatre of cruelty; however, an ontological pessimism reigns: 'when we speak the word life, it must be understood that this does not pertain to life as we know it from its factual exterior, but rather from that sort of fragile and fluctuating core untouched by forms' (*OC* IV: 18).

The psychological effects of this double-bind system upon Artaud are explained by Guy Rosolato:

> Expulsion, for Artaud, was to be situated neither on the exterior nor in the interior of the system, as ineluctable as it might be; neither on the side of life nor on the side of death: but, through the quest for total mastery, by maintaining what became for him the impasse, the double-bind, of the simultaneous and absolute *injunctions to live and to die*, that is to say by means of the single thought incarnate in the infinite instant of passage within the circumscribed immensity of the theatre: a scream.
>
> (Rosolato 1978: 141–2)

The scream is the expulsion of an unbearable, impossible internal polarisation between life's force and death's negation, simultaneously signifying and simulating creation and destruction. Parallel to the antithetical sense of excrement for the infant – gift or weapon – the scream, as the non-material double of excrement, may be both expression and expulsion, both a sign of creation and frustration.

In one of the first texts written after his release from Rodez, '*Suppôts et suppliciations*' ('Henchmen and Torturings' 1946), Artaud poses the question: '. . . isn't the mouth of the current human race, following the anatomical survey of the present human body, this hole of being situated just at the outlet of the haemorrhoids of Artaud's ass'? (*OC* XIV*: 153). This conflation of humanity's mouth with Artaud's asshole is not simply a scabrous affront; this anatomical symbolism also reveals the desublimatory trajectory of Artaud's expression, of a body caught within the symbolic web and wishing to escape, of an anatomy trying to undo its own destiny. Psychoanalytic theory teaches us that speech is invested with narcissistic libido; this is true in regard to both the meaning of enunciations and the psychophysical manifestations of the speech act itself. The pleasures of speech are not merely phatic, communicative, seductive, but also autoerotic; the oral play of sensations, the very grain of the voice, creates and indicates the various pleasures and displeasures of vocal acts of expression.

Spoken sounds have a primary libidinal value, for both speaker and (through identificatory introjection) auditor, before ever becoming meaningful: rhythm, harmony, euphony, even dissonance and cacophony have a passional, often erotic, quality. Ultimately, this question reaches beyond the differences between logocentrism and melocentrism, with the latter being only a trope (musication) of the former. Rather, Artaud's poetics is formed beneath the thresholds of both, in the sensate body worked through by the active libido.

What Roland Barthes spoke of as the 'grain of the voice' reveals the very materiality of the body within that sublimation known as speech, or song. The scream is the desublimation of speech into body, in opposition to the sublimation of body into meaningful speech. Barthes insists that, 'there is no human voice in the world that is not the object of desire, or of repulsion; there is no neutral voice, and if occasionally this neuter, this whiteness of the voice appears, it is a great terror for us, as if we were to fearfully discover a frozen world, where desire is dead' (Barthes 1982: 247). For Artaud, death is not heard in the voice through such a 'white terror'; Artaud's terror was dark, filthy, emanating from the deepest recesses of his body, a body which his discourse tried, always unsuccessfully, to rejoin.

Reducing the mouth/anus conflation to the purely physiological level, Artaud notes: 'The hone kernel of the cyst of the lingual gum of the anal tongue of the hard palate, glottis, larynx, pharynx' (*OC* XXIII: 328).

Here the connection is not merely symbolic: contemporary psycho-linguistics teaches that the pronunciation of glottal occlusives (sounds created by closure of the glottis) creates a direct sub-glottal pressure on the diaphragm and the intestines, thus facilitating defecation.[6] This vortex of force is indicated by Artaud in the corporeal trajectory of gums, tongue, palate, glottis, larynx, pharynx, which explains the meaning of the apparent oxymoron of an 'anal tongue' (where the translation of '*langue anale*' by 'anal language' would be linguistically more logical, but would break the physiognomic chain of expression). Thus glottal sounds are a symbolic – and physiognomic – reflection of defecation: speech, as *flatus voci*, is the ejection of a dematerialised substance, the inverse of the anal *flatus*. Such a relation is often found in psychopathological symptoms, as in the following case of a patient of Sandor Ferenczi, cited by Istvan Fonagy:

> Another patient (a hysteric) suffered from two symptoms, simultaneously and with the same intensity: a glottic spasm and a spasm of the anal sphincter. If he is in a good mood, his voice is strong and flows freely and his defecation is normal, 'satisfying'. During a state of depression – especially if it is due to an insufficiency – or in his relations with his superiors, there is simultaneously aphonia and tenesmus.
>
> (Fonagy 1983: 91)

The glottic sphincter permits the physical and symbolic articulation of oral and anal rejection (and retention). This is primally and hyperbolically expressed by the glottal occlusive /k/, universally signified in its popular scatological form of *kaka* or *caca*. Whence the general condemnation of the sound /k/ as ugly, filthy;

this is a direct result of the corporeal displacement of anal libido directly onto such sounds.[7]

As such, these glottal vocalisations are screams of the entire body, and not just the mouth. Yet these screams never fall below the threshold of meaning, since even the sub-glottal regions of the body are full of signification and overtly expressive. The interior of the soul speaks through the interior of the body. The realisation of the intimate ties between body and language became central to Artaud's poetics:

> I don't give a damn if my sentences sound French or Papuan, but if I drive in a violent word, I want it to suppurate in the sentence like a hundred-holed ecchymosis; a writer is not reproached for an obscene word because it is obscene, but because it is gratuitous, flat gris-gris.
>
> But who will say that it suffices for a word to sweat out its violence in the severed sentence which trails it like a severed living member; within infinity it is perhaps a fine skewer for a poet to burst forth a scream, but this is comforting only from the day that he succeeds in barding his words in such a manner that, parting from him, they would respond within the sentences of a written text as if without him, and when in rereading them he feels that these words summon him to them just as he called them to him.
>
> (*OC* XXIII: 46, 47)

Rhetorically creating a 'body' of the text (with its corresponding diseases and torments), Artaud wishes to recuperate a poetic or literary level to his work, beyond the raw, brutal scream. In itself, screams might be effective to jolt us out of our commonplace literary and linguistic habits, but they in no way suffice to create a style, nor a poem. Ultimately, the poetic text (including its screams) must distance itself from the poet (i.e. it must go beyond the level of sheer expression), only to return to him as an external summons. It is only in leaving the poet that the word can call out to the other, and attain its own destiny.

18 Denis Hollier

'The death of paper, part two: Artaud's sound system'*

This article begins as a reflection on the Artaud *Works on Paper* exhibition at MOMA, New York, in 1996, but becomes a millennial piece on sound culture, theatre and the visual in which Hollier argues that, for Artaud, theatre and film were vehicles for a radical experiment in 'phonic disarticulation' – sounds produced and received in such a way that we forget about the conventional means of communicating and representing our desires and our thoughts but discover new uses for our senses and our sound systems (theatres). Hollier argues that Artaud used sound as a device for short-circuiting representation, for bridging 'street' and 'theatre'. This playful cross-pollinating piece is written with wit (see the passage on 'technological coitus', with Artaud's infamous horror of sexuality as its subtext), and style. It is a provocation to think beyond disciplinary boundaries.

> Music has an effect on snakes, not by means of the mental ideas it induces in them, but because snakes are elongated, coil up langorously on the ground, and touch the earth along almost the entire length of their bodies; thus the musical vibrations transmitted to earth affect these bodies as a very subtle and very long massage; well, I propose to treat the public like snakes.
>
> (Artaud 1938)[1]

Our century, one hears, is wrapping itself up under the sign of visual culture. This might be a mere effect of the melancholic mood that easily allows the distancing ingrained in visual experience to side with some kind of sense of an ending. Man, after all, was given sight in order to be sad. However, at the other end of the century, when it was young and future-oriented, artists and thinkers, at least an impressive number of them, were adamant that they were moving in the opposite direction, away from the visual. The nineteenth century, they claimed, had been the century of vision; the twentieth was going to be the century of sound.[2] Man had just discovered that he was given hearing to listen to the future.

Artaud's recent entry in the Apollonian serenity of the museum (due homage paid to the MOMA show) is, no doubt, a long overdue posthumous recognition, his first successful escape from a rather unwelcoming publishing industry. One might wonder, however, if this escape from literature into the museum echoes in any way what he was fighting for when he was fighting his way out of the space of the written sign. From 'Le Théâtre de la cruauté' to 'Les Voix du silence' something got lost. The sound track.

Think for a moment about the title of the show: *Antonin Artaud: Works on Paper*.[3] In an artist's *catalogue raisonné*, the expression 'work on paper' refers to that part of his or her oeuvre that the artist hasn't put on a major, canonical support, canvas if a painter is in question, bronze or marble if a sculptor. Internal to the plastic arts, this taxonomy doesn't apply to literature, however. Artaud, to my knowledge, has never painted on canvas. The slight, if poetic, *détournement* that applies this rubric to Artaud's drawings, to the plastic production of a writer, thus entails interesting semantic effects: the expression 'works on paper' no longer referring primarily to the support of the work, but to the type of signs traced on it. If plastic, they are on paper. If graphic, they aren't. The museum has in the most elegant way asserted its monopoly over paper. Literature, deprived of its support, no longer belongs to the rubric work on paper. The death of paper, act two. Literature, we know, doesn't rest on anything.

Artaud, it is true, is a major voice in our century's many campaigns for the death of paper. However, his transgressions of the space of the book do not lead into the museum, the written sign being substituted, not by the image, but by sound. In other words, the writing versus drawing competition for ownership of paper as support, the text/image problematic, is not decisive here; and what is, doesn't happen on paper: it is the acoustic deconstruction of the voice, the liberation of sound from the tyranny of speech. Artaud's theatrical utopia, a transgression of literariness indeed, has nothing to do with admission into the museum; it is primarily what I call a sound system.

*

Sound is the main object of Artaud's back-and-forth negotiations between cinema and theatre during the 1920s and '30s.

He started his career as an actor in the early '20s, when he moved from Marseille to Paris. Both the production of *Les Cenci* and the publication of *Le Théâtre et son double* date from the mid- and late '30s. During the almost twenty years in between, he performed on stage and, as long as movies remained silent, on screen, both in France and in Germany, but was also involved in various ventures, theatrical and cinematographic, such as the Alfred Jarry Theatre in the late '20s and the theatre of cruelty in the mid-'30s, these two episodes being separated by his unsuccessful attempts at putting together, once again with the financial patronage of his shrink and his shrink's wife Yvonne Allendy, a film production company. To give a complete listing of his career in sound, one should also mention here the kind of Walter Rutman half-urbanistic, half-cosmic science-fiction extravaganza he sketched in 1933 with the Franco-American composer Edgar Varese, and for which he wrote the unfinished script 'There Is No More Firmament' (*OC* II: 106–24). Successful or not, and generally not, these experiments inscribe Artaud's theories of the theatre within a dialectic of the stage and the screen that, to my view, is much more important and productive than the tiresome cliché opposing the stage and the book.

Of course, Artaud's early interest in silent movies as well as his later opposition to talking pictures may seem to go against my emphasis on sound. These positions, however, need to be reframed in the context of Artaud's lifelong fight against the reduction of theatre to a series of on-stage recitations of literary dialogues. Artaud's siding with silent movies was part of a larger tactical alliance aimed at upstaging a theatre that spoke too much. And such an alliance was far from being counter-nature, since silence and sound have one important feature in common: they are not articulated. He thus approached silent movies as a first, paradoxical, and negative experiment in sound, a linguistic tabula rasa. But this was only a first step. The destruction of speech by silence was supposed to provide a springboard for the subsequent occupation of silence by noise.

In other words, Artaud was not attracted to the cinematic medium, *positively*, for its optical potential, the addition of movement to the static image of photography, but, *negatively*, for its way of silencing human chat, of breaking theatre's plight of allegiance to speech. Its being liberated from speech mattered infinitely more for him than its liberation of the visual. The silent movie was less a (positive) opto-event than a (negative) audio-event. Visuality as such, in any case, was never Artaud's major concern. In the first published presentation of his views about theatre and stage direction, the 1924 essay 'The Evolution of the Stage Setting', Artaud goes even as far as suggesting that one could very well forget about (cancel) 'the whole visual side of theatre' (*OC* II: 15).

The same indifference applies to his interest in the movies. Artaud did not positively care for their visual aspect. But he did not positively care for their silence, either. As I said previously, his involvement with the new medium was primarily tactical. Silence had no value per se; it was simply the first step in the deconstruction of speech: clearing the space for the unarticulated sounds whose production would follow later. In other terms, for Artaud, early cinema was not silent, it was speechless, or, as Lacan would say in another context, it was *infans*, without speech.

One might recall here that the first manifestation of the Alfred Jarry Theatre was the performance of a play written for the occasion by one of its directors, Roger Vitrac's *Power to the Infants* – a beautiful play, indeed, and probably the closest approximation to what a surrealist play could be – whose main protagonist, Ida Mortemart, is a woman both beautiful and afflicted by a grotesque phonic infirmity, worse than a speech impediment: she farts constantly. The reviewers did not miss such an opportunity: 'Un rôle qui fera du bruit' (a part that will hit a high note).[4]

*

This, somehow, leads me to Artaud's second move, which was prompted by the development of the talking picture. Like most of his fellow avant-gardists, he opposed the new art form. But, unlike them, his grievance was not acoustic pollution, he did not blame the sound track for disturbing a supposed quintessential visuality of the moving image. But he immediately foresaw that the phonic vacuum of the early movies was going to be filled in, not by the nonarticulated sounds of the future, but by the articulated speech of the past. He immediately foresaw that the sound track, becoming a speech track, would be used primarily as a barrage against the rising tide of the inarticulate. Here again, for Artaud, the border between the visual and the aural was less decisive than that between sound and speech. And this is one of the reasons why, leaving the studios and the screen, he went back to working for and thinking about the stage.

In a letter written to Yvonne Allendy in March 1929, Artaud discusses the opportunity for their still virtual production company to consider entering the talking-picture market and, more pointedly, to follow the new technological fad, 'synchronisation'. (The term, I recall, referred to the fact that, with the talkies, the image was irreversibly glued on speech, tied to its temporality: what you hear is what you see, and you see it and hear it at the same time.) Artaud's personal account of his experience of the sound track strikes today's reader with, even more than its insightfulness, the bad will it betrays toward the medium. It is hard to sort out what is descriptive or prescriptive (not to say proscriptive) in these comments. It is hard to decide if, for Artaud, sound and image cannot or should not mix. In any case, he writes, this mix does not work. And he explains why: 'However well synchronised, sound does not come from the screen, from this virtual, absolute space that the screen deploys in front of us. Try as we may, our ear will always hear it *in the theatre*, while our eye will perceive what's happening on the screen *elsewhere than in the theatre*' (*OC* III: 162).

Proximity of the sound. Distance of the image. Artaud's description refers, of course, to the still rudimentary technology of the theatres, where images were projected on a screen flanked by two loudspeakers. Hence the perception of a sound that, synchronous or not, was not coming from the image. Image and sound were, so to speak, split by the edges of the screen, each happening on one side of the frame, the image within and the sound without. The face of the speaker and his or her voice were separated by the frame of the picture.

This was, at least, what Artaud emphasised in his experience. What some analysts have described as a phonic umbilical cord (or chord) has been severed: there was an image and there was sound, but the vessels didn't communicate. Sound did not come from the floodlit rectangular space of the screen, but from the darkness that surrounded it. The question we might ask here is, was that good or bad? or, what was good and what was bad in such a sound system? But, to start with, before trying to answer, we should remark that Artaud was wrong. The separation between the acoustic and the visual source of the sound, between the face within the screen and the loudspeaker without, didn't prevent, in any case not for long, the public from 'suturing': it didn't take long for viewers to adjust and correct this perception. But this, which probably Artaud himself suspected, does not matter. It wouldn't change anything if, by means of whatever technological *tour de force*, images were finally taught to speak convincingly, since what he was opposing was, precisely, the return of speech as such – no matter where, no matter on which side of the screen, no matter if on-screen or offscreen. His critique was not of a technological order. He was not asking engineers to improve the techniques of recording or projecting. ('This is science and it does not interest me', he goes on in his letter to Allendy (*OC* III: 163)). His resistance was of another, more radical order. His was not a critique of tools. It was a critique of aims. He did not blame the machines, he blamed their purpose. He was never able to figure out why reterritorialising the voice within the screen should be such a cause for triumph. This being said, as far as the sound track was concerned, Artaud was rather intrigued by its potentialities. The letter continues: 'If I have an idea for a movie that would offer sound or musical possibilities, and I am going to think about it, I'll let you know. BUT I WON'T PUT ANY WORDS IN IT' (*OC* III: 163). This last sentence written in capital letters.

I would like to insert here two remarks concerning this resistance to the ideal of synchronisation. What motivates Artaud's resolute hostility to the ideal of a voice that would emerge from the image and merge with it, of an image that would speak as if from within, that would have found a voice, its own voice? Synchronisation has often been praised as the climax of a technological grand narrative culminating in the orgasmic union of voice and face, speech and phenomenon coming on screen at the same time. First we saw them speak, now we can hear them speak. But, progress or not, this perfect technological coitus was nothing more, according to Artaud, than a deeply regressive move.

But, here again, the significant divide does not run between sound and image: it splits the sound track itself. For sounds are either centripetal or centrifugal, flowing inward or outward, producing in one case an intimacy effect, in the other an outsider effect. The sound track itself has become the battlefield between speech and noise, between articulated and nonarticulated sounds, i.e. between the sounds that want to be in and those that are committed to stay off. Baudelaire once wrote about the tyranny of the human face. With the regressive coalescence of face and voice in the talkies, this is multiplied by the tyranny of human speech. The talkies implement the taming of the sound by the dialogue; they reterritorialise the voice within the face on screen by means of personalising the sound.

Let's go back for a moment to the loudspeakers. The loudspeaker itself, not the rendering of the voice, is what interested Artaud in these experiments in sound. It is offscreen and should stay there. Synchronisation misses the most significant step owed to the sound track: not the grafting of voices back onto faces, but the sudden opening of the beholder's space to an acoustic outside. Not the possibility of hearing what one sees, but the exact opposite, the possibility of hearing what one doesn't see. Instead of folding the sound track back onto the surface of the screen, the sound unfolds as its outside, provides it with an outside. Film technicians call *voice-over* (in French: voice *'off'*, i.e. *offscreen*) a sound whose source does not appear on-screen. The overblown import given by Artaud to the technological detail of the loudspeakers hanging outside the screen is a direct expression of what is, for him, an ontological *parti pris*: sound is by essence and should remain offscreen. He does not blame the loudspeakers for being off. He blames the talkies for pretending that they could be on.

There is thus a radical heterotopia of sound and image. Images remain out of the reach of sound, and sounds, at best, only manage to inhabit images as so many squatters. It is not simply that they occupy different places. They happen and move in different spaces. Somehow, a sound always comes, not only from outside the frame or the picture, but from outside the field of vision. A sound always comes from where one doesn't look. It occurs, as Freud would have said, on another *Schauplatz*, or rather *ein anderes Höreplatz*. There is, in sound, a spaciousness that prevents it from ever being framed. As for synchronisation, who really cares if sound and image are happening at the same time, since they are not in the same space? Sound and image can be simultaneous: their simultaneity can only reinforce their heterogeneity.

*

Artaud's emphasis on the volumetric potential of the 'offscreenness' of sound – the way the frontal perpendicularity of the Cartesian camera obscura is punctured and twisted by the zoom effect induced by the sound track – recalls in many ways *Being and Nothingness*'s most brilliant and fecund pages, those in which Sartre describes the experience of the other's gaze. In both cases (Artaud's and Sartre's) a visual experience is disturbed by an acoustic event. Sartre's description, one recalls, is primarily a critique of spectatorship: Through a keyhole, a subject is gazing at what is happening behind the door. He watches, totally absorbed by what he sees unfolding in front of his very eyes. All his fluids and thoughts concentrated in his field of vision, his body is reduced to what Jean Starobinski has called *un oeil vivant*, a living eye. But suddenly, says Sartre, 'I hear footsteps in the hall', or, in another *Being and Nothingness* description, one hears branches crackling (Sartre 1956: 349).[5] The other's gaze has punctured the visual mastery of the viewer. The gaze of the other, as Lacan praised Sartre for emphasising, has entered the voyeur's field of non-vision: it is an (offscreen) *acoustic* gaze, one experienced not visually, but acoustically; through the surprise of hearing another presence, of feeling him there acoustically, through one's ears. Paul Claudel gave his book on Dutch painting the title *L'Oeil écoute*, listening with one's eye. Here, however, the eye doesn't listen to what the so-called 'voices of silence' want to say in the pictures; it's plugged into the crackling of a gaze offscreen. This interest in sound, not as an emanation of an inner self but as the trace of the other, is precisely what led Artaud from the movies back to the theatre. If the movies, no longer silent, do not tolerate anything but articulated speech, the field for experiments in phonic disarticulation will have to move to the stage.

Sartre's voyeur doesn't perceive sound frontally. There is someone behind him. A presence lurking where he does not look.[6] Or where he cannot see. He is caught unawares, off guard. I've said that in the early sound theatres the screen was flanked by loudspeakers. I should have said outflanked. And if I may briefly reopen the worn-out topos of contrasting Artaud with Brecht, I'd suggest that Brechtian distantiation is primarily meant to restore the epistemological comfort of the camera obscura setting. The *Verfremdungseffekt* is meant to prevent the spectator from ever feeling outflanked. Literally as well as metaphorically, it tells the spectator to sit back, as far as possible from the stage, to fill in the buffer zone behind, so that he could safely look at the stage, sure that whatever happens will happen in front of him, between him and the stage, allowing him to watch the play without having to worry about being taken off guard, to be put in the embarrassing position of Sartre's voyeur.

Artaud uses theatre in the exact opposite way. He wants the spectator to be brought to feel uneasy, to worry that during the performance of what he thought was going to be nothing more than a spectacle, something compromising may unfold. Brought to worry that he may be caught watching. The spectator, for example, should be led suddenly to realise that, if he were to be discovered, if his gaze were to be returned to him, if instead of merely seeing he were also to be seen here, if he himself were to become the spectacle, or at least part of the spectacle, if (as Lacan said) he were to be in the picture, that could be quite embarrassing for him. Artaud wants his spectator to feel vulnerable, framed like a politician caught in the act, discovered during a police raid in a place where he shouldn't have been. It is no longer just for fun. No More Play.

And when time comes for Artaud to give a precise description of what the state of mind of his spectator should be when leaving the performance, the situation he comes up with is interesting in this regard. It is to be found in the first manifesto for the Alfred Jarry Theatre. The model he offers is that of the feelings stirred by a police raid in a brothel. 'Our emotion and our awe are at their highest pitch. Never has a more beautiful staging led to such a denouement. Guilty we surely are in equal measure as these women and cruel in equal measure to these policemen. This is truly a total spectacle. And, such a spectacle, that's the ideal theatre' (*OC* II: 21).

I'll go back, in conclusion, to some of the implications of such a choice, of giving such an exemplary value for the theatre to such a violent closure of a 'maison clos' (brothel). But first I'd like to return briefly to the sound track, since in Artaud's account of that scene, the other's gaze, here that of the police, manifests itself by means of what he describes as the 'lugubrious' sound of their professional whistles.

*

What do we know about Artaud's sound tracks? After the performance of *Les Cenci*, Artaud, in an interview, expressed regret at not having been able to install on stage 'bells ten metres high that would have surrounded the public in the middle of a swirl of vibration and forced it to surrender' (*OC* V: 299). This fantasy is the exact description of Artaud's ultimate cathartic sound effect: it occurs when the spectator feels surrounded to the point of surrendering. *Le Théâtre et son double* is filled with references to such an enveloping and powerful curvature of the sound space. 'We advocate a rotating kind of spectacle that, instead of turning the stage and the public into two worlds, sealed with no communication between them, would spread its visual and sonorous burst on to the entire mass of the public' (*OC* IV: 103). Or, again: 'The spectator is in the middle while the spectacle surrounds him' (*OC* IV: 98).[7] 'Once the stage is eliminated, the spectacle can spread to the entire theatre and, taking off the ground, will surround the spectator in the most physical ways, leaving him immersed in a constant pool of lights, images, movements, and sounds' (*OC* IV: 150). The structure of the camera obscura crumbles when the sound is liberated from the tutelage of speech. In Artaud's version, the deconstruction of the frontal subject–object relationship described by Jonathan Crary is primarily induced by means of sound effects. Soundwaves manage to circumvent the linear transitivity of visual confrontation.

I would like now to conclude by returning to some echoes of the scene of the police raid on the red-light district. Artaud's experiments in sound, we remember, were aimed at preventing it from being sucked in by the face on-screen. Sound is always offscreen; it opens up to an outdoors. And it does it in the most literal way: in real space.

Throughout Artaud's manifestos for the stage, but even more in his notes as a stage director, one is struck by how obsessed he was by what was going on outside. How impatient he was not only with the separation between the stage and the seating rows, but between theatre and street. And this wall is where Artaud's sound system was ultimately aimed: at its being transgressed, trespassed, crossed, by reinscribing street noises within the space of the theatre. By opening the theatre to the outdoor noises, Artaud's sound system was meant to force the life outside, the sound of life outside, into the space of the theatre.

Many of his notes give an impression of what could be described as a strange but fascinating barometric competition. As if the walls of the theatre, like an eardrum, were threatened by the near catastrophic difference between the high pressure of noise in the street and the silence inside the building. The task of the stage director thus consists first in raising the level of the noise within the theatre so that it matches the acoustic pressure of the street on the walls, a pressure that, in the '30s, was growing dangerously fast. For example, in the stage directions he noted for another play by his co-director at the Alfred Jarry Theatre, Vitrac's 1931 *Trafalgar's Trick*, Artaud wrote: 'From the very beginning of the act, a background noise will be established in order to make one feel the constant presence of life outside' (*OC* II: 147).

This ear for what's going on in the street is time specific. It refers explicitly to the increasing street violence of the early '30s, to the demonstrations and clashes between extreme-right and extreme-left, or between both or either of them and the riot police. Hence Artaud's mention of 'the urgent need for a theatre that events wouldn't upstage' (*OC* IV: 101), his call for a theatre that could revive 'the kind of poetry one breathes in the fairs and the crowd, on those days, all too infrequent in our times, when the people surge onto the street' (*OC* IV: 102). 'Today, in Paris, the question is one of knowing whether, before the cataclysms that have been predicted erupt, we will be able to put together the means of production, financial and otherwise, that would allow such a theatre to come to life, one which would survive in any event, since it is the future. Or if we will have to shed some real blood, right now, in order for that cruelty to be revealed.' A date is inscribed next to these lines: *May 1933* (*OC* IV: 105). And, in July 1934, in the notes that Paule Thévenin has collected under the title 'About a Lost Play', Artaud evokes a theatrical event that would exploit, he says, the nervousness 'that the public generally displays only on the occasion of extra-theatrical events, such as collective unrest, nervous collapses, casualties and triumphs of the kind that turns life itself into the most colossal tragedy' (*OC* II: 205).

It is no longer the individual spectator, but the theatrical institution itself that, being surrounded, is on the verge of surrendering. For Artaud clearly expected from the thirties that they would bring about events that would force theatre to surrender, to leave the space of representation for that, precisely, of the event (*OC* II: 19). He expected from upcoming revolutionary events that they would force theatre into staging and performing the closure of representation, force theatre off the stage, or offstage, forced to leave the stage for the street. A theatre directly tattooed, as it were, on the skin of the world, woven onto the world's own fabric – *un théâtre sur fond de monde*.

In other words, offstage but not backstage. Between stage and street, there should be no space, no gap, no third term between offstage and out-of-doors, between in and out. Artaud's scene has no margin, and his theatre no reserve. When he reviewed Pitoëff's production of *Six Characters in Search of an Author*, he praised Pirandello for having brought the wings into the middle of the stage: nothing happens behind the scene when the scene's behinds are exposed (*OC* II: 180). Conversely, when describing the type of sound effects I just referred to, Artaud was adamant that the loudspeakers should in no way suggest a backstage sound effect. It shouldn't give the impression that, behind the backdrop, there is a buffer zone, a fake outside, neither scene nor street. 'The noise background is what theatre lacks the most', Artaud asserted,

> and this is why the noises and screams that come from backstage are so ridiculously mangy and grotesque . . . One should never try to have ten extras sound like a ten-thousand-men crowd. To produce such an effect, one must use recordings of real noises whose intensity could be regulated at will by means of amplifiers and loudspeakers disseminated all across the stage and the theatre.

(*OC* II: 148–9)

*

I'll use this project for a closure of representation as my conclusion. How to exit representation? Maybe by returning to Gilles Deleuze's opposition between theatre and factory, between spectacle and production. That is, in our case, by returning theatre itself to production, by chiasmatically inscribing the spectacle within the space of production. Such a closure has a name; it is a strike. And it seems that for Artaud, indeed, at least in the early '30s, there was no better way to strike representation than forcing it into a strike.

In May 1932, the *Nouvelle revue française* had a short piece by him. Its title: 'Theatres on Strike' ('La grève des théâtres'). Artaud wrote it on the occasion of the April 5, 1932, twenty-four-hour strike of Paris's theatres; in many regards, as you will see, his characterisation of the event and of its affective resonance rings a note that is strangely similar to the previously mentioned raid of the police implementing the closure of what French people used to call 'maisons closes':

> During the past month, theatres, movie houses, dance halls, and whorehouses all over Paris began the shadow of a strike, in a purely demonstrative gesture that allowed one nevertheless to anticipate the benefits true theatre would gain from the eradication of the small-trade mentality pervasive among those involved in spectacle, all types of which, whether theatre, music hall, cabaret, or whorehouse, deserve to be wrapped in exactly the same package. In any case, for a few hours, one had the chance to witness a prodigious lift of the atmosphere, both in terms of barometer and of theatre.
>
> (*OC* II: 191)

19 Mikhail Yampolsky

From 'Voice devoured: Artaud and Borges on dubbing'*

Mikhail Yampolsky[1] is a Russian scholar of cinema and the image and author of
The Memory of Tiresias: Intertextuality and Film (University of California Press,
1998). Here he discusses Artaud's cinema writings, in particular his text on
dubbing and his lost screenplay *The Dybbuk*, in a way which goes to the question
of the relation between language and the body. These texts describe Artaud's
aversion to dubbing as the dramatised invasion of the body by foreign elements, an
invasion which he felt to be a generalised problem, not simply in the cinema but in
any use of symbolic language, and especially analogous to the way in which
language is acquired by children. It is therefore a pivotal phenomenon for Artaud.
Yampolsky makes use of a notion which he dubs 'somatic solecism' to explain the
perceptual and physical error which dubbing performs on the body of the visible
actor and for the spectator. The second half of Yampolsky's essay is not included
here, as it deals closely with a similar idea in the fiction of Borges.

Antonin Artaud's article 'Les Souffrances du dubbing' (The torments of dubbing)
appears to have been written in 1933 (*OC* III: 85–7). Discovered soon after his
death, it was published posthumously. At first glance it appears to be a
straightforward vindication of those French actors who sold their voices for
pittances to American film companies engaged in dubbing their own productions
for the foreign market. A closer look at the text will, however, reveal a connection
between 'Les Souffrances du dubbing' and a whole constellation of aesthetic
issues that transcend the narrow limits of the essay's ostensible topic.

On April 19, 1929, Artaud wrote to Yvonne Allendy to inform her that he was
completing work on the screenplay for the film *The Dybbuk* which was to contain
'sound fragments': 'I have decided to introduce sound and even *talking* portions
into all my screenplays since there has been such a push towards the talkie that in
a year or two *no-one* will want silent films any more' (*OC* III: 151). The script of
The Dybbuk did not survive, but its very title is highly suggestive. A *dybbuk* is a
character of Jewish folklore, a person inhabited by the spirit of someone who has
died and who speaks through the mouth of that person. The ghost of the deceased

torments the living person, causing him to writhe and to rave, forcing him to blaspheme against his will. This folkloric character obviously recapitulates, in its own way, the problematic of dubbing though in an inverted form: in dubbing, the film star divests the live actor of his voice; through the *dybbuk*, the voice of the deceased inhabits a living body. Nevertheless in both cases the situation remains much the same; the voice resides in someone else's body. Given his love of anagrams and glossolalia Artaud might well have identified one with the other, purposely retaining the foreign English spelling of the word *dubbing*: dubbing – dibbouk.[2] The overtly satanic subtext of an article about dubbing, which is about something 'thoroughly ghoulish' – the snatching of the personality, of the soul – is crucial.

The question of the reciprocal alienation of voice and body was by no means an academic one for Artaud; rather it struck to the very core of the artistic problems that confronted him, tormented him, and, in the end, drove him to insanity. For Artaud, the mistrust of the audible word – the word that exists prior to its utterer – is central. Its origins are obscure, for it is as if prompted and spoken by someone else – a predecessor – and in it the speaker loses his identity. The word is always a repetition; it never originates from within the body of the speaker. If Artaud strives to implant the word in the body, in breathing, in gesture, it is in order to restore the corporeality and individuality of its source. We must prevent 'the theft of the word'. Jacques Derrida describes Artaud's dilemma as follows: 'If my speech is not my breath, if my letter is not my speech, this is because my spirit was already no longer my body, my body no longer my gestures, my gestures no longer my life. The integrity of the flesh torn by all these differences must be restored in the theatre' (Derrida [1967b] 1978: 179).

In dubbing, however, the focus on eliminating the difference between word and gesture, between voice and flesh – an integral part of Artaud's poetics – confronts its antithesis: the conscious separation of voice and body, with repetition as the principle according to which words are translated from one language to another, seemingly ceasing to be their own, mechanically reproduced. The removal of differences to which Derrida refers creates a particular 'speech-affect', which originates directly from within the body and attains its fullest realisation in the scream, the howl, or the groan, as in the behaviour of the writhing *dybbuk*. Gilles Deleuze observes: 'It is a question of transforming the word into an action by rendering it incapable of being decomposed and incapable of disintegrating: *language without articulation*' (Deleuze 1990: 89).

The 'speech-affect' is to a large degree utopian; it is possible only insofar as it is linked to the presence of the body itself. Dubbing, which is decried by Artaud, blocks its manifestation, due not only to the absence of the speaker's visible body, but also to the peculiar technique of dubbing, exclusively oriented toward a maximally exact imitation of speech articulation. Artaud devotes particular attention to the articulatory technique of synchronisers – to the play of 'the facial muscles of the actors', to 'the simultaneous opening of the mouth', and to 'an equivalent quivering of the face' (*OC* III: 85–7).

At first glance this muscular technique, this cult of enunciation, binds speech to the body, to the actor's physiognomy. However, Artaud sees it principally in the method of articulation of speech, the hypertrophy of the articulatory moment. In 1931 he published a review of a film by Jean Kemm, *Le Juif polonais* (The Polish Jew, 1931), starring the famous actor Harry Baur, in which he harshly criticised the protagonist's detailed facial expression:

> One should see how this head suddenly and as if accidentally experiences a monstrous avalanche of muscular movements, as though amid the moral expression of suffering, remorse, obsessions, [and] fear, appeared only the play of muscles, bolting like horses . . . Life resonates when it reaches a certain degree of tragic expressiveness; it is the sound of the wildest frenzy, not serene in the least, and is inevitably directed outward. True dramatic acting is not a kaleidoscope of expressions displayed first with one, then another muscle, or by crudely spaced individual shrieks.
>
> (*OC* III: 80)

The soma for Artaud begins where differentiation and articulation end. Thus, the body itself becomes just as indivisible as speech. Deleuze defines such a soma as schizophrenic. Its model is a body with no extremities, a body with no organs, characterised by a lack of surface. The nondifferentiation of the body's integument, its lack of divisions or boundaries, corresponds to the indissolubility of sound. In the assessment of Baur's acting, this is particularly evident: Artaud will accept neither the discreetness or divisibility of sounds (screams) nor the dissociation of facial movements. The denial of surface is apparent in yet another signal observation: 'the sound of life', according to Artaud, is not directed outward; it is as if consumed by the body, swallowed whole. Deleuze describes the 'schizophrenic' language of the body in Artaud's conception thus:

> The first schizophrenic evidence is that the surface has split open. Things and propositions have no longer any frontier between them, precisely because bodies have no surface. The primary aspect of the schizophrenic body is that it is a sort of body-sieve. Freud emphasised this aptitude of the schizophrenic to grasp the surface and the skin as if they were punctured by an infinite number of little holes. The consequence of this is that the entire body is no longer anything but depth – it carries along and snaps up everything into this gaping depth which represents a fundamental involution. Everything is body and corporeal. Everything is a mixture of bodies, and inside the body, interlocking and penetration.
>
> (Deleuze 1990: 87)

This is why the sound of life is not directed outward and the facial integument is deprived of its play of muscles on the surface. The horror experienced by Artaud from the very sight of a dubbed film arises as a reaction against the fundamental contradiction between the external, articulatory nature of the technique of synchronisation, the fanatic attention to the micromovements of the mouth divined in the actors' speech, and a property of the actor's body such as the ability to assimilate and to swallow up the voice of another. This ability to absorb voice, to draw it inside, is captured nicely in the final metaphor of the article, the image of Moloch, 'who absorbs everything'.

Significant in Artaud's text is a particular physiological attention to the shape and movements of the actor's mouth. Indeed, if the main locus of the visual code of montage lies in the eyes (the direction of the gaze to a large degree is responsible for the spatial orientation of the scene), then the code of dubbing has as its principal locus the mouth and the synchronisation of its movements with audible speech. Artaud, striving to create an image of a mouth that is separate from the face and body, has recourse to strange epithets: 'the heavy mouth of Marlene Dietrich, the pulpy and hard mouth of Joan Crawford, or the equine mouth of Greta Garbo'. Each of the mouths of these elegant stars is heavy and pulpy; they are the mouths of cannibals, more suited to speaking than to eating.

By referring to the heavy pulpiness of the mouths of these female faces, Artaud evokes a sense of their incongruity with the ideal beauty of a star, a feeling of their carnivority, and their isolation as 'autonomous' alimentary organs. Artaud's epithets introduce a strange shift in the appearance of these beauties: it is analogous to that which can be observed when sound and articulation do not correspond, when 'the American star would scream with her mouth closed', while 'in the sound system you would hear a burst of profanity', or when 'the star, pursing her lips, would emit what seemed to be a whistle', but instead 'you would hear a cavernous bass, a whisper, or who knows what'. The discrepancy between mouth and face appears as a somatic analogue of the discrepancy between sound and articulation. An extraneous sound is analogous to a face with someone else's mouth on it.

Pierre Klossowski, in the novel *The Revocation of the Edict of Nantes*, discusses the solecism or syntactic error of gesture: 'But if solecism there be, if it is something *opposite* which the figures *utter* through this or that gesture, they must say something in order that this opposition be palpable; but painted, they are silent; does the spectator speak on their behalf, in such a way as to sense the opposite of the gesture he sees them performing?' (Klossowski 1969: 97, 98). The discovery of the somatic solecism (the discrepancy, the violation, the semantic paradox) in Klossowski comes about through an original method of dubbing, the voice-over of painted characters. In this case, exactly what the viewer says is not important. What is at issue is only that this is someone else's speech, speech imposed on the characters in the canvas from the outside. The alienness of the speech is sufficient to violate the integrity of the body, in such a way that Greta Garbo gets someone else's 'equine mouth'.

The solecism of gesture in Klossowski is the opposite of the facial articulatory movements to which Artaud took exception. If, in Artaud, the facial expressions are subordinate to the precise logic of the articulation of speech, in Klossowski, the microgesture contradicts itself and the gesticulatory syntagm of body as a whole. It is realised as the negation of articulation or, to be exact, negative articulation. In dubbing, however, the mouth's main solecism consists of the contrast in its functions. Because it is an organ of speech, it exhales sound, directs speech outward. Being an organ of ingestion, a body cavity absorbing the body, the word, or another's voice, it is as if it draws sound in, devouring the voice. Hence we see its duality: the organ of speech reveals itself to be an organ of ingestion, 'heavy', and 'pulpy'. The fundamental solecism consists in this duality. As Sigizmund Krzyzanowski ironically remarked, 'there is not enough room' for the same meanings 'in one mouth'. [. . .]

[I]n dubbing, facial expressions are already primordially distorted with respect to sound, and the face is already subject to a barely visible deformation. Everything happens as if according to a model described by the thirteenth-century cabbalist Abraham Abulafia, who maintained that to every sound of speech there corresponds a specific organ of the body: 'One has to be most careful not to move a consonant or vowel from its position, for if he errs in reading the letter commanding a certain member, that member may be torn away and may change its place or alter its nature immediately and be transformed into a different shape so that in consequence that person may become a cripple' (Scholem 1946: 138). According to the description of Abulafia's disciples, speech in some instances was accompanied by spasmodic facial contortions. Such distortive speech is primordially construed as broken, torn out of the circuit of the body – in a word, alien.

Dubbing can be described as the intrusion of foreign acoustical matter into the body, causing deformities on the surface of the body that can be defined as the 'events' of dubbing. 'Events' in this case are the changes occurring on the visible surface.

The history of psychiatry has preserved an example of such somatic changes associated with sound in *Memoirs of My Nervous Illness* by Daniel Paul Schreber, which is renowned for its subsequent interpretation by Freud and Lacan. Schreber was convinced that his body, by the will of some higher form of predestination, was being turned into a woman's and that this transformation was taking place in conjunction with the actual assault of voices and souls dwelling within his body and attempting to subjugate him to their will. One form of such domination consisted in speech coercion. It was as though the patient's mouth had been cinematically dubbed, and in terms not unlike those described by Artaud: '[I] counted out loud, particularly in French – because questions were also constantly directed at whether I could still speak "foreign languages"' (Schreber 1968: 162). The very form of the counting and the senseless repetition manifesting themselves in speech coercion are physical embodiments of the concept of the alien word, toward the transcending of which Artaud's somatic strategies were similarly directed.

The forcible transformation of one's native speech into a foreign language is only a minor episode in the possession of Schreber's mouth. Noises from the outside world penetrate his head, vibrating in unison with his words and, in essence, shaping his speech. On the pattern of the *dybbuk*, 'the lower God Ariman' penetrates his body and discourses in language 'spoken into my head', etc. (Schreber 1968: 151). This vocal obsession reaches its culminating point in the 'bellowing miracle' which occurs 'when my muscles serving the process of respiration are set in motion by the lower God (Ariman) in such a way that I am forced to emit bellowing noises' (Schreber 1968: 165).

Schreber's case history shows a few peculiarities. First of all, there is a connection between the voices and food. Ariman, tormenting the patient, resides somewhere in the depths of his stomach. The souls that enter Schreber and speak within him penetrate his body by way of his mouth; they are essentially eaten by him. 'In quite a number of other instances later I received souls or parts of souls in my mouth, of which I particularly remember distinctly the foul taste and smell which such *impure* souls cause in the body of the person through whose mouth they have entered' (Schreber 1968: 92).

This psychophagia, this vocal cannibalism, causes trouble with food, which Schreber also imputes to miracles and supernatural intrigues:

> I have had (and sometimes still have) great difficulty with meals . . . While I was eating, miracles were continually produced inside my mouth; and even the nonsensical questions continued: 'Why don't you say it (aloud)?', etc., although speaking aloud is impossible when one has one's mouth full of food . . . Frequently during meals a miracle was effected of biting my tongue. The trains of my moustache were almost regularly miracled into my mouth with the food.
>
> (Schreber 1968: 160)

Eating and the extortion of sound here are closely linked, but the extortion of sound occurs without hindrance and even without involving the speech organs, whereas eating becomes torture. However, Schreber struggles no less against the forcible extraction of sound outward than for the right to take matter inward. The 'eater's block' appears as a somatic correlate of speech coercion. The mouth is at the centre of this struggle, this 'fundamental solecism'. In Schreber's case the morbidity of this solecism can be explained by the narcissistic withdrawal of contact from the Other. Schreber does not want to assimilate the Other and speak with someone else's voice. This is precisely why ingestion and eructation of the voice turn out to be equally dramatic processes.

Lacan observed that drawing God closer and taking him away influenced Schreber's verbal behaviour. The farther removed God is in space the more laboured and nonsensical the speech of the patient becomes. Placing God – the Other to which the existence of the subject is bound – at some remove can mean 'emptying the places in which the murmur of the words is deployed' (Lacan 1977a: 204). This is precisely why the assimilation of the Other is marked in the form of speech. All speech is based on that of the Other, but with Schreber this situation assumes all the symptoms of hallucination and paranoid dementia.

Still another feature linked to Schreber's dementia is his transmutation into a woman: the literal physical transformation of his body into that of the Other which enables him to have coitus with God. Dozens of professional papers have been devoted to this delusion of transformation and its roots in paranoia, homosexuality and narcissism so that there is no need to touch upon this issue in any detail here. The special role of the mouth in this transformation should however be pointed out. Melanie Klein has shown that through contact with the mother's breast in the nursing process the mouth becomes the organ of the interiorisation of the female body. The breast as the source of infantile pleasure 'is taken in and becomes part of the ego and the infant who was first inside the mother now has the mother inside himself' (Klein 1977: 179). But this same mouth can also appear as the symbolic 'equivalent' of the anus or vagina 'transforming' the body of a man into the body of a woman. This is why the fixation on the oral region associated with the tormenting 'miracles' of sound-extortion and eating is in part responsible for the delusional feminisation of Schreber's body. His speech coercion is inseparable from this fundamental 'event' of the body's transformation. Freud observed that the magical speaking bird-souls filling Schreber's body were women penetrating his body's integument (Freud 1963: 134–55).

The case study of Schreber returns us to the problematic of dubbing in Artaud. It is significant that in the beginning of Artaud's article the examples of poor synchronisation are based precisely on the discrepancy between the sex of the visible star and that of the audible voice. In the dubbing the 'burst of profanity' and 'booming bass' correspond to a female image of the star. The voice is not presented merely as someone else's but as the voice of a man inhabiting a woman's body. This situation, incidentally, is typical of the myth of the *dybbuk*. Here is how Isaac Bashevis Singer describes the behaviour of a woman possessed by a *dybbuk*:

> And when all the elders of the town and its leaders gathered together they could not recognise her; for her shape was completely changed and her face was a chalk and her lips were twisted as with seizure (God save us) and the pupils of her eyes were turned back after an unnatural fashion; and her voice was a woman's voice and the dybbuk cried with the voice of a man with such weeping and wailing that terror seized all that were there and their hearts dissolved with fear and their knees trembled.

> (Singer 1955: 221, 222)

The change in sex appears as the final stage of the deformation of the body, initiated by eating someone else's voice, and in its own way can be inscribed into the linguistic situation of dubbing: the forcible entry of the alien voice unconsciously presents the maximal conceivable difference – the sexual –

between the speaker and the Other, the one to whom the audible speech belongs. The co-presence of man and woman in one body transforms that body into that of a Chimera, whose linguistic status will be examined below.

In Artaud's article, another aspect is worthy of note: all the characters in the article – the American stars and the unfortunate French actresses – are women. It is possible that this predominance of the female body is tied to the specific characteristic of the female voice suggested by Theodor Adorno. Analysing phonographic recordings of voices, Adorno found the following:

> Male voices can be reproduced better than female voices. The female voice easily sounds shrill – not because the gramophone is incapable of conveying high tones, as is demonstrated by its adequate reproduction of the flute. Rather, in order to become unfettered, the female voice requires the physical appearance of the body that carries it. But it is just this body that the gramophone eliminates, thereby giving every female voice a sound that is reedy and incomplete. Only there where the body itself resonates, where the self to which the gramophone refers is identical with its sound, only there does the gramophone have its legitimate realm of validity: thus Caruso's un-contested dominance. Wherever sound is separated from the body – as with instruments – or wherever it requires the body as a complement – as is the case with the female voice – gramophonic reproduction becomes problematic.
>
> (Adorno 1990: 54)

Adorno's observations were made in 1927. Today's level of sound recording technology would probably necessitate certain modifications, but they are entirely applicable to early sound film. Once they are granted in relation to the specific stage of technology, the properties of the female voice have an inade-quacy that requires a body, that requires the Other. These properties are therefore especially easily ascribed into the dramatic collision of dubbing and the somatic 'events' associated with the process. The female voice, by contrast with the male's, 'is incapable' of sounding natural without a visible body. By virtue of its inherent 'inadequacy', it is as if the female voice clamours for cannibalism, for an alien body, for pulpy, heavy mouths just waiting to devour. According to Adorno, the female voice requires a supplemental body.

The [. . .] voices inhabiting Schreber feminised the body of the German madman, the American stars of Artaud began speaking in a booming bass – and their mouths became heavy, evincing the male in female form. The devoured voices transformed his sex and distorted his sense of body by introducing the Other, the alien, into it. This somatic solecism of sound film with the paradoxical power revealed by dubbing may provide a clue to some fundamental characteristics of film as such, in which meaning arises in the barely perceptible distortion of the surface, in the somatic event. But this meaning-bearing somatic event arises on the frontier between plane and depth, around the gap – the 'mouth' – simultaneously absorbing and expelling. It is here that the illusion of transition from plane to depth and vice versa, intensified around the edges of the somatic gap, appears in the forms of the metamorphosing surface, the semantic event.

20 Francis Vanoye

'Cinemas of cruelty?'*

This brief text serves as an up-to-the-minute register of the various approaches to the cinema of cruelty under Artaud's name and after. It deals with Truffaut's collection of Bazin's writing under the heading *Cinemas of Cruelty* (a collection which relies on Artaud's ideas, but fails to mention him at all). Francis Vanoye discusses Artaud's disappointment with the 'precocious old age of the cinema' and argues, importantly, that any attempt to remain close to Artaud's ideas of cruelty in cinema (as in other media) must exclude any representations of cruelty or reductions of it to violence or schlock, as in, for example, the splatter film genre or the work of Quentin Tarantino. The piece links Artaud's thought on cinema with that of Roland Barthes and Christian Metz.

To include a programme of films and a paper on cinema in a symposium on 'The Theatres of Cruelty' seems to make perfect sense. Various film titles and the names of a number of auteurs and directors immediately come to mind. Then the doubt comes. Isn't this just dealing in the implicit? What do we understand exactly by the term 'cruelty' insofar as the cinema and its relation to Artaud are concerned? Is the cinema even compatible with Artaud's cruelty?

Artaud and the cinema, or: on disappointment

Without rehearsing the well known facts (Artaud as actor, critic, scriptwriter, aspiring director), let's examine for a minute Artaud's disappointments in relation to the cinema. Not so much in terms of the personal, insofar as these may have affected the man, but more in terms of the larger context in which they may be placed, that of the literary, artistic and cultural life of the time (roughly speaking the years 1920 to 1925 through 1935). In that perspective, Artaud's disappointment, or what Camille Dumoulié calls his 'disillusion', is, as far as cinema goes, nothing special. First, because it is the disappointment of a poet. As with a number of French poets and writers born along with the cinema (Cendrars

1897, Morand 1888, Giono 1895, Soupault 1897, Audiberti 1899), Artaud (1896) lived his relation to the cinema in three stages (or according to three states).

First, enthusiasm; the establishment of an extravagant critical/theoretical discourse: that the cinema is a new language, all the more powerful in that it does without words, a revolutionary art, articulating the real and the dream, an instrument which lays bare things the world keeps hidden. Things like the functions of thought and the depths of the psyche. According to Artaud, as well as Cendrars, Soupault, Aragon, and Epstein, the cinema is the total art form (combining music, painting, poetry). It is the modern art form par excellence in its speed, montage and interiority, but always on condition that it evade the grip of both the literary model (the novel or psychological theatre) and the temptations of a 'pure' cinema (on this point Artaud manifests the originality of his point of view).

The second phase is the confrontation with the real, with the materiality of cinema in its technical and economic aspects: being an actor (with Dreyer, Gance or Herbier), writing screenplays, selling them, attempting to shoot a film, participating in the adventure of cinematographic production. Artaud would shine for ten years, as an actor as much as a critic, though he didn't get the role he coveted in *The Fall of the House of Usher* (Epstein 1928), nor did he direct the film of his screenplay *The Seashell and the Clergyman* (Dulac 1928). In the end, he felt somehow betrayed.

Thus we come to the disappointment, the rejection of the loved object. Artaud deplored *The Precocious Old Age of the Cinema* (1933) and accused the talkie of reducing cinema's poetry and magic powers to nothing and even doubting the existence of these powers. The familiar phenomenon of invalidation: an idealised object is suddenly perceived in its always disappointing reality, and is summarily rejected. Only the Marx brothers find favour in Artaud's eyes for their 'dangerous aspect' and their propensity for bothering women . . . The same progression can be seen with Cendrars and Soupault and, in more nuanced form, with Giono or Morand, all writers having lived similar misadventures. The lost object: silent cinema. The lost illusion: that poets will take over the cinema, rescue it from the producers and the suits, so as to reach the people, to educate and move them. But the people are too distant, too alienated by the Demon of industrial and commercial cinema. So sound film serves as the scapegoat: after all it reintroduced text, literature, psychology, bad theatre and paralysed the movement of images. [. . .]

In any case with Artaud we are dealing with a hegemonic conception of dramatic art and poetry, with militant, not to say revolutionary, aims, and yet, as the cinema transparently demonstrates, it is itself a powerful instrument of suggestion which always escapes the control of the poets.

Artaud's disappointment is again nothing unusual if we take into account his position as a theoretician and practioner of the theatre. In this regard he reconnects with Bertolt Brecht, with whom he has, no doubt, little in common if not a passion for theatre and a stormy relationship to the cinema. Brecht therefore

– born in 1898, admirer of Chaplin, unsuccessful but obstinate screenwriter (*The Threepenny Opera* in 1928, *Hangmen Also Die* in 1943: two 'disappointments'), interrogated in Hollywood by the Commission for Anti-American Activities in 1947 – broke definitively with the cinema in 1948. In both cases the divorce from cinema was rationalised in two ways, after two convergent groups of arguments (I say rationalised because it is clear that both invested their time, energy and talent in the cinema, ultimately at their loss, and that it is necessary to analyse these investments with instruments other than their own, but this is not my object here). In broad terms these arguments are as follows: 1. Films are merchandise, the cinema is only a distraction from the laws of the market and the grip of capitalism on the industry; 2. Cinema is an alienating device in that it solicits the identification of the spectator with the character through emotional participation and plunges them into a hypnotic state. For Brecht this is clearly incompatible with the idea of the V-effect (distanciation) and the didactic, reflexive and political goals of his theatre. For Artaud 'everything there is of the active, of the magical' in these technical deployments of the cinema is wasted, lost because it is placed in the service of the 'ineffectual numbing' of the spectator (*OC* IV: 82).

But perhaps that which most radically condemns the cinema in relation to theatre is that it does not place the actor and the action in a real and direct co-presence with the spectator. There is too much deferral, too much representational mediation to satisfy a dramaturg, theatre director or actor. In the end the cinema thwarts both Brecht's and Artaud's projects: Brecht's in provoking immediately and collectively the movement of reflection and awareness in the audience and Artaud's affirmation that the theatre operate directly in both an organic and controlled way, structured around dreams and erotic obsessions, savagery and utopia: 'It is impossible to compare a cinematic image which, however poetic, is confined to the skin, with an image from the theatre which obeys all the demands of life' (*OC* IV: 95).

Keeping this in mind – and even if the description of *The Conquest of Mexico* in 1933 forces us to think of Eisenstein's *Que Viva Mexico!* shot in 1931, a resonance which bears witness to Artaud's fecund cinematographic imagination – we have to assume an element of betrayal in evoking the possibility of a cinema of cruelty, unless it becomes a featureless generic category.

Cinemas of cruelty

In 1975 François Truffaut collected a number of articles by André Bazin in an edition bearing the title *The Cinema of Cruelty* (Bazin 1987). Their content concerns Eric Von Stroheim, Carl T. Dreyer, Preston Sturges, Luis Buñuel, Alfred Hitchcock and Akira Kurosawa. In his preface, Truffaut only weakly justifies his choice of title, arguing that these six film-makers share 'a very particular style and a subversive cast of mind'. No reference to Artaud.

Bazin's texts, while not mentioning Artaud, focus on the notion of cruelty both indirectly and overtly. The indirect references to cruelty are made by way of discussing acting and the close up in Stroheim (*Les Rapaces* 1923) and Dreyer (*La Passion de Jeanne d'Arc* 1928) revealing the 'upheavals in the human soul', 'sexual frenzy' and 'carnal incantation'. The more direct references are made *à propos* of Buñuel and *Los Olvidados* (1950) which shows 'the objective cruelty of the world', 'the pulsating, burning affectivity' of the dream: 'the thick blood of unconsciousness which surrounds and drowns us like an open artery in a pulsing mind'. For Bazin, Buñuel touches the 'real problem': 'to probe the cruelty of creation', 'to reach the bottom of reality'. We would not have been too far from Artaud's *Letters on Cruelty* ('life is always the death of someone else', 'evil is the permanent law') (*OC* IV: 98–100), if Bazin – rushing straight from having recuperated Don Luis into a Christian ideology – hadn't pretended that Buñuel returns 'to cruelty, dialectically, in the acts of love and charity'.

If we want to stay close to Artaud while betraying him, as we must, since we are trying to promote a cinema of cruelty, we must exclude all pure and simple representations of cruelty (Sergio Leone?), all reductions of cruelty to violence, crude sadism and blood, we must therefore exclude a good part of the cinematographic production of the past and especially the present. Quentin Tarantino, for example, and his emulators, French or American, who make of cruelty an object of representation and of spectatorial pleasure. Whereas cruelty for Artaud is situated very evidently on the side of *jouissance*, if you want to refer to that perhaps too practical construction of Roland Barthes. *Jouissance* means to 'place in a state of loss', to 'shake historical, cultural or psychological foundations' (Barthes 1973: 25), to touch what Christian Metz theorised as 'filmic displeasure', the moment where the 'Id' is either insufficently or excessively stimulated (Metz 1977). Cruelty here would be found in the latter, in an excess of dream, of crime, of savagery, of terror, of energy, of nothingness, *unbounded*, to borrow a term from Artaud, or revealed, to shatter the spectator.

Barthes wrote: 'The asocial character of jouissance . . . the extreme depths of the clandestine, the dark of the cinema' (Barthes 1973: 63). What Artaud styled as 'blunt jolts', 'the diminished role of understanding', 'the encircling space of images and sounds' (*OC* IV: 84) constitutes ordinary cinema today. This is what we ask artists to produce, and what cinematographic pleasure institutes and articulates in technological and mediated culture. Cruelty can only be elsewhere.

But it can no longer be said to reside where cineastes pretend to play with the spectator's pleasure, to render them complicit in the cruelty of the world or the spread of evil. Such a puritan posture, not exempt from perversity, is beautifully illustrated by Alfred Hitchcock (see in particular *Rear Window,* 1954, or *The Birds,* 1963) and, more crudely, by Oliver Stone in *Natural Born Killers* (1999) or Michael Haneke (*Funny Games*, 1997).

Cruelty is here envisaged in a moral perspective, it doesn't speak of 'appetite for life' or 'cosmic rigour' and doesn't call forth 'an impassioned and convulsive life' as Artaud indicated (*OC* IV: 98–118), neither does it seek to reactivate great myths: it screens the torturer and the victim so as to trap the spectator.

So where are the cinemas of cruelty to be found . . . ?

In the work of those film-makers adventuring towards the depths and forcing themselves to deal with gaps, obscurities, violence, disconnections, *jouissances* which are the everyday experience of the unconscious. With the Buñuel of *Los Olvidados*, or of *Tristana* (1970). With the Bergman of the extreme films, the most stripped down, the most heavily inscribed with the theatricality of that 'other scene' (the unconscious): in films like *The Ritual, The Communicants, Hour of the Wolf, Shame, From the Life of Marionettes,* where the close-ups, the minimalist sets, the over-exposed images, carbonised and grainy, participate in the depriviliging and the ultimate dispersion of characters and actors, in the *mise-en-scène* of a vital swarming. One could add the David Lynch of *Eraserhead* or the first part of *Lost Highway.*

Also with those film-makers who, without moralising or sentimentalising too much, deal straightforwardly with the world's cruelty, as an immediate given but one which is always striking in its brazen indifference. I think of Mikio Naruse (*Floating Clouds, Sound of the Mountain*), of nearly all the work of Maurice Pialat (who discovered Artaud through Van Gogh in Artaud's text 'Van Gogh, ou le suicidé de la société'), of *Mes Petites amoureuses* by Jean Eustache, of the ends of certain films confronting us with powerful images of solitude, indifference or powerlessness (*Vivre sa vie* from J.L. Godard, *Les Parapluies de Cherbourg* by J. Demy, *Fox and His Friends* by R.W. Fassbinder . . .).

Finally, with those who, having recourse to a more sumptuous, sometimes stylised, even ideographic and hieroglyphic language, theatricalise the archetypal, and animate before our eyes and deep within us the obscure forms, the 'great shadows of destiny' after the expression of Robert Abirached (Abirached 1978): the Dreyer of *Gertrud*, the Kurosawa of *Kagemusha*, the Greenaway of *The Baby of Mâcon*, the Bresson of *Lancelot du Lac.*

But, it may be argued, what about provocation . . . and the cruelty in the situation where the spectator's comfort is disturbed? And what of Godard in *Le Weekend* and *Le Camion* by Marguerite Duras, and Bellochio, Ferreri and Garrel . . . ? and the badly treated actors – i.e. the stars, the tortured celluloid, the distorted sound? I concede a certain amount of anger, violence or rage in evidence here, the desire to shock the spectator. I don't necessarily see the cruelty proper to Artaud, at least as I perceive it, and which must go deeper to where the filmic apparatus can attain the sense of the inexorable (here we are at the antipodes of Brecht), Artaud's 'implacable necessity' (*OC* IV: 98). If it is through beauty that film carries us in that 'kind of rigid direction, the submission to necessity', then beauty is really a quasi-cruelty (see the *Van Gogh* of Pialat or *Le Vent de la nuit* of Maurice Garrel).

However, *Salo or the 120 days of Sodom* by Pier Paolo Pasolini (1975) is a separate case. This work links the implacability of the apparatus (that of libertines/assassins and that of the film) to the impassiveness of the ritual of death, and the scenography of phantasm to the stylisation of quotidian horror. Its *jouissance* (bliss/ecstasy) is inseparable from murder, including the bliss of the spectator, constrained to live the extreme experience of cinematographic insecurity since he/she is exposed to desire the point of view of the libertines. Not in the perspective of a moral or moralising reversal as in Michael Haneke (*The Piano Teacher* (2001) ES), but simply in that of experiencing at the deepest level what bliss means. *Salo* is perhaps the only film entirely relevant to a cinema of cruelty, one reason why, apparently, one must defend oneself against it (see the texts which Roland Barthes and Michel Foucault have devoted to it), to such an extent that it can no longer be incuded in the screenings at the University of Paris X . . . But it is still a matter of a cruelty in the style of cruelty. The cruelty of Artaud dates roughly to 1933, that of *Salo* comes after the camps.

Notes

Introduction

1 Thanks to Agnese Trocchi, Candida TV and DocDivago for information regarding the committee's activities.
2 Artaud describes his admiration for the transgressive themes of incest and catastrophe in this image in his chapter 'La Mise en scène et la métaphysique' (*TD*: 49–72).
3 See Nin (1966) for a powerful evocation of this event.
4 Singleton's new edition of *Artaud on Theatre* provides a welcome updating of the record in this respect. His argument that Artaud's work in theatre therefore constitutes an 'anti-theatre' is, I think, an apt summation (Artaud 1989; 2nd edn 2001: xi).
5 (*AA*: 38, 39). I use Clayton Eshleman's characteristically lively and enthusiastic translation here as it emphasises the point about the tension between scholarly processes and creative abandon in its every phrase.
6 This is a criticism that could also be made of a number of other scholars, for example Julia Kristeva's reading is similarly eager to avoid some of these aspects of Artaud: Artaud's occultism is strangely glossed in 'Le sujet en procès' as a materialist social critique (1977: 104–6). She reads Artaud's texts from Mexico as socialist revolutionary texts when Artaud is explicitly describing spiritual transformations, etc.

1 André Breton with André Parinaud

* Trans. Mark Polizzotti, New York: Paragon House, 1993 (originally published as *Entretiens radiophoniques (1913–1952)*), Paris: Gallimard, 1969).
1 *Une Vague de rêves* (*A Wave of Dreams*) was the title of a 1924 surrealist manifesto by Aragon.

2 André Breton

* In *Free Rein*, trans. Michel Parmentier and Jacqueline d'Amboise, Lincoln: University of Nebraska Press, 1995 (originally published as 'Hommage à Antonin Artaud', in *La Clé des champs*, Paris: Jean-Jacques Pauvert, 1967).

3 Georges Bataille

* In *The Absence of Myth: Writings on Surrealism*, trans. and ed. Michael Richardson, London and New York: Verso, 1994.
1 Fraenkel had written the 'Letter to the directors of the insane asylums' from the third issue of *La Révolution surréaliste*, edited by Artaud. (ES)

4 Sylvère Lotringer

* Trans. Edward Scheer.

1 This interview remains unpublished in English in its entirety. However, sections have appeared in *Impulse*, Spring 1988, 14.1: 17, 18 and *Grand Street*, Spring 1997, 15.4: 251–60, trans. Deborah Treisman. These represent only a fragment of the total text, which runs to some 60 pages in French.

2 This text has also not yet appeared in full in English, but is available in German along with the full text of the interview. See Lotringer (2002).

3 Dr Jacques Latrémolière, 'I talked about God with Antonin Artaud', *La Tour de feu*, 69, April 1961: 10–31.

4 The event was called 'The lived history of Artaud the momo' and took place at the Vieux-Colombier theatre in St Germain-des-Près. It was attended by about 900 people. Artaud spoke for four hours, without a text and often abusing the audience.

5 Actually, when Artaud was released from Rodez, he went to stay at a clinic in Ivry-sur-Seine, where he had a two-room pavilion at the edge of the property. He lived there until his death in March 1948. Earlier he had been interned at Ville-Evrard near Paris for four years from February 1939. It was from there that he came to Rodez in February 1943.

5 Gilles Deleuze

* In *The Logic of Sense*, trans. Mark Lester with Charles Stivale, ed. Constantin V. Boundas, New York: Columbia University Press, 1990 (originally published as *Logique du sens*, Paris: Minuit, 1969).

1 This chapter in *Critique et clinique* is a Deleuzian amalgam of readings of Artaud with D.H. Lawrence, Kafka, Nietzsche and, of course, Baruch Spinoza, and offers a fundamental insight into Artaud's modus operandi.

2 In an interview from 1972, Deleuze and Guattari do not deny that their approach is romantic and irresponsible; indeed, they affirm that aspect of their work (Deleuze 1990: 37, 38).

3 'Perspendicace' is a schizophrenic portmanteau word designating spirits which are held above the subject's head (*perpendiculaire*, perpendicular) and which are very perspicacious (perspicaces) (Dumas 1946: 303).

4 Antonin Artaud, 'L'Arve et l'aume, tentative antigrammaticale contre Lewis Carroll':
 Il était roparant, et les vliqueux tarands
 allaient en gibroyant et en brimbulkdriquant
 Jusque là lò la rourghe est à rouarghe a rangmbde
 Et rangmbde a rouarghambde:
 Tous les falomitards étaient les chats-huants
 Et les Ghoré Uk'hatis dans le Grabugeument.

5 Freud, 'The Unconscious', in *Metapsychology* (1915). (This can be found in Freud, *SE* XIV, p. 161. (ES)). Citing the cases of two patients, one of whom perceives his skin, and the other his sock, as systems of little holes which are in perpetual danger of becoming enlarged, Freud shows that this is a properly schizophrenic symptom which could not fit either a hysteric or an obsessed.

6 With respect to letters-organs, see Artaud 1963: 26–32.

7 See in *84*, 1948c: 'No mouth No tongue No teeth No larynx No oesophagus No stomach No intestine No anus I shall reconstruct the man that I am.' (The body without organs is fashioned of bone and blood alone.)

8 In a very fine study, Gisela Pankow has taken the examination of signs in schizophrenia very far. In connection with the cases related by Mrs Pankow, special notice should be made of the analysis of fixed alimentary words which explode into phonetic bits: 'CARAMELS', for example (Pankow 1956: 22). Also of particular

interest is the dialectic of the container and contained, the discovery of polar opposition, and the theme of water and fire which is tied to it (Pankow 1956: 57–60, 64, 67, 70); the curious invocation of fish as the sign of active revolt and of hot water as a sign of liberation (Pankow 1956: 74–9); and the distinction of two bodies – the open and the dissociated body of the man-flower, and the head without organs which serves as its complement (Pankow 1956: 69–72).

9   It is in this sense that, in Carroll, invention is essentially vocabular, rather than syntactical or grammatical. As a consequence, portmanteau words can open up an infinity of possible interpretations by ramifying the series; nevertheless, syntactical rigour eliminates a certain number of these possibilities. The same holds true in Joyce, as Jean Paris has shown in *Tel Quel* 1967, 30: 64. The opposite is the case with Artaud, but only because there is no longer a problem of sense properly speaking.

6 Jacques Derrida

*   In *Writing and Difference*, trans. Alan Bass, London: Routledge, 1978 (original version published as 'Le Théâtre de la cruauté et la clôture de la représentation', in *Critique* 230: July 1966).

1   On the integral spectacle, see *CW* 2: 31. This theme is often accompanied by allusions to participation as an 'interested emotion': the critique of aesthetic experience as disinterestedness. It recalls Nietzsche's critique of Kant's philosophy of art. No more in Nietzsche than in Artaud must this theme contradict the value of gratuitous play in artistic creation. Quite the contrary.

2   Brecht is the major representative of the theatre of alienation. Trans.

3   These questions receive an extended treatment in Derrida 1967a: 235.

4   The theatre of cruelty is not only a spectacle without spectators, it is speech without listeners. Nietzsche: 'The man in a state of Dionysean excitement has a listener just as little as the orgiastic crowd, a listener to whom he might have something to communicate, a listener which the epic narrator, and generally speaking the Apollonian artist, to be sure, presupposes. It is rather in the nature of the Dionysean art, that it has no consideration for the listener: the inspired servant of Dionysus is, as I said in a former place, understood only by his compeers. But if we now imagine a listener at those endemic outbursts of Dionysean excitement then we shall have to prophesy for him a fate similar to that which Pentheus the discovered eavesdropper suffered, namely, to be torn to pieces by the Maenads ... But now the *opera* begins, according to the clearest testimonies, with the *demand of the listener to understand the word*. What? The listener *demands*? The word is to be understood?' (Nietzsche 1964a: 40–41).

5   *Répétition* also means 'rehearsal' in French. Trans.

6   Letter to Jean Paulhan, 25 January 1936: 'I think I have a suitable title for my book. It will be *The Theatre and its Double*, for if theatre doubles life, life doubles true theatre ... This title corresponds to all the doubles of the theatre that I believe to have found over the course of so many years: metaphysics, the plague, cruelty ... It is on the stage that the union of thought, gesture and act is reconstituted' (*OC* V: 272–3).

7   To attempt to reintroduce a purity into the concept of difference, one returns it to nondifference and full presence. This movement is fraught with consequences or any attempt opposing itself to an indicative anti-Hegelianism. One escapes from it, apparently, only by conceiving difference outside the determination of Being as presence, outside the alternatives of presence and absence and everything they govern, and only by conceiving difference as original impurity, that is to say as *différance* in the finite economy of the same.

8   Nietzsche again. These texts are well known. Thus, for example, in the wake of Heraclitus: 'And similarly, just as the child and the artist play, the eternally living fire

plays, builds up and destroys, in innocence – and this game the artist plays with himself . . . The child throws away his toys; but soon he starts again in an innocent frame of mind. As soon however as the child builds he connects, joins and forms lawfully and according to an innate sense of order. Thus only is the world contemplated by the aesthetic man, who has learned from the artist and the genesis of the latter's work, how the struggle of plurality can yet bear within itself law and justice, how the artist stands contemplative above, and working within the work of art, how necessity and play, antagonism and harmony must pair themselves for the procreation of the work of art' (Nietzsche 1964b: 108).

7 Helga Finter

* Trans. Matthew Griffin, *TDR*, 41.4, Winter 1997, 15–40.
1 As, for example, in Pina Bausch's *1980* or in the work of the Canadian group Lala Human Steps.
2 As, for example, in the 1993 production *Law of Remains*.
3 Artaud produced three works for radio after World War II. In 1946 he recorded two pieces for *Club d'Essai*, a local Parisian radio station: on 8 June he recorded his text 'Les malades et les médecins', which was followed on 16 July by the reading from 'Aliénation et magie noire'. Both programmes, which were broadcast on the day after they were recorded, could until 1995 only be consulted in the archives of Radio France. These radio pieces could be said to be precursors (see Finter 1990: 130–1, 133–8) of 'Pour en finir avec le jugement de dieu', which Artaud recorded for Radio France with Maria Casarès, Roger Blin, Paule Thévenin and a *bruitage* of percussion instruments, which was edited as a tape by Virmaux in 1986. All three of the radiophonic works from 1946 to 1948 are available today on four CDs from the INA, edited together by André Dimanche (Paris, 1998) and with the title *Antonin Artaud*.
4 This represents an expansion of Derrida's thesis (in *Writing and Difference*; see Finter 1982).
5 See the work of Istvan Fonagy (1983), Françoise Dolto (1984), Denis Vasse (1974), Didier Anzieu (1985), and Julia Kristeva (1977).
6 Wolfgang Rihm, the German composer who wrote music for an opera and a ballet with Artaudian material, should also be mentioned in this context.

8 Jerzy Grotowski

* In *Towards a Poor Theatre*, trans. M. Buszewicz and J. Barba, London: Methuen, 1968.

9 Jane Goodall

* *Modern Drama* 33, December 1990, 529–42.
1 In this chapter *TD* refers to the version of Antonin Artaud, *Le Théâtre et son double*, in *Oeuvres Complètes*, IV, Paris, 1978. All quotations from Artaud's work translated by the author.
2 The first French translation of *Totem and Taboo* appeared in 1924 and the correlation between its vocabulary and that of Artaud's Preface to *Le Théâtre et son double* is remarked upon by the Gallimard editors. Artaud's own experience of psychoanalysis with René Allendy (a founder member of the Freud-inspired Psychoanalytic Society of Paris) is likely to have intensified his awareness of Freudian theory and his reactions to it.
3 See Goodall (1994).

10 Herbert Blau

* In *The Dubious Spectacle: Extremities of Theatre, 1976–2000*, Minneapolis/London: University of Minnesota Press, 2002 (originally published in 2000).

11 Susan Sontag

* In Artaud (1976) *Antonin Artaud: Selected Writings*, New York: Farrar, Strauss and Giroux, republished 1988, Los Angeles: University of California Press (originally published in *The New Yorker*, 19 May 1973).

12 Leo Bersani

* In *A Future for Astyanax: Character and Desire in Literature*, Boston and Toronto: Little, Brown and Co., 1976.
1 All the translations from Artaud are the author's.
2 *Any* code is, of course, unthinkable without repetition. In a sense, Artaud's project is obviously absurd, but the devaluation of verbal language has important consequences for the theatre. Repetition can't be abolished, but the psychology supported by rational discourse can be replaced by a purely scenic psychology already pointed to in the *Illuminations*.
3 Birth is the origin of derivation in an individual's life, although this is obviously not the same thing as saying that it is the origin of Artaud's traumatised interpretation of birth. The (hypothetical) origins of an obsession inevitably get lost in our enactments of it. Artaud's horror of being born may, after all, be the retroactive effect on his memory of birth of a view of defecation as a loss of self. But such causal origins are, in fact, impossible to locate. Artaud's hatred of derivation and repetition exists nowhere apart from his performances of that hatred; there is no unperformed source from which all versions of the theme proceed.
4 They may also be meant to seduce reality into conforming to desire. Our very willingness to admit the fictive status of our stories about the world suggests a wish to strike a bargain with the world. More secretly, we hope that fiction will have an energy sufficient to transform the world and thus return us to that harmony between desire and reality which would make fictional narratives obsolescent …

13 Maurice Blanchot

* In *The Blanchot Reader*, trans. Ian MacLachlan, ed. Michael Holland, Cambridge, MA: Blackwell, 1995 (originally published in *Nouvelle Revue Française*, 47, November 1956, 873–81).

14 Julia Kristeva

* In *The Tel Quel Reader*, trans. Patrick ffrench, London: Routledge, 1998 (originally published 1972).
1 This notion of the *chora* first appears in Plato's *Timaeus*, in the section dealing with the descriptions of that which existed prior to the formation of the cosmos (Plato 1970: 219). Kristeva adapts this concept to the formation of the subject. Her footnote, which is a small essay in itself, details her use of the idea and suggests its indebtedness to Derrida.

2   (*SW:* 26). In this translation the subject of the sentence is mistakenly given as Rimbaud, not Mallarmé. Trans.

15   Jacques Derrida

*   In *The Secret Art of Antonin Artaud*, trans. Mary Ann Caws, Cambridge, MA, and London: MIT Press, 1998 (originally published as 'Forcener le subjectile' 1986).
1   A fragment of this has been previously translated by Mary Ann Caws as 'Maddening the subjectile' in *Yale French Studies*, 84, 1994, pp. 154–71.
2   Derrida refers the reader here to 'Recherche d'un monde perdu' (The Search for a Lost World), published in the same volume in which this essay appeared (most recently *The Secret Art of Antonin Artaud*, Cambridge, MA, and London: MIT Press, 1998), and to a number of Thévenin's other publications notably 'Entendre/voir/lire' (Hearing/Seeing/Reading), *Tel Quel*, 39 (Fall 1969) and 40 (Winter 1970). (ES)
3   Derrida lists three definitions here which, for reasons of economy, have not been included. (ES)
4   At the moment when these pages were written they were supposed to appear first, in fact only, in German translation. Trans.
5   The translation here is from A. Artaud (1976) *Antonin Artaud: Selected Writings*, ed. Susan Sontag, trans. Helen Weaver, New York: Farrar, Strauss and Giroux, p. 234.
6   Artaud does to the French language what he does to the subjectile. [. . .]
    'We have to vanquish French without leaving it, For 50 years it has held me in its tongue. Now I have another tongue under [sic] tree.' [. . .]
       We will verify it later, you have to repair the sick body, make it as new, really, take it back to the very beginning as an egg, have it born again. And that will be true for the subjectile as much as for French:
       'As for French, it makes you sick, it is the sickest, with a sickness, tiredness, that makes you believe that you are French, that is to say, finished, a person finished.' [. . .]
7   The *trajectory* (as well as the spurt or the eject of a projectile), in other words the path (sent, *set*) of the *forcènement* is what we will try to follow here among a number of languages.
8   This translation is from A. Artaud (1976) *Antonin Artaud: Selected Writings*, Susan Sontag (ed.), p. 499.
9   This translation is from A. Artaud (1976) *Antonin Artaud: Selected Writings*, Susan Sontag (ed.), p. 500.

16   Umberto Artioli

*   Trans. Edward Scheer and Jane Goodall (originally published in *Europe*, 667, 668, November–December 1984, 132–47).
1   See Artioli and Bartoli (1978). Their book, *Theatre and the Glorious Body*, identifies three phases in Artaud's 'theatrology': the juvenile, the metaphysical and the materialist. The first part of this essay is concerned with the shift from the second to the third of these.

17   Allen S. Weiss

*   In *Art and Text*, 37, September 1990, 56–9.
1   'Pour en finir avec le jugement de dieu' was commissioned by Radiodiffusion française in November 1947, and recorded between 22 and 29 November of that year, with sound effects added later. It was scheduled for broadcast on the evening of

2 February 1948, but the broadcast was cancelled at the last moment by the director of French radio, Wladimir Porché, who claimed that the public had to be spared from such a vicious, obscene, anti-American and anti-Catholic work. Despite the protestations of numerous French intellectuals who heard the tape in a private audition, the interdiction held, and the tape was not aired until approximately 30 years later. (The text of 'Pour en finir avec le jugement de dieu' appears in *OC* XIII: 65–104.) All translations are the author's.

2 On glossolalia, see the works cited in Weiss (1989). See also the two issues of *Le Discours psychanalytique* (March and June 1983), edited by Jean-Jacques Courtine; and the issue of *Langages*, 91, Paris: Larouse, 1988, also edited by Courtine.

3 Artaud's pronunciation of his glossolalia (whose written phonetic structure is borrowed from Turkish and Greek, his mother's 'mother tongue') was not quite French, as Paule Thévenin explains in a note to *Artaud le Mômo*: 'For the most part his pronunciation was closer to the Italian than to the French. For example, the /h/ is never mute; /u/ is pronounced /ou/; /z/ is pronounced /dz/; /g/ is always hard, and slightly general when followed by /h/; the final /ch/ is pronounced somewhat like the German /ch/' (*OC* XII: 276). These transformations of the French language become pertinent and distinctive features of Artaud's written and spoken texts, thus a highly marked feature of his theatrical (and not only psychopathological) enunciations.

4 On the scatological implications of early modernist poetic glossolalia, see Michelson (1982).

5 On the excremental symbolism and surrealist poetics, see Weiss (1989).

6 The section on psycho-phonetics in this article is deeply indebted to Fonagy (1983), which provides an excellent synthesis and rich interpretation of current research.

7 See Fonagy (1983) for the empirical research on the relations between sound and meaning; this statistical research provides strong evidence for the non-arbitrary relation between signifier and signified, in contradistinction to Saussure's linguistic model.

18 Denis Hollier

* *October*, 80, Spring 1997, 27–37.

1 Due to the author's dissatisfaction with the existing English translations of Artaud's writings all quotations within this essay have been translated by the author and are cited to the French.

2 Jean-Richard Bloch, for example, writes that the past century 'was the century of sight. Our twentieth announces itself as its opposite, on these as well as other matters. With talking machines, wireless, sound movies, one has to anticipate that the ear will take its revenge' (Bloch 1930: 198–9). In April 1931, Artaud wrote to Bloch asking for his support (*OC* V: 53–4).

3 Margit Rowell (curator), *Antonin Artaud: Works on Paper,* New York: MOMA, 1996.

4 Pierre Lazareff, in *Paris-Midi*, December 18, 1928, qtd in *OC* II: 315.

5 'A rustling of branches, or the sound of a footstep followed by silence' (Sartre 1956: 346).

6 The canonical text for how to focus on what escapes sight is Jean Paulhan's 1938 'La demoiselle aux miroirs' (see Paulhan 1966).

7 See also 'placed in the middle of the action, the spectator is shrouded and so to speak grooved by it' (*OC* IV: 115).

19 Mikhail Yampolsky

* Trans. Larry P. Joseph, *October*, 64, Spring 1993, 57–77.

1 An alternative spelling of the author's name is Iampolski. I am using the spelling from the original translation. (ES)
2 For a discussion of Artaud's anagrams, see Yampolsky (1991: 129–33).

20 Francis Vanoye

* Trans. Edward Scheer (originally published in *Les Théâtres de la cruauté: Hommage à Antonin Artaud*, ed. Camille Dumoulié, Paris: Desjonquères, 2000, 198–204).

Bibliography

Abirached, R. (1978) *La Crise du personnage dans le théâtre moderne*, republished (1994), Paris: Gallimard.

Adorno, T. (1990) 'The curves of the needle', trans. Thomas Y. Levin, *October,* 55: 49–55.

Anzieu, D. (1985) *Le Moi-peau*, Paris: Dunod.

Artaud, A. (1927) *L'Ombilic des limbes suivi de Le Pèse-nerfs et autres textes*, Paris: Gallimard nrf.

—— ([1938] 1964) *Le Théâtre et son double*, Paris: Gallimard; trans. Mary Caroline Richards (1958) *The Theatre and its Double*, New York: Grove Press.

—— (1946) *Lettres de Rodez*, Paris: G.L.M.

—— (1947) 'L'Arve et l'aume, tentative antigrammaticale contre Lewis Carroll', *L'Arbalète*, 12.

—— ([1947] 1979) 'Dix ans que le langage est parti . . .', *Luna Park*, 5: 8.

—— (1948a) 'Aliéner l'acteur' ('To alienate the actor'), *L'Arbalète*, 13.

—— (1948b) 'Le Théâtre et la science' ('Theatre and science'), *L'Arbalète*, 13.

—— (1948c) 'Le Théâtre de la cruauté', *84,* 5–6: 109–24.

—— (1958) 'Letter to Pierre Loeb, 23th April 1947', in *Les Lettres nouvelles* 59: 481–6.

—— (1961) *Collected Works*, vols 1–4. Vols. 1, 2, 4 trans. Victor Corti; vol. 3 trans. Alastair Hamilton, London: Calder and Boyers.

—— (1963) 'Le Rite du peyotl', in *Les Tarahumaras*, Paris: Arbalete.

—— (1965) *Artaud Anthology*, ed. Jack Hirschman, San Francisco: City Lights Books.

—— (1968) 'Lettres à André Breton, 28 February 1947', *L'Éphémère*, 8: 319, 20–5.

—— (1969) 'Lettre à André Breton, 23 April 1947', *L'Éphémère*, 11: 50.

—— (1971) 'Notes pour une "Lettre aux Balinais"', *Tel Quel*, 46: 10–34.

—— (1976) *Antonin Artaud: Selected Writings,* trans. Helen Weaver, ed. Susan Sontag, New York: Farrar, Strauss and Giroux, republished 1988, Los Angeles: University of California Press. See especially the following: 'Alfred Jarry Theatre, first season, 1926–7' (*SW*: 157–9); 'Rimbaud and the moderns' (*SW*: 26); 'Dinner is served' (*SW*: 103); 'Letter to René Allendy' (*SW*: 168–71); 'Manifesto in clear language' (*SW*: 108, 109).

—— (1976–) *Oeuvres Complètes*, 26 vols (of 30 prepared), Paris: Gallimard. See especially the following: 'Van Gogh, ou le suicidé de la société' (*OC* XIII: 9–64); *Suppôts et suppliciations* (comprises volume 14 of the *OC* in two parts: XIV* and XIV**); 'Pour en finir avec le jugement de dieu' (*OC* XIII: 65–104); *Héliogabale ou l'anarchiste couronné* (*OC* VII: 13–137); *Ci-gît* (*OC* XII: 75–100); *Les Cenci* (*OC* IV); *Cahiers de Rodez (May–June 1945)* (*OC* XVII); 'À propos d'une pièce perdue' (*OC* II:

159–61); 'À Jean Paulhan, 16 December 1932' (*OC* III: 285–90); *Le Théâtre et son double* (*OC* IV).

—— (1977) *Nouveaux Écrits de Rodez*, Paris: Gallimard.

—— (1989; 2nd edn 2001) *Artaud on Theatre*, trans. and ed. B. Singleton and C. Schumacher, London: Methuen Drama.

—— (1995) *Watchfiends and Rack Screams: Works from the Final Period*, ed. and trans. C. Eshleman with B. Bador, Boston: Exact Change.

—— (1996) 'Letter to André Breton, 28 February 1947', trans. Yvonne Houlton, *Interstice*, 2: 33–4.

Artioli, U. (1984) 'Production de "réalité" ou faim d'impossible?', *Europe*, 667, 668: 132–47.

Artioli, U. and Bartoli, F. (1978) *Teatro e corpo glorioso*, Milano: Feltrinelli.

Barber, Stephen (1993) *Antonin Artaud: Blows and Bombs,* London and Boston: Faber and Faber.

Barthes, R. (1973) *Le Plaisir du texte*, Paris: Seuil.

—— (1977) 'From work to text', *Image – Music – Text*, ed. and trans. Stephen Heath, London: Fontana.

—— (1980) *Le Chambre claire: Note sur la photographie*, Paris: Seuil.

—— (1982) 'La Musique, la voix, la langue', *L'Obvie et l'obtus*, Paris: Seuil.

—— (1994) *Oeuvres Complètes: 1966–1973*, vol. 2, Paris: Seuil.

Bataille, G. (1970) *Oeuvres Complètes: Écrits posthumes 1922–1949,* vol. 2, Paris: Gallimard.

—— (1987) *Eroticism*, trans. Mary Dalwood, London: Boyars.

—— (1994) *The Absence of Myth: Writings on Surrealism*, trans. and ed. Michael Richardson, London and New York: Verso.

Baudrillard, J. (1983) *Simulations*, trans. Paul Foss, Paul Patton and Philip Beitchman, New York: Semiotext(e).

Bazin, A. (1987) *Le Cinéma de la cruauté*, Paris: Champs, Contre-Champs, Flammarion.

Bersani, L. (1976) *A Future for Astyanax: Character and Desire in Literature*, Boston and Toronto: Little, Brown and Co.

Blanchot, M. (1959) 'Artaud', *Le Livre à venir*, Paris: Gallimard.

—— (1969) 'La Cruelle Raison poétique', *L'Entretien infini*, Paris: Gallimard.

Blau, H. (2002) *The Dubious Spectacle: Extremities of Theatre, 1976–2000*, Minneapolis/London: University of Minnesota Press.

Bloch, J.-R. (1930) *Destin du théâtre,* Paris: Gallimard.

Boulez, P. (1966) *Relevé d'apprenti*, Paris: Seuil.

Boulez, P. and Cage, J. (1991) *Correspondence*, ed. Jean-Jacques Nattiez, Paris: Bourgois.

Brecht, B. (1964a) 'Alienation effects in Chinese acting', in *Brecht on Theatre: The Development of an Aesthetic*, ed. and trans. John Willett, New York: Hill and Wang.

—— (1964b) 'A short organum for the theatre', in *Brecht on Theatre: The Development of an Aesthetic*, ed. and trans. John Willett, New York: Hill and Wang.

Breton, A. (1967) 'Hommage à Antonin Artaud'; trans. Michel Parmentier and Jacqueline d'Amboise (1995) 'Homage to Antonin Artaud', in *Free Rein,* Lincoln: University of Nebraska Press.

—— (1969; 2nd edn 1972) *Manifestoes of Surrealism*, trans. Richard Seaver and Helen R. Lane, Ann Arbor: University of Michigan Press.

Breton, A. and Parinaud, A. (1969) *Entretiens radiophoniques (1913–1952)*; trans. Mark Polizzotti (1993) *Conversations: The Autobiography of Surrealism*, New York: Paragon House.

Brunel, L. (1982) 'Avec John Cage', *Avant-Scène: Ballet/Danse*, 10: 66–73.

Castarède, M.-F. (1987) *La Voix et ses sortilèges*, Paris: Les Belles Lettres.

Chemana, R. (1993) *Dictionnaire de la psychoanalyse*, Paris: Larousse.

Chion, M. (1990) *L'Audio-Vision*, Paris: Nathan.

Deleuze, G. (1969) *Logique du sens*; trans. Mark Lester with Charles Stivale (1990) *The Logic of Sense*, ed. Constantin V. Boundas, New York: Columbia University Press.

—— (1979) 'The schizophrenic and language: surface and depths in Lewis Carroll and Antonin Artaud', *Textual Strategies*, ed. and trans. Josué Harari, New York: Cornell University Press.

—— (1990) *Pourparlers*, Paris: Minuit.

—— (1993) 'Pour en finir avec le jugement', *Critique et clinique*, Paris: Minuit.

Deleuze, G. and Guattari, F. (1972) *L'Anti-oedipe*; trans. Robert Hurley, Mark Seem and Helen R. Lane (1977) *Anti-Oedipus*, New York: Viking Press, reprinted 1983 Minneapolis: University of Minnesota.

—— (1980) *Mille plateaux*; trans. Brian Massumi (1988) *A Thousand Plateaus*, London: Athlone Press.

Derrida, J. (1967a) *De la Grammatologie*; trans. Gayatri Spivak (1976) *Of Grammatology*, Baltimore and London: Johns Hopkins University Press.

—— (1967b) 'La Parole soufflée', trans. Alan Bass (1978) in *Writing and Difference*, London: Routledge.

—— (1967c) 'The theatre of cruelty and the closure of representation', trans. Alan Bass (1978) in *Writing and Difference*, London: Routledge.

—— (1986) 'Forcener le subjectile'; trans. Mary Ann Caws (1998) 'To unsense the subjectile', in *The Secret Art of Antonin Artaud*, Cambridge, MA, and London: MIT Press.

Dolto, F. (1984) *L'Image inconscient du corps*, Paris: Seuil.

Dumas, G. (1946) *Le Surnaturel et les dieux d'après les maladies mentales*, Paris: PUF.

Dumoulié, C. (1996) *Antonin Artaud*, Paris: Seuil.

Esslin, M. (1976) *Artaud*, Glasgow: Fontana/Collins.

Finter, H. (1982) 'Die soufflierte Stimme. Klangtheatralik bei Schoenberg, Artaud, Jandl, Wilson und anderen', *Theater Heute*, I: 45–51.

—— (1990) *Der Subjektive Raum,* vols 1 and 2, Tübingen: Narr.

—— (1994) 'Disclosure(s) of re-Presentation: performance hic et nunc', in *REAL: Yearbook of Research in English and American Literature 10*, Tübingen: Aesthetics and Contemporary Discourse.

—— (1996) 'Der Körper und sein Doubles'; trans. Matthew Griffin (1997) 'The body and its doubles: on the (de-)construction of femininity on stage', *Women and Performance,* 9.2.

—— (1997) 'Antonin Artaud and the impossible theatre: the legacy of the theatre of cruelty', trans. Matthew Griffin, *TDR*, 41.4: 15–40.

Fonagy, I. (1983) *La Vive voix: Essais de psycho-phonétique*, Paris: Payot.

Foucault, M. (1961) *Folie et déraison. Histoire de la folie à l'âge classique*, Paris: Plon, republished 1972 as *Histoire de la folie à l'âge classique*, Paris: Gallimard.

—— (1966*) Les Mots et les choses*, Paris: Gallimard.

ffrench, P. and Lack, R.-F. (eds) (1998) *The Tel Quel Reader,* London and New York: Routledge.

Freud, S. (1953–75) *The Standard Edition of the Complete Psychological Works of Sigmund Freud,* Vol. XIV, trans. and ed. James Strachey, Anna Freud, Alix Strachey and Alan Tyson, London: Hogarth Press.

—— (1963) 'Psychoanalytic notes upon an autobiographical account of a case of paranoia (dementia paranoides)', in P. Rieff (ed.) *Three Case Histories,* New York: Collier Books.

—— (1985) *Totem and Taboo,* in *Pelican Freud Library,* vol. 13, ed. and trans. James Strachey, Harmondsworth: Pelican.

Girard, R. (1977) *Violence and the Sacred,* trans. P. Gregory, Baltimore: Johns Hopkins University Press.

Goebbels, H. (1993) *Les Nouvelles maladies de l'âme,* Paris.

Goodall, J. (1990) 'The plague and its powers in Artaudian theatre', *Modern Drama,* 33: 529–42.

—— (1994) *Artaud and the Gnostic Drama,* Oxford: Clarendon Press.

Greene, N. (1970) *Antonin Artaud: Poet Without Words,* New York: Simon and Schuster.

Grotowski, J. (1968) *Towards a Poor Theatre,* trans. M. Buszewicz and J. Barba, London: Methuen.

Hayman, R. (1977) *Artaud and After,* Oxford: Oxford University Press.

Hegel, G.W.F. (1971) *The Phenomenology of Mind,* trans. J.B. Baillie, London and New York: Allen and Unwin.

Heidegger, M. (1959) *Unterwegs zur Sprache,* Pfullingen: Neske.

Henric, J. and Thévenin, P. (1992) 'Paule Thévenin. Ma rencontre avec Antonin Artaud', *Art Press,* 155: 59–61.

Hollier, D. (1997) 'The death of paper, part two: Artaud's sound system', *October,* 80: 27–37.

Jonas, H. (1963) *The Gnostic Religion,* Boston: Beacon Press.

Kaufmann, V. (1993) 'Life by the letter', trans. Caren Litherland, *October,* 64: 91–105.

Klein, M. (1977) *Envy and Gratitude and Other Works, 1946–1963,* New York: Delta.

Klossowski, P. (1969) *Roberte ce soir and the Revocation of the Edict of Nantes,* trans. Austryn Wainhouse, New York: Grove Press.

Knapp, B. (1971) *Antonin Artaud: Man of Vision,* New York: Discus Books.

Kristeva, J. (1974) *La Révolution du langage poétique*; trans. Leon S. Roudiez (1984) *Revolution in Poetic Language,* New York: Columbia University Press.

—— (1977) *Polylogue,* Paris: Seuil.

—— (1980a) *Desire in Language,* trans. Leon S. Roudiez, Oxford: Basil Blackwell. This is a translation of some of the chapters comprising *Polylogue.*

—— (1980b) *Pouvoirs de l'horreur*; trans. Leon S. Roudiez (1982) *Powers of Horror: An Essay on Abjection,* New York: Columbia University Press.

—— (1986) 'A question of subjectivity – an interview', *Women's Review,* 12: 19–21.

Lacan, J. (1966) *Écrits,* Paris: Seuil.

—— (1977a) 'On a question preliminary to any possible treatment of psychosis', in *Écrits: A Selection,* trans. Alan Sheridan, New York: Norton.

—— (1982) 'Hamlet, le desir de la mère'; trans. (1977b) 'Desire and the interpretation of desire in Hamlet', in S. Felman (ed.) *Literature and Psychoanalysis: The Question of Reading Otherwise,* New Haven, CT: Yale French Studies.

Laporte, R. (1975) *Quinze Variations sur un thème biographique,* Paris: Flammarion.

Latrémolière, J. (1961) 'I talked about God with Antonin Artaud', *La Tour de feu*, 69: 10–31.

Lotringer, S. (2002) *Antonin Artaud und der gute Mensch von Rodez*, Vienna: Schlebrügge.

Lotringer, S. and Latrémolière, J. (1988) 'I talked about God with Antonin Artaud' (interview), *Impulse*, 14.1: 17, 18; trans. Deborah Treisman (1997) *Grand Street*, 15.4: 251–60.

Maeder, T. (1978) *Antonin Artaud*, Paris: Plon.

Martin, J. (1991) *Voice in Modern Theatre*, London: Routledge.

de Mèredieu, F. (1983) *Antonin Artaud: portraits et gris-gris*, Paris: Blusson.

—— (1992) *Antonin Artaud, les couilles de l'ange*, Paris: Blusson.

Metz, C. (1977) *Le Signifiant imaginaire*, Paris: Union Générale d'éditions, republished (1993) by Christian Bourgois.

Michelson, A. (1982) 'De Stijl. Its other face: abstraction and cacophony, or what was the matter with Hegel?', *October*, 22.

Moissi, A. (1927) 'Der Erlkönig', *Sound recording No. 60 U 24/528584*, Frankfurt a.M.: Deutsches Rundfunkarchiv.

Nietzsche, F. (1963) *Par-delà le bien et le mal*, trans. G. Bianquis, Paris: Aubier.

—— (1964a) 'On music and words', in *Early Greek Philosophy*, trans. Maximilian Mugge, New York: Russell and Russell.

—— (1964b) 'Philosophy during the tragic age of the Greeks', in *Early Greek Philosophy*, trans. Maximilian Mugge, New York: Russell and Russell.

Nin, A. (1966) *The Diary, 1931–1934*, New York: Harcourt, Brace and World.

Pankow, G. (1956) *Structuration dynamique dans la schizophrénie,* Bern: Verlag Hans Huber.

—— (1969) *L'homme et sa psychose*, Paris: Aubier.

Paulhan, J. (1966) *Oeuvres Complètes*, vol. 2, Paris: Cercle du Livre précieux.

Plato (1970) *The Dialogues of Plato, vol. 3: Timaeus and Other Dialogues*, trans. Benjamin Jowlett, ed. R.M. Hare and D.A. Russell, London: Sphere Books.

Poe, E.A. (1985) 'The masque of the red death', in *The Complete Tales of Mystery and Imagination*, London: Octopus Books.

Rey, J.-M. (1991) *La Naissance de la poésie: Antonin Artaud*, Paris: Éditions Métailié.

Rosolato, G. (1978) 'L'Expulsion', in *La Relation d'inconnu*, Paris: Gallimard.

Rousseau, J.-J. (1960) *Letter to M. d'Alembert*, trans. Allan Bloom, Glencoe: Free Press.

Sartre, J.-P. (1956) *Being and Nothingness*, trans. Hazel E. Barnes, New York: Washington Square Press.

Scheer, E. (ed.) (2000) *One Hundred Years of Cruelty: Essays on Artaud*, Sydney: Artspace and Power Publications.

Scholem, G. (1946) *Major Trends in Jewish Mysticism*, New York: Schocken Books.

Schreber, D.P. (1968) *Memoirs of My Nervous Illness*, trans. Ida MacAlpine and Richard A. Hunter, Cambridge, MA: Harvard University Press.

Seneca (1953) *Thyestes*, in *Seneca's Tragedies*, vol. 2, trans. Frank Justus Miller, London: The Loeb Classical Library.

Shyer, L. (1989) *Robert Wilson and His Collaborators*, New York: Theatre Communications Group.

Singer, I.B. (1955) *Satan in Goray*, New York: Noonday Press.

Singleton, B. (1998) *Artaud: Le Théâtre et son double*, London: Grant and Cutler.

Sollers, P. (1968) *Logiques*, Paris: Seuil.

—— (1973) 'L'État Artaud', in P. Sollers (ed.) *Artaud* (proceedings from the 1972 Cerisy conference), Paris: 10/18, Union Générale d'éditions.

Thévenin, P. (1969) 'Entendre/Voir/Lire', *Tel Quel*, 39, 40: 1–91.

—— (1993) *Antonin Artaud, ce deséspéré qui vous parle*, Paris: Seuil.

Tourneur, C. (l967) *The Revenger's Tragedy*, ed. B. Gibbons, London: Benn.

Vanoye, F. (2000) 'Cinémas de la cruauté?', in Camille Dumoulié (ed.) *Les Théâtres de la cruauté: Hommage à Antonin Artaud*, Paris: Desjonquères.

Vasse, D. (1974) *L'Ombilic et la voix*, Paris: Seuil.

Virmaux, A. and Virmaux, O. (1976) 'La Séance du Vieux Colombier (ou le discours abandonné)', in R. Borderie and J.J. Pauvert (eds) *Obliques 10, 11*, Paris: HAR/PO.

—— (1979) *Artaud: un bilan critique*, Paris: Belfond.

—— (1980) *Artaud vivant*, Paris: Nouvelles éditions Oswald.

Weiss, A. S. (1989) *The Aesthetics of Excess*, Albany: SUNY Press.

—— (1990) 'K', *Art and Text*, 37: 56–9.

—— (1992) *Shattered Forms: Art Brut, Phantasms, Modernism*, New York: SUNY Press.

—— (1994) 'Radio, death and the devil. Artaud's *Pour en finir avec le jugement de dieu*', in Douglas Kahn and Gregory Whitehead (eds) *Wireless Imagination: Sound, Radio and the Avant-Garde*, Massachusetts, London: MIT Press.

—— (1995) *Phantasmic Radio*, Durham and London: Duke University Press.

—— (2000) *Feast and Folly: Cuisine, Intoxication, and the Poetics of the Sublime*, Albany: SUNY Press.

—— (2002) *Breathless: Sound Recording, Disembodiment, and the Transformation of Lyrical Nostalgia*, Middletown, CT: Wesleyan.

Winnicott, D. (1971) *Playing and Reality*, London: Tavistock Publications.

Wolff, P. (1960) 'The natural history of crying and other vocalisations in early infancy', in B.M. Foxx (ed.) *Determinants of Infant Behaviour IV*, London: Methuen.

Wright, E. (1989) *Postmodern Brecht: A Re-presentation*, London, New York: Routledge.

Yampolsky, M. (1991) 'O stat'e Grashiny Shimchik-Kliushchchinskoi', *Kinovedcheskie zapiski*, 9: 129–33.

—— (1993) 'Voice devoured: Artaud and Borges on dubbing', trans. Larry P. Joseph, *October*, 64: 57–77.

—— (1998) *The Memory of Tiresias: Intertextuality and Film*, Los Angeles: University of California Press.

Index

Note: the notes have not been indexed.

Abirached, R. 182
abomination 75
'About a Lost Play' 167
Abramovic, M. 49
abstract theatre 40
Abulafia, A. 173
ac/dc 95
acting 85, 160, 179
action-word 33
Adorno, T. 176
alchemy 139
Alfred Jarry Theatre 84, 93, 160, 161, 165, 166
'all critical commentary is pigshit' 7–8
Allendy, R. 4, 89
Allendy, Y. 89, 160, 162–3, 169
'another form of civilization' 92
Anti-Oedipus 69, 117, 137, 142, 144, 145, 146
anti-representational performance 2
'Antonin Artaud and the impossible theatre: the legacy of the theatre of cruelty' 47–58
Antonius and Cleopatra 49
'Approaching Artaud' 83–95
Aragon 179
Aran Islands 95
Arden of Feversham 94
Ariman 174
Arnim 15
Arrabal 94
art 3, 84, 85, 86, 87–8, 89, 90
'Artaud' 109–15
Artaud at 1987 documenta 56
'Artaud, defecation and birth' 96–106
Artaud and the Gnostic Drama 65
Artaud le Mômo 47

Artioli, U. 137–47
Atlas, C. 49
Audiberti 179
Aurélia 15

Baby of Mâcon, The 182
Bacchae, The 94
Balcony, The 79
Balinese theatre 61–2, 91, 97
Barber, S. 4, 6
Barthes, R. 6–7, 53, 81, 157, 178, 181, 183
Bataille, G. 16–20, 47
Baudellaire 10, 88, 163
Baudrillard, J. 77, 81
Baur, H. 171
Bazin, A. 178, 180–1
Beard, The 95
Beckett 102
being 42
Being and Nothingness 164
Bellochio 182
Bene, C. 94
Benjamin, W. 79, 88
Bergman 182
Bersani, L. 96–106
Beyond Good and Evil 144
Birds, The 181
birth 100–2, 104
Birth of Philosophy, The 42
Birth of Tragedy, The 91
Blanchot, M. 19, 109–15
Blau, H. 5, 77–82
Blin, R. 41
body of the voice 53–6
body without organs 6, 145–6
Bosch 138

Boulez, P. 56
Brando, M. 78
Breathless: Sound Recording, Disembodiment and the Transformation of Lyrical Nostalgia 151
Brecht, B. 59, 62, 78–9, 81, 90–1, 95, 165, 179–80, 182
Bresson 182
Breton, A. 5, 11–13, 14–15, 48, 92
Breughel 138
Brook, P. 5, 24, 59, 106
Brunel, L. 56
Brunius 29
Büchner 94
'Buddhist Schools, Letter to the' 12, 92
Bun, R. 95
Buñuel, L. 180, 181, 182
'Bureau of Surrealist Research' 12
Butoh 6

Cage, J. 2, 56
Calderon 94
Cambodian theatre 91
Camion, Le 182
Capitalisme et schizophrénie 27, 28
Capture of Jerusalem, The 94
Carroll, L. 3, 27, 29, 30–1, 33, 34–5, 99
Castellucci, R. 6
Cenci, B. 61
Cenci, The 3–4, 67–9, 71–2, 74, 94–5, 160, 165–6
Cendrars 178
Centre Mother and Boss-Pussy 48
'century no longer understands the fecal poetry, the intestinal ills, of that one, Madam Death, The' 152–3
Chaikin, J. 106
Chaplin, C. 180
Chinese acting 78–9, 81
Chion, M. 52
chora 116, 118, 121–4
cinema 2, 85, 159, 160, 178–80; immolation 4; silent movies 161; talking pictures 161, 162
'Cinemas of cruelty' 178–83
Claudel, P. 134, 164
Cocteau 90
Committee for the Beatification of Antonin Artaud 1, 2, 5
committee work 1–3
Communicants, The 182
Conquest of Mexico, The 94, 180

consciousness 89
Conversations: The Autobiography of Surrealism 11–13
'Coquille et le clergyman, La' 3
cosmic trance 60, 62
Crary, J. 166
critic 179
Critique et clinique 28
'Cruelle raison poétique, La' 110
cruelty of subject's performance 48–9
cultural revolution 93
cultural theatre 41

Dadaists 23, 90, 94
'Dalai lama, letter to the' 12
Daumal, R. 91–2
De Chirico 12
Deafman Glance 95
Death of Empedocles, The 94
'death of paper, part two: Artaud's sound system, The' 159–68
'Declaration of January 27, 1925' 12
'decomposition of Paris, the' 4
defecation 100–2, 104
Deleuze, G. 6, 27–36, 70, 71, 75, 82, 168, 170, 171; *Anti-Oedipus* 117, 137, 142, 144, 145, 146
Delusional 49
Demy, J. 182
Derniers vers 97–8
Derrida, J. 8, 39–46, 109, 126–36, 170; Artaud's rebellion 103; faithful rendering 5; murder 104; repetition 79, 98, 102; speech and voice 54; theatre of dreams 77–8
Descartes, R. 130
Desire in Language 116
Desnos 13
Devereux, G. 71
Dialectics 42
Diderot 49
Dionysus in 69 77
disappointment 179
discipline 62
double-bind 155–6
Dream Play 94
Dreyer, C.T. 4, 179, 181, 182
drive 137
dubbing *see* 'Voice devoured: Artaud and Borges on dubbing'
'dubious spectacle of collective identity, The' 77–82
Duchess of Malfi, The 94

Dulac 179
Dullin, C. 85
Dumoulié, C. 178
Duras, M. 182
Dybbuk, The 169–70, 174, 175

Écriture et la différence, L' 39
Eisenstein 180
electro-shock treatments 21
Eliade 77
Eliot 82
Elle était et elle est, même 49
Eluard 10
enthusiasm 179
Entretien infini, L' 110
Epstein 179
Eraserhead 182
Erlkönig 54
Esslin, M. 109
Eugénie de Franval 94
Euripides 94
Eustache, J. 182
'Evolution of the Stage Setting, The' 161
excrement 154
Expérience intérieure, L' 17–18
expulsion 121, 122, 123

Fabre, J. 49, 50
faith 5
Fall of the House of Usher, The 179
Fargue, L.-P. 12
Fargue, V. 12
Fassbinder, R.W.
Feast and Folly: Cuisine, Intoxication and the Poetics of the Sublime 151
Feral, J. 3
Ferdière, G. 18–19, 21, 22, 24, 26
Ferenczi, S. 157
Ferreri 182
festival of cruelty 43
Fichte 129
Fiends and Torturings 134
Finter, H. 47–58
Floating Clouds 182
Fonagy, I. 157
force 155
forcené 130–1
Ford 67
Foreman, R. 51
Foucault, M. 8, 16, 109, 117, 183
Fraenkel 17
Fragments of a Diary from Hell 89
France 2

Frankenstein 95
Freud, S. 69, 70, 117, 145, 164, 171, 173, 175; Oedipus myth 72–3; schizophrenia 31; 'symptoms' and 'sublimations' 103; taboo and totemism 16, 68, 74–5
From the Life of Marionettes 182
Funny Games 181
Fura dels Baus, La 50

Gachet, Dr 140
Gallimard 21
Gance, A. 4, 179
Garrel, M. 182
Genealogy of Morals, The 43
Genet 94
Gerard, F. 12
Gertrud 182
Gide, A. 48
Giono 179
Girard, R. 71, 73–4, 75, 79
glossographia 153
glossolalia 152–3, 154
gnostic literature 75–6
God 55, 99, 156, 174
Godard, J.L. 93, 182
Goethe 54
Goodall, J. 2, 65–76
grafted transference 121, 122
grain de la voix 53
Gramsci, A. 93
'Grande Oeuvre' 139
Greenaway 182
Greene, N. 109
Grotowski, J. 6, 24, 59–64, 93
Group I Magazzini 56
Guattari, F. 6, 27, 28, 70, 71, 75; *Anti-Oedipus* 117, 137, 142, 144, 145, 146

Haneke, M. 181, 183
Hangmen Also Die 180
Hayman, R. 109
'He wasn't entirely himself' 59–64
'heads of insane asylums, to the' 12
Hegel, G.W.F. 80, 119, 120, 131, 146
Heidegger, M. 129–30
Heliogabalus 92
'Henchmen and Torturings' 156
Herbier 179
Hercules Furens 71
Hesse 91
Histoire de la folie à l'âge classique 109
Hitchcock, A. 180, 181

Hitler, A. 24
Hölderlin 33, 94, 115
Hollier, D. 159–68
'Homage to Antonin Artaud' 14–15
Hour of the Wolf 182
Hum, D. 89

ideological theatre 41
Illuminations 98, 103
impossibility of thinking which is thought 111–13
incest 68–9, 70
Indian Culture 48
Inner Experience and Eroticism 16
Innommable, L' 102
interpretive theatre 41
intrafamilial violence and murder 68–9, 70
Invocation à la Momie 47
Ireland 24
'is God a being? If so, he's a shit' 153–5

'Jabberwocky' 27, 29, 30, 33, 99
Janouch, G. 58
jetée 133–4
Jonas, H. 76
jouissance 181, 182
Jouvet, L. 93

'K' 151–8
Kafka 58
Kagemusha 182
Kemm, J. 171
King Ubu 94
Klein, M. 146, 175
Klossowski, P. 172–3
Knapp, B. 109
Knowles, C. 56
Kristeva, J. 50, 57, 67–8, 69, 75–6, 116–24, 126
Krzyzanowski, S. 173
Kurosawa, A. 180, 182

Laboratory Theatre of Jerzy Grotowski 93
Lacan, J. 53, 117, 145, 164, 165, 173, 174
Lancelot du Lac 182
language 3, 4, 98, 99, 116
'language' without exteriority 118–24
Laporte, R. 109
Latrémolière, J. 21–6
Lauwers, J. 49
Lawrence, D.H. 93, 101, 1045
lectures 4
leitmotiv 132–3

Letter for Queen Victoria 56
Letter to M d'Alembert 41, 87
Letters on Cruelty 181
Letters from Rodez 16, 18, 29–30
Leyden, L. Van 3
Life is a Dream 94
Living Theatre 5, 24, 94–5
Livre à venir, Le 109
Logique du sens 27
Lombardi, S. 56
Lost Highway 182
Lotringer, S. 21–6
Lucrèce Borgia 4
Ludlam, C. 106
Lynch, D. 182
Lyotard, J.-F. 50

Macbeth 94
McClure, M. 95
Maeder, T. 49
magic theatre 60, 62, 92
Mallarmé 115, 120
Manet, E. 95
Marinetti 90, 93
Marx brothers 179
Marx, K. 80
Marxism 92
'Masque of the Red Death, The' 66–7, 76
Mei Lan-fang 78
Memoirs of My Nervous Illness 173
Memory of Tiresia: Intertextuality and Film 169
Mes Petites amoureuses 182
Metz, C. 178, 181
Mexico 24, 92, 95
Meyerhold 61
Miller 145
Misanthrope, The 87
mise-en-scène 182
Moissi, A. 54
Molière 87
Momie attachée, La 47
Morand 179
motif 131–2, 135, 140, 145, 146
Mounet-Sully 40
myths 2, 62

Nadeau, M. 19
Naruse, M. 182
Natural Born Killers 181
Nerve Metre, The 89, 114
Nerve-scale, The 15
Nietzsche, F. 40, 41, 42, 62, 91, 93, 144

Nin, A. 151–2
'No More Masterpieces' 79
'Nobody in Europe knows how to scream anymore' 151–2
non-political theatre 41
nonsense 33–4
Novalis 15
Nuns, The 95

Oedipus 70–1
Oedipus Complex/myth 70, 71–2, 73, 74, 75
Oedipus Rex 70
Oeil écoute, L' 164
Oeuvres Complètes 3, 21, 27
Olvidados, Los 181, 182
Ombilic des limbes, L' 103
'On biography: madness and language' 7
'On Suicide' 155
'Open the Prisons! Disband the Army!' 12
opus 138–9, 141–2, 145
Order of Things, The 116
Oresteia 80
Orient of Buddhism 92
Other 54–8, 67, 68, 72, 76, 174–6
Overmeir, M. Van 50

paintings/drawings 2; *see also* 'To unsense the subjectile'
Pankow, G. 121–2
Parapluies de Cherbourg, Les 182
Parinaud, A. 11–13
Parisot, H. 18, 29, 33, 99
'Parole soufflée, La' 8, 39, 109
Pasolini, P.P. 182–3
Passion de Jeanne d'Arc, La 4, 181
passion-word 33
Phaedra 71
Phaedrus 43
Phantasmic Radio 151
phonetic elements 31–2
phonic disarticulation 159
Pialat, M. 182
Piano Teacher, The 183
Pirandello 93, 167
Pitoëff 85, 167
'plague and its powers in Artaudian theatre, The' 65–76
Plato 42–3, 67, 68, 86, 87, 88
poetry 2, 85
Poland 24
Polish Jew, The 171
'Pope, to the' 12

post-structuralism 2
Pound 85, 93
'Pour en finir avec le jugement' 27
Power to the Infants 161
Powers of Horror 116
Precocious Old Age of the Cinema, The 179
primary order 34
primitive cultures 92, 95
primitive theatre 44
'Production of reality or hunger for the impossible?' 137–47
Proust 101
psychoanalysis 35, 117, 156
psycholinguistics 116
psychology 97–8, 99, 102, 103, 104–5

Que Viva Mexico! 180
Quinze Variations sur un thème biographique 109

Racine 24
radio 2, 6
Rapaces, Les 181
Real 48, 49–52, 57, 58, 179
Rear Window 181
'Recherche de la fécalité, La' 155
Recherche du temps perdu, À la 101
'rectors of European universities, to the' 12
Reich, W. 83, 145
Reinhardt 61
repetition 41–3, 44, 45, 98, 99, 101–2, 104, 170
representation 41, 45–6, 50–1, 52, 137–8, 139
Republic 88
Return of Artaud the Mômo, The 48
revelation 75
Revenger's Tragedy, The 67, 68–9, 74
Revocation of the Edict of Nantes, The 172
'revolt against poetry' 85
Révolution surréaliste, La 13, 15
Reza Abdoh's theatre 50
Richard II 94
Rilke 110–11
Rimbaud 15, 97–8, 99, 105, 134
'Rimbaud and the Moderns' 119
ritual 78, 79–82
Ritual, The 182
Rivière, J. 63, 85, 99, 109, 110, 111, 113–14
Rolland de Renéville, A. 126

Rosolato, G. 156
Rousseau, J.-J. 41, 87
Russell 29
Rutman, W. 160

sacrificial crisis, theory of 73
Sade 83, 94, 114
Salo or the 120 days of Sodom 182–3
Sartre, J.-P. 164, 165
Scheer, E. 1–8
schizophrenia 27, 28, 29, 31, 32, 34, 121, 171
'schizophrenic and language: surface and depths in Lewis Carroll and Antonin Artaud, The' 27
Scholem, G. 173
Schreber, D.P. 173–4, 175, 176
Seashell and the Clergyman, The 85, 179
Season of Cruelty 5
'Second Manifesto of Surrealism' 10
'Second Manifesto of the Theatre of Cruelty' 86
secondary organisation 34
Self 72
Seneca 65, 67, 70–1, 73, 74, 94
sense 34
Shame 182
Shelley 3, 67
Shepard, S. 94
'Short Organum' 78
signifiance 122
signifier/signified 117–18
simultaneous theatre 61
Singer, I.B. 175
Singleton, B. 7
Six Characters in Search of an Author 167
Social Contract, The 41
Societas Raffaello Sanzio 6
solecism 172–3, 174
Sollers, P. 55
Sontag, S. 83–95, 109
Sophocles 70, 71
sound 160–4, 166–7
Sound of the Mountain 182
Soupault 179
Southeast Asia 91
speech coercion 173, 175
speech-affect 170
Spengler 93
spontaneity 62
Stanislavski 59, 61, 62
Starobinski, J. 164
Stone, O. 181

Strindberg 94
Stroheim, E. Von 180, 181
structuralism 35
struggle, description of a 113–15
studio recording 2
Sturges, P. 180
subconscious 78
'subject in process, The' 116–24
subjectile *see* 'To unsense the subjectile'
subjectivity 116, 117
subjects onstage 52–3
suffering 115
Suppôts et supplications 142
surrealism 88–9, 90, 92, 161
'Surrealism from day to day' 16–20
Surrealist Documents 19
synchronisation 162–4, 170–1, 172, 175
Syrkus 61

taboo 16
Tansk 146
Tarahumara Indians 92
Tarantino, Q. 178, 181
Tatlin 93
Taylor, E.B. 69
theatre 3, 85–6, 87, 89, 90, 99, 159, 160
'Theatre: acts and representations' 7
theatre of alienation 40
theatre of cruelty 3, 53–6, 59, 74, 92, 93, 99, 160; Bataille, G. 16; *Cenci, The* 4, 94; Derrida, J. 43, 44; passive-word/action-word 33; Poe, E.A. 66, 68; 'superstition of texts' 103; *Theatre and its Double, The* 152–3
'theatre of cruelty and the closure of representation, The' 39–46
'Théâtre et la culture, Le' 3
Theatre and its Double, The 5, 43, 59, 70, 91, 151, 160; attack on theatre 87; cruelty and metaphysics 39, 152–3; cultural analysis 78; force/form 3; Latrémolière on 24; metaphysics and the concrete 98; Platonic imagery 88, 89; 'pure' theatre 86; sound space 166; totemism 69
'theatre and the plague, The' 4, 57, 65, 69, 73, 151
Theatre of the Ridiculous 94
theatre of terror or passion 33
theatre writings 3
'Theatres of Cruelty, The' 178
'Theatres on Strike' 168
theatrical language 97–8

theoretical encounters 6–7
'There Is No More Firmament' 161
Thévenin, P. 27, 126, 167
thinking 115
'Thirteenth series of the schizophrenic and
  the litte girl' 27–36
Threepenny Opera, The 180
Thyestes 67, 68–9, 72–3, 74, 94
Tiezzi, F. 56
'Tis Pity She's a Whore 67, 68–9, 74
Titus Andronicus 94
'To have done with the Judgement of
  God' 6, 48–9, 53, 56, 152, 155
'To unsense the subjectile' 126–36
Torment of Tantalus, The 72, 74; *see also*
  Thyestes
'torments of dubbing, The' 169
Totem and Taboo 69, 70, 74, 75
Tour de feu, La 31
Tourneur, C. 67, 75, 76, 94
Trafalgar's Trick 166
Tristana 182
Truffault, F. 178, 180
Turn to the East 92

Umbilicus of Limbo, The 15, 114
Unconscious/Conscious schema 117–18
Under the Sign of Saturn 83
Une Saison en enfer 97
United Kingdom 24
United States 2, 24

Vakhtangov 61
'Van Gogh, the man suicided by society'
  22, 131–4, 137–47, 182

Vanoye, F. 17–83
Varese, E. 161
Vauthier, J. 94
Vawter, R. 50
Vent de la nuit, Le 182
Verfremdungseffekt 40
Vertov 92
Virmaux, A. 5, 48, 49
Virmaux, O. 5, 48, 49
Vitrac, R. 161, 166
Vivre sa vie 182
'Voice devoured: Artaud and Borges on
  dubbing' 169–77
'Voix du silence, Les' 160

Wagner 86, 91
Webster 94
Weekend, Le 182
Weiss, A.S. 151–8
White Devil, The 94
Who Shall Speak My Thought 50
Williams, H. 95
Wilson, R. 6, 51, 56, 95, 106
Women in Love 101
'Works and Men' 134
Works on Paper exhibition 159, 160
Woyzeck 94
Wright, E. 3
Writing and Difference 126

Yampolsky, M. 169–77
Yoga 92